The Victorian Short Story

Frontispiece: Sidney Paget's drawing of Sherlock Holmes locked in mortal combat with Dr. Moriarty, accompanying *The Adventures of Sherlock Holmes No. XXIV*, "The Adventure of the Final Problem," by A. Conan Doyle, in *The Strand Magazine* (November 1893)

THE
VICTORIAN SHORT STORY

Development and Triumph of
a Literary Genre

HAROLD OREL

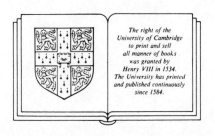

The right of the
University of Cambridge
to print and sell
all manner of books
was granted by
Henry VIII in 1534.
The University has printed
and published continuously
since 1584.

CAMBRIDGE UNIVERSITY PRESS

Cambridge

London   New York   New Rochelle
Melbourne   Sydney

Published by the Press Syndicate of the University of Cambridge
The Pitt Building, Trumpington Street, Cambridge CB2 1RP
32 East 57th Street, New York, NY 10022, USA
10 Stamford Road, Oakleigh, Melbourne 3166, Australia

First published 1986

Printed in Great Britain at the University Press, Cambridge

British Library cataloguing in publication data
Orel, Harold
The Victorian short story: development and
triumph of a literary genre.
1. Short stories, English – History and criticism
2. English fiction – 19th century – History and
criticism
I. Title
823′.01′09   PR871

Library of Congress cataloguing in publication data
Orel, Harold, 1926–
The Victorian short story.
Bibliography: p.
Includes index.
1. Short stories, English – History and criticism.
2. English fiction – 19th century – History and
criticism. I. Title.
PR829.07   1986   823′.01′09   85-25534

ISBN 0 521 25899 5

Contents

List of illustrations   *page* vi

Preface   ix

Acknowledgements   xi

Introduction: problems in defining a genre   1

1 William Carleton: elements of the folk tradition   14

2 Joseph Sheridan Le Fanu: developing the horror tale   33

3 Charles Dickens: establishing rapport with the public   56

4 Anthony Trollope: baking tarts for readers of periodicals   79

5 Thomas Hardy: an older tradition of narrative   96

6 Robert Louis Stevenson: many problems, some successes   115

7 Rudyard Kipling: the Anglo-Indian stories   138

8 Joseph Conrad and H. G. Wells: different concepts of a
   short story   160

Epilogue: the triumph of a genre   184

Notes   193

Index   204

Illustrations

Sidney Paget's drawing of Sherlock Holmes locked in mortal combat with Dr. Moriarty, accompanying *The Adventures of Sherlock Holmes No. XXIV*, "The Adventure of the Final Problem," by A. Conan Doyle, in *The Strand Magazine* (November 1893)   *frontispiece*

1   Portrait of William Carleton by John Slattery (courtesy of the National Gallery of Ireland)   *page* 15

2   Title page of William Carleton's *Traits and Stories of the Irish Peasantry*, edition of 1843   19

3   Joseph Thomas Sheridan Le Fanu, c. 1843 (portrait owned by Mrs. Susan Digby-Firth. Reproduced by permission of W. J. McCormack, from his book *Sheridan Le Fanu and Victorian Ireland* (Oxford: Clarendon Press, 1980))   35

4   Illustration by "Phiz" of Le Fanu's "The Watcher," from *Ghost Stories and Tales of Mystery* (Dublin: James McGlashan, 1851)   39

5   Portrait of Charles Dickens by D. Maclise   58

6   D. Maclise's design for the title page of *The Chimes* by Charles Dickens (London: Chapman & Hall, 1845, 9th edition)   70

7   Cover of *Mugby Junction*, the Christmas number of *All the Year Round*, by Charles Dickens (1866)   75

8   Portrait of Anthony Trollope by S. Laurence, 1865 (courtesy of the National Portrait Gallery)   81

9   Portrait of Thomas Hardy by Augustus John (reproduced by permission of the Fitzwilliam Museum, Cambridge)   98

10 Portrait of Robert Louis Stevenson by W. B. Richmond, 1887 (courtesy of the National Portrait Gallery)   116

11 Portrait of Rudyard Kipling by P. Burne-Jones, 1899 (courtesy of the National Portrait Gallery)   140

List of illustrations

12 Cover of the Indian Railway Library edition of *Soldiers Three* by Rudyard Kipling. Design supervised by John Lockwood Kipling (Mayo School of Art, Lahore)   142
13 Title page of the Indian Railway Library edition of *Soldiers Three* by Rudyard Kipling   143
14 Cover of the Indian Railway Library edition of *The Phantom 'Rickshaw* by Rudyard Kipling. Design supervised by John Lockwood Kipling (Mayo School of Art, Lahore)   155
15 Photograph of Joseph Conrad   162
16 H. G. Wells, from *The Graphic* (7 January 1899)   174
17 Drawing of *The Country of the Blind* by H. G. Wells, from *The Strand Magazine*, vol. xxvii (April 1904)   180
18 Another drawing of *The Country of the Blind* by H. G. Wells, from *The Strand Magazine*, vol. xxvii (April 1904)   181

To Desmond Hawkins

Preface

The Victorian Age, a richly productive literary period, is notable for (among other things) its nurturing of the short story. The genre had been ill-defined in earlier centuries, and for much of the nineteenth century attracted little critical attention as a new and increasingly popular reading diversion. Many Victorian authors regarded it with suspicion, as a diversion from more profitable novels and plays; even when prospering periodicals paid them decent wages for short stories that pleased readers, authors usually neglected to collect them and reprint them in hard covers.

Two points must be made at the outset. The first is that this review of the development and triumph of a literary genre is based upon stories written only in England, Scotland, and Ireland. Histories of the short-story tradition in the United States have often enough been written, and studies of the briefer fictions of Edgar Allan Poe, Nathaniel Hawthorne, Herman Melville, Mark Twain, Bret Harte, and Stephen Crane (to name only the more prominent of nineteenth-century authors) abound. The market for such stories was established earlier, and the rationalizing of their aesthetics was defined more fully, in the United States than in the United Kingdom. Yet the very few available histories that concentrate on the stories treated in this volume at the expense of, or to the exclusion of, American examples have not adequately accounted for the reasons why the English short story developed independently of Poe's philosophy of composition, or why, for that matter, so many of the greatest writers in England turned enthusiastically to the writing of short stories in the final decades of the century. I have written my book to fill what I consider to be a real gap in literary history, and to suggest that Victorian writers of short stories may be best understood in terms of an English context, and of English historical development, rather than in relation to an American – or even a Continental – influence.

The second point has to do with the absence of relatively minor writers such as Douglas Jerrold and Ouida. Readers will miss discussions of many of their favorites: "George Egerton" (Mrs.

Preface

Golding Bright), Ernest Dowson, George Gissing, "Saki" (H. H. Munro), George Moore, Arthur Symons, Israel Zangwill, Hubert Crackanthorpe, Ella D'Arcy, and a large number of mid-Victorian novelists who also, on occasion, wrote short stories. The introductory chapter outlines problems confronting all literary historians who seek to define the genre as it was understood and practiced at the beginning of the Victorian Age; the major part of the book consists of essay-chapters dealing with the short stories of major authors. To some extent the reasons for doing so resemble those which militate against trying to discuss both English and American short stories in the same volume: I am trying to avoid superficiality in covering too much ground, identifying too many literary figures, naming (and not analyzing adequately) too many short stories. Equally important, however, the particular authors chosen may be thought of as being, at one and the same time, representative of a larger group of short-story writers, and as individuals who contributed something special and specific to the development of our understanding of the genre. My book is not intended to be the definitive history of the English short story up to the outbreak of the Great War; it should not be mistaken for a reference work that seeks to catalogue and characterize all the periodicals, important short stories, and Victorian writers who specialized in this field. My primary aim is to say what needs to be said about why and how short stories became so popular in England over a period covering (roughly) seven decades, and to suggest new ways of thinking about some of the contributions of some of our best writers. In Seneca's words, there is no satisfaction in any good without a companion – in this case, the companion being the curious reader interested in a fascinating aspect of Victorian literary culture.

Acknowledgements

Special thanks are due to Dr. Eoin McKiernan, editor of *Éire-Ireland*, for permission to reprint portions of the text of the two chapters on William Carleton and Joseph Sheridan Le Fanu that appeared in that periodical; Mrs. Pam LeRow and Mrs. Sandee Kennedy for their impeccable typing of individual chapters and of the final draft; Mr. Andrew Brown of the Publishing Division of Cambridge University Press, for his intelligent, sympathetic, and indispensable editing of the manuscript; and to the University of Kansas General Research Fund, Allocation Number 3059–20–0038, which provided some released time for the writing of this manuscript.

Introduction: problems in defining a genre

Remarkably little is known about the history of the short-story genre in England. Even as we accept as truisms the ancientness of narrative and the wide variety of forms that a piece of fiction might assume, we are confronted by the knowledge that during the eighteenth century at least 15,000 brief narratives ("brief" meaning less than 12,000 words) appeared in periodicals; that their publication accompanied the appearance of anthologies of short novels, episodic romances, separable short narratives within novels, sketches, translations of foreign short stories, character studies, extended anecdotes, and tales emphasizing wondrous locales and action; and that never once did an author attempt to analyze the aesthetics of abbreviated fiction. Benjamin Boyce, one of the few modern critics who has looked into the subject of how English short stories developed as a genre, has been able to differentiate several major recurring types: the character-sketch of a representative person (often satirically embellished); the Oriental tale, frequently allegorical (the first English translation of *The Arabian Nights* began in 1704); humorous, serious and shocking, or pitiable passions dominating plots not necessarily marked by believability; Shandean fragments aiming at a single striking effect; enlargements of a fugitive moment of experience; and exposures of flaws in social organization and lapses in individual moral behavior. But even Boyce despairs of bringing order to so fragmented a picture: "With no conception of a genre (unless a *Tatler–Spectator* genre may have been in authors' minds), writers handled any idea in any way that pleased them. One of the fortunate circumstances in this period of development in prose fiction was that in the realm of story-telling there were few generally recognized rules and no undisputed models, ancient or modern. The amateur spirit reigned in a way to shock modern dogmatists."[1]

It is vaguely appreciated that short stories matured as a genre during the Victorian Age. Their growing popularity was related to the development of general-interest periodicals and a substantial need to fill columns of white space with agreeable reading-matter. Nevertheless, for much of the nineteenth century concepts of the nature and aim of a short story were not significantly more sophisticated than those known to the eighteenth century. Relatively brief narratives were often used, during the first half of the century, as a means of enlivening longer narratives (as in Dickens's *Pickwick Papers*). Dante Gabriel Rossetti, in "Hand and Soul," and Walter Pater, in the "The Child in the House," saw no need to differentiate between a sketch and a story. Novels were the central commodity, and short stories a by-product, filler material; the latter did not pay well, and printers and publishers often preferred works with lapsed copyrights, for which the payment of fees were unnecessary; books that collected short stories of a single author were chancy undertakings throughout the entire century. Novelists were certain, for a very long time indeed, that they might prosper if they wrote novels, but suffer financially if they concentrated on stories that took fewer than 30,000 words to tell. George Eliot's *Scenes of Clerical Life* (1858), a fairly substantial volume, contained only three stories. In his short stories William Makepeace Thackeray needed an equal amount of space, and of a reader's leisure time. George Meredith, in one of the brilliant comic stories of the age, "The Case of General Ople and Lady Camper," a supposedly short narrative, demanded from his reader the better part of an evening.

Indeed, the "normal" length of a story that might be called *short* seems not to have been agreed upon until the late 1870s. By then magazine editors, familiar with the tastes of their audiences, and aware of contemporary commercial realities, were writing to their contributors, in considerable detail, about the most suitable themes, vocabulary, and types of characterizations in serialized novels, and were denying space to those who refused to accept their advice. Thomas Hardy's disgust with the strictures of grundyism – which he regarded as unwarranted editorial interference – finally reached such a blazing intensity that he could no longer continue writing fiction. (Most of the remarks made by Hardy in his essays "Candour in English Fiction," 1890, and "The Science of Fiction," 1891, were applicable no less to short stories than to novels.) But for those who were willing to abide by the conventions, and who took the trouble to master the tricks of satisfying the audience for a given periodical, the rewards could be substantial. "Dr. A. C. Doyle" of 2 Devonshire Place, W., submitted two short stories, "A Scandal in Bohemia" and "The Red-Headed League," to *The Strand Magazine*, in 1891, its first year of publication, and was paid thirty guineas each for his first set of Holmes stories; fifty guineas each for the second series. Other examples of high pay for well-written short stories may be cited. The 1890s, after all, was the decade of Stevenson, Kipling, and Wells.

We still have to explain why writers did not agree on any definition of the short story even as they discussed "new" things, and the possibility of making a fresh start in all the arts (a common theme in the 1890s). Wendell V. Harris, in his useful survey *British Short Fiction in the Nineteeth Century* (1979), points out that the most immediate problem he faced in writing his work was terminological. Distinctions among such terms as "sketch," "tale," "story," or even "novel" mean more to us in this century than they ever did in Victorian England. Harris was understandably bemused by the discovery that any of these kinds of narratives "might or might not be intended primarily for moral edification," and that Victorians never satisfactorily defined the distinction between "factual accounts, imaginative essays, and fictional narratives."[2] Edgar Allan Poe's no-nonsense views on what a short story should do were not much discussed, and certainly not subscribed to, by Victorian authors for most of the century. Henry James, after worrying, at some length, about the problems of novelistic form in "The Art of Fiction" (1884), finally sighed, perhaps not unhappily: "But the only condition that I can think of attaching to the composition of the novel is, as I have already said, that it be sincere." His confession of frustration – the novel was too baggy a form to be satisfactorily measured by "rules" – did not hold up the writing of his own creative fictions, to be sure; but neither writers of fiction nor literary critics were interested in debating the aesthetics of the short story as a genre, particularly since efforts to define the novel all too easily foundered.

Before I look more closely at the conditions governing the publication of short narratives in the first half of the nineteenth century, a word of caution. The materials needed for a publishing history are in disarray, and a great deal of essential information is missing. The maturation process of Victorian short stories cannot easily be determined, and perhaps cannot be satisfactorily determined, from an examination of books about editors, publishing houses, and periodicals. The number of journals published between 1824 and 1900 exceeds 50,000, and the state of research in this field is not far advanced for a large number of both principal and secondary literary figures. The levels and kinds of audience reached by various periodicals have not been identified, for the most part; this problem is only one of several confronted by social and cultural historians interested in writing histories of the trade (journals, weeklies, family papers, annuals, etc.). *Victorian Periodicals: A Guide to Research*, edited by J. Van Dann and Roseman T. Van Arsdel and published by the Modern Language Association (1978), notes that much still needs to be done before any history can be considered definitive.

Hence, a procrustean definition will not account for all the irregularities of Victorian short stories, and since this critical study does not concentrate on theoretical considerations, I will concern myself with the careers and short-story achievements of individual writers: William Carleton and Joseph Sheridan Le Fanu (two Irishmen emerging from an oral tradition of story-telling), Charles Dickens, Anthony Trollope, Thomas Hardy, Robert Louis Stevenson, Rudyard Kipling, H. G. Wells, and Joseph Conrad. Each essay reviews the author's work in this particular genre; considers relevant biographical and socio-cultural factors; and says something (whenever possible) about the relationship of each writer to editors and periodicals. Working backward, through the examination of individual authors, makes more sense, and is more feasible, than attempting to write a formal history of the evolution of the genre.

Finally, the confession of a bias. I believe that the best Victorian short stories are astonishingly honest and dry-eyed in their examination of human problems that, all too easily, might have been treated sentimentally, or with condescension. They impress us by their economy of means; in them, the questions of why things happen as they do, and why people behave as they do, remain unanswered. Much that is taken as "modern" may be traced back to Victorian story-telling techniques. If this study satisfies a reader looking for information about Victorian short stories, it will be – I hope it will be – a worthwhile contribution to literary history.

The taxes on knowledge that inhibited the growth of the periodicals press in the nineteenth century trace back to 1710, when a duty on printed matter was first proposed as a revenue measure, and to 1712, when the first Stamp Tax replaced the regulation of the Printing Acts, which had lapsed. The tax rapidly became a means of controlling and regulating the press, and various versions of the legislation which authorized it were to last until they were repealed in 1855. The steepness of the duty – a halfpenny on every paper contained in half a sheet or less, and a penny on every *copy* between half a sheet and a whole sheet (i.e. four pages) – led to several unforeseen consequences, as well as the easily foreseeable one that a large number of publishers, driven to the wall, ceased publication of their newspapers. Since a duty of two shillings had been fixed for each edition of a pamphlet, and every advertisement was taxed at one shilling, it became economically sensible for the first time to increase the size of periodicals to at least six pages so that they could be classified as pamphlets. As a consequence, two shillings would be levied on the whole edition rather than a halfpenny on each copy. Mastheads increased in size. So did the type. It became feasible to include letters and essays in each issue. Under the eye of the fretful censor, many newspapers swiftly converted themselves into periodicals.

A revised Stamp Act was passed in 1725 to end these attempts to evade duties, but the struggle between the government and publishers was to last fully a century and a half, and to assume considerable importance in the history of press freedom. The government might insist that periodicals which included public news were liable to duty, but judges frequently found it difficult to differentiate between "public news" and "class news." (The latter, referring to information of particular interest to one category of readers, was not dutiable.) They encountered problems in deciding which periodicals were entitled to be sent through the Post Office in exchange for payment of a stamp tax. There were no clear guidelines – for publishers or for government officials – governing the number of copies of a liable journal that should pay the stamp tax (for the sake of transmission to outlying sections of the country), and how many should be printed on unstamped paper so that they might be privately delivered. These, and a host of related issues, are not completely tangential to the history of the short-story genre.

The desire to avoid taxes encouraged the development of periodicals aimed more at entertainment than edification. Writers of short fictions were not ignorant of the implications (for their free expression of political commentary) inherent in stamp duties, which for more than a century fell heavily on advertisements and pamphlets as well as on the paper on which periodicals were printed. The primary market of these writers – indeed, their only market – was periodicals. If they wanted to write political commentary, they either had to learn how to place the didactic message within an innocent-seeming or allegorical wrapping, or run the risk of government displeasure.

Until 1800 apologues or tiny moral tales outnumbered all kinds of serial stories in the miscellanies by ten (or at least eight) to one.[3] Indeed, 1800 has been chosen by more than one historian as marking a great divide in the history of English periodicals. Walter Graham, whose history of English literary periodicals is now more than half a century old (though not yet superseded), found that the typical magazine before 1800 might be described as a storehouse of miscellaneous information, a storehouse of all sorts of facts and fancies; but it definitely was not primarily literary. After 1800, however, it became increasingly hospitable to original works of the imagination.

No historian should attempt to lightly define the short-story genre in the latter half of the eighteenth century. If we review the years between 1740 and 1815, we can identify only nine periodicals that specialized in prose fiction; all appeared between 1780 and 1810. To settle for such a generalization would be misleading, inasmuch as during these 75 years some 470 different periodicals, with circulations ranging from 100 to 15,000 per month, printed fiction of some kind.[4] Some of these pieces were reprints of classics; others were redactions of Gothic romances and sentimental adventure stories. Well over half of these stories were plagiarized, or adapted or translated without payment. We should be wary of any judgment that places major blame on the unscrupulous practices of editors because of this heavy emphasis on "lifted" materials. Contributors often claimed, as their own, stories that had appeared years before, in other periodicals; the more obscure, the better. Moreover, a new title did not necessarily mean an original story; both contributors and authors freely rebaptized their pieces.

And what was a short story anyhow? A pseudo-biography of a real person? An anecdote based on history? A dramatic novel? A story that in some vague measure might be founded on fact? A dramatic novel? An Ossianic prose poem? A moral essay that incorporated a long illustrative story? A travel book or a "tour" with a slight fictive element? A "character" or a "scene" extracted from a new novel? A summary of a play or an opera? An essay-series that, on closer examination, turned out to be a collection of short stories?[5]

I have spoken of the influence, more inhibitory than liberating, of the taxes on knowledge on the free exercise of the imagination. Some additional external factors operated to encourage the production of shorter pieces of fiction, and these deserve to be listed. Ireland offered creative writers surprising freedom during the years when the stamp tax acted as a depressing weight on periodical publishers in England; Dublin printing houses were outside the law, and took full advantage of their freedom from censorship. Technical improvements that reduced the cost of printing – such as the first printing machine that produced part of the *Annual Register* in 1811 – helped to expand the market for writers of fiction. The cost of paper, which seriously cut into the publishing plans of countless editors, had been outrageously high during the Napoleonic Wars: thirty-four shillings a ream, in addition to the threepence-a-pound tax and wastage caused by imperfect sheets. A paper-making machine invented by John Gamble in 1801 cut this cost by more than fifty per cent, produced better paper, and made possible larger sizes for periodical production. Opposition by vested interests delayed a widespread adoption of the machine until 1820, but its improvements over hand-produced paper were plain for all to see, and the economic benefits were irresistible. The introduction of the rotary steam press followed soon after.[6]

It is no disservice to the literary quality of John Galt's *Ayrshire Legatees*, a serial that began to run in *Blackwood's* in 1820, to note that it benefited from such developments; it was the first serial novel deliberately written for a popular miscellany since Smollett's *Sir Launcelot Greaves* came out in 1760–1. (George Saintsbury confessed himself unsure whether Smollett's work was the first magazine story ever published in parts.) Nor is it fanciful to see, in the handsome payments made by the *Edinburgh Monthly* for contributions to its "Original Communications" section, the fertilizing soil of an entirely new class of professional writers. (After the fifth number, the *Edinburgh Monthly* changed its name to *Blackwood's Edinburgh Magazine*, and John Wilson ["Christopher North"], James Hogg, and John Gibson Lockhart became its editors.)

Perhaps all these factors, taken together, help to suggest rather than demonstrate the development of favorable economic circumstances for a professional author wishing to concentrate on fiction. But the question of why a short story might suit everybody's taste – the author's, the publisher's, and the reading public's – is not easily answered. Many readers, of course, disliked then – as they do today – a long story subdivided into numerous installments, an attitude not uncongenial to many editors who remembered the editing practice of such eighteenth-century periodicals as the *Tatler*, the *Spectator*, and the *Rambler*, whereby no tale might be stretched out for more than three installments. And there was an economic factor. The majority of miscellanies were bound and sold as collected editions, twice a year, or only once; these volumes became part of a book-seller's stock; for understandable reasons, they sold better if the stories could be described as self-contained, complete within an individual volume. A magazine novelette gradually settled into a "normal" length of between five and twelve thousand words, printable in two to six parts, and usually complete by the end of a single semi-annual volume, or at most a single annual volume. (Novels already in print remained largely untouched by the mania for plagiarizing or "adaption" that raged during the second half of the eighteenth century; they were too long to be chopped up into installments that might conclude within a half-year's time, and their copyright was, by and large, respected.)

The most important magazines specializing in fiction during the first half of the nineteenth century include John Aikin's *Athenaeum* (1807–9); the *Dublin and London Magazine* (1825–6); the *Cambrian Quarterly Magazine* (1829–33); the *Dublin University Magazine* (1833–80), which printed fiction by Samuel Lover, William Carleton, G. P. R. James, and Joseph Sheridan Le Fanu; *Blackwood's Edinburgh Magazine*, which encouraged the fiction of John Galt, Bulwer Lytton, and George Eliot; the *London Magazine* (1820–9); the *Literary Magnet of Belles-Lettres, Science, and the Fine Arts* (1824–6), which printed mostly tales and romances; the *Metropolitan* (1831–57), which specialized in light fiction such as Captain Frederick Marryat's *Peter Simple*, and paid sixteen pounds a sheet; *Fraser's Magazine for Town and Country* (1830–82), which printed Thackeray's *The Luck of Barry Lyndon* in 1844; the *Shilling Magazine* (1845–8), which became the favorite journal for Douglas Jerrold's wide-ranging pieces of fiction; Sherwood's *Monthly Miscellany* (later to be called the *London Monthly Magazine*), which printed all its stories signed beginning in 1838; *Bentley's Miscellany* (1837 on), for which Dickens served as first editor, and which printed more fiction than any other genre (the stories of Samuel Lover, Thackeray, and "Thomas Ingoldsby," or R. H. Barham). The 1830s were a particularly active decade in the history of English periodicals. From 1815 on, cheap periodicals specializing in fiction, included *Chambers's Edinburgh Journal Magazine* (1832–4); and any number of periodicals that sold for a penny or for a penny and a half, such as *Christian's Penny Magazine, Ladies Penny Gazette, London Penny Journal, Girl's and Boy's Penny Magazine, Dibdin's Penny Trumpet,* and the *Penny Comic Magazine.* The *Penny Magazine,* appearing weekly and printing its "parts" in monthly installments, reached a circulation of 200,000 by the end of its first year (the first issue sold 50,000 copies; five readers looked over every copy).[7]

But there remain to this day a number of mysteries about the multiplication of periodicals that regarded short fictions as suitable material for their pages. Despite several scholarly investigations of the growth of a new urban class, the rise in literacy, the educational work of the National Society from 1811 on and the British and Foreign School Society from 1813 on, the development of libraries, etc., we cannot state with certainty which social classes purchased periodicals for their fictional content, i.e., for pleasure rather than intellectual content. Prejudices *against* fiction cut across several social classes; it was never a simple matter of one entire class against another. Moreover, a number of periodicals specializing in short stories carried advertisements of commodities that ranged in price from a few pence to *very* expensive sums. And it has become apparent that the growth of a market for semi-pornographic fiction was not a reaction against – did not follow, but accompanied – the growth of a mass market for periodicals whose editors saw, as their primary function, the purveying of information about religion, science, politics, and cultural developments; popular fiction did not come into existence to satisfy a taste for titillation that high-brow publications refused to recognize, but was there from the very beginning. The Religious Tract Society and the Society for the Propagation of Christian Knowledge printed chap-books by the tens of thousands; bluebooks that abridged or imitated Gothic novels (either 36 or 72 pages covered in cheap blue wrapping) were popular at least until 1820; almanacs, broadsides, and crime-obsessed publications enjoyed wide circulation even before 1832, the year in which the three eight-page periodicals – the *Penny Magazine*, the *Saturday Magazine*, and *Edinburgh Journal* – commenced publication.[8]

In brief, efforts to appeal to the reading tastes of a large public proceeded on the assumption that those tastes needed improvement. I have already noted the popularity of the *Penny Magazine* at the beginning of its run. The *Saturday Magazine* sold some 80,000 copies a week. *Chambers's* rapidly climbed to 50,000 copies (by the third issue); within a few years, 80,000. The flavoring of all three was educational. Short fiction was regarded as a useful (though not an essential) sugaring. None of it reached a high literary standard, and none has added permanent lustre to English literature. But sober, self-consciously edifying fictions appealed to at least substantial fractions of the readership of these periodicals. The editors – Charles Knight, acting on behalf of the Society for the Diffusion of Useful Knowledge; literary men at the Society for the Propagation of Christian Knowledge; and William Chambers, a bookseller, publisher, and businessman who sought to avoid becoming entangled in debatable questions of politics and theology – were, from the beginning, concerned with the problem of how to broaden a circulation base.

The creation of a mass reading public was the indispensable *preliminary* to editors' recognition that fiction was their most saleable commodity. This point must be appreciated if we are to make sense of the relentless efforts to share information in the columns of the periodicals of the 1830s; because the common reader wanted information, publishers and editors were supplying it. A genuine intellectual revolution took place in the half-century that culminated in the 1840s. (It may not be minimized by patronizing.) Cheap books, cheap periodicals, cheap cyclopedias were appearing in quantity for the first time; their publishers learned how to operate on the narrowest of profit margins, and to reap large profits from the sales of their merchandise when the numbers passed the break-even point. (The economic sophistication required for knowledge of where to place that break-even point was not easily acquired; Charles Knight, a shrewd analyst of his own business, consistently neglected to include overheads as part of his continuing costs, and believed that 60 to 70 thousand copies of the *Penny Magazine* were all he needed to sell before profits accrued, whereas in fact he needed to sell more than 100,000 copies.)

The book trade – both wholesale and retail – was the primary medium whereby low-priced periodicals found their market. Not without some opposition from booksellers who preferred to deal in parts rather than in individual numbers of periodicals; who kept their circulation figures secret, thus hindering intelligent assessment of future print orders; or who refused to cooperate with schemes to create new channels of distribution, even though their own facilities were over-stretched. Still, specially commissioned agents helped to distribute periodicals and related works, and itinerant pedlars, carrying publications in their packs, disseminated them far and wide. Moreover, the astounding demand for printed materials selling for hitherto-unknown low prices meant that the old concept of a "cent per cent profit" (making a penny profit for every cent invested) was obsolete; a dealer could make more money than ever before by selling each penny copy for a fraction of a cent profit.[9]

The success of mass-circulation periodicals was not as linear as this brief history suggests. Both the *Saturday Magazine* and the *Penny Magazine* expired in the mid-1840s because of increasing competition from an over-supply of cheap periodicals. The market for edifying and informational literature proved to be less permanent and stable than the Society for the Diffusion of Useful Knowledge (along with other publishing houses) had assumed. Also, the natural desire of publishers to avoid demagoguery in political and religious issues led, perhaps inevitably, to greyishness and dullness whenever such issues were treated. Dr. Arnold had scoffed at the *Penny Magazine* as "all ramble-scramble," and readers of the 1980s who return to the bound files of these trail-blazing periodicals will find vast expanses of sand, with fewer meandering rivulets of entertaining or stylistically exciting prose than periodicals of the second half of the nineteenth century regularly supplied.

Nevertheless, the success of these periodicals must be measured in terms of their circulation (ten million copies of the *Penny Magazine* sold in 1833 alone); the number of imitators they inspired; their ability to satisfy a hunger for cheap literature and for knowledge, and to liberate millions of Englishmen, women, and children, who ascended to new levels of understanding of ideas and values. If the short fictions which then overwhelmed the pages of mass-circulation periodicals did much to deaden this excitement – this new-found freedom of sharing in a universal literacy – and thereby helped to debase taste, they also made possible the emergence of a new literary genre, and the development of some of the finest story-telling talents in the history of English literature.

Let us now review the careers of eight writers of short stories published (for the most part) during Queen Victoria's reign. We can trace, through their changing attitudes toward the kinds of fiction they found most congenial to their own talents and to the pragmatic judgments of editors and readers whom they sought to please, a history of the development of the genre. This history is not intended to be a revisionist reading of the past. The conventional, even platitudinous, view that the English short story triumphed as a genre in the 1880s, after most of the great Victorian novelists had died or exhausted their desire to write the three-deckers demanded by patrons of circulating libraries, is substantially correct. The importance of an author's understanding of the story-telling perspective, or point of view, became clear very late in the century, as literary historians have long understood. And the Epilogue will confirm, ruefully, our general impression that the exploding popularity of short stories in mass-circulation, general-interest periodicals was not inspired by, and not accompanied by, much serious analysis of the aesthetics of the genre by critics or, for that matter, creative writers themselves.

What I hope to demonstrate, however, is that the Victorian short story was affected by some important extrinsic considerations. In Ireland, for example, the short story, much more than the novel, was indebted to oral tradition and to identification of the story-teller with "the folk"; certainly this was the case with William Carleton, the greatest fiction-writer of his time and place, and the generalization applies, in almost equal measure, to his contemporaries and successors for fully half a century. Joseph Sheridan Le Fanu, more self-consciously literary than Carleton, was writing about Ireland even when his diabolical characters seemed to lack both habitation and name; it is inconceivable that a debt-free, happily-married Le Fanu could have written the tales contained in *In a Glass Darkly*. For the two mid-Victorian novelists considered, Dickens and Trollope, changes in the relationship between an author and his public were paramount: they frequently affected content as well as tone in the short stories that both men wrote (and handled, in their capacity as editors of successful magazines); in the case of Dickens, such factors as serial publication, Christmas Books, and tours providing the opportunity to give dramatic readings were new to the Victorian scene; and Trollope's willing acceptance of Thackeray's view that they were both in the business of baking tarts for the reading public – a view that might be interpreted as either affectionate or cynical – signified a new understanding of what kind of business story-tellers had blundered into. Thomas Hardy's insistence on older, more traditional modes of narrative became, in the 1890s, a stubborn refusal to accept experimentation for its own sake; after all, his novel-writing career had largely ended before he began writing his short stories, when he was over fifty years old. But Hardy, like Dickens and Trollope, was writing for a specific market of readers, and the kinds of fiction he wrote were influenced – inevitably – by his experiences with editors and periodicals during the previous two decades.

Robert Louis Stevenson, like Hardy, suffered in his relations with editors, but may have been more tormented by self-doubt; over-willing to accept the criticism of his friends, not always able to reject the advice of editors whose judgments he respected, he satisfied himself on relatively few of his short-story efforts; fewer, at any rate, than his large public knew at the time. Rudyard Kipling's literary debut in London, explainable in terms of a rising fervor for imperialism, growing respect for India as the largest jewel in Queen Victoria's crown, and public awareness of an extraordinary personality helped to insure readers' interest in anything Kipling brought with him from the Orient, or would write once he had established himself in Villiers Street, Strand. Finally, Joseph Conrad and H. G. Wells, writers of diametrically opposing concepts of what a short story should do, and how it should be written, won their first public favor for stories that appealed to a sense of wonder at worlds both remote and hitherto unknown.

To some extent, then, the short-story genre defines itself as a consequence of several crucial (and often slighted) developments in the publishing industry. My essays on the shorter fictions of Carleton, Le Fanu, Dickens, Trollope, Hardy, Stevenson, Kipling, Conrad, and Wells will record mundane information on such matters as relationships between periodicals and authors, and prices paid for individual stories. The quarrel with a publisher that leads Dickens to devise new business arrangements for the marketing of his fiction, or the usefulness of press syndication for Kipling and Wells, is not only interesting in itself, but – I believe – has value as an element in the history of a literary genre that has given pleasure to millions of readers.

William Carleton: elements of the folk tradition

I begin with William Carleton because he represents a critical moment in the history of an emerging awareness. Behind his back, an oral tradition, the acknowledged presence of an audience, an emphasis on colorful incident and verbal exaggeration; ahead of him, the more formal cadences of written prose, the weight of English literary tradition, the importance of style and formal design. Carleton moved between these two worlds, never permanently joining either. There are reasons why he never satisfactorily defined the short-story genre for his successors (these will be discussed). He was followed by Joseph Sheridan Le Fanu, Fitz-James O'Brien, and Bram Stoker, whose developments were indebted to his example; and by an astonishing number of splendid story-tellers who exploited Irish folklore in far more sophisticated ways than he did – Somerville and Ross, George Moore, James Joyce, Seamus O'Kelly, Daniel Corkery, Liam O'Flaherty, Frank O'Connor, Sean O'Faolain, Samuel Beckett, and Mary Lavin.

Given his placement in time, Carleton might have accomplished more. He could have placed in his debt English short-story writers as well as Irish. But he lived in Ireland, and it is not unfair to note that – at the end of the eighteenth century – the Irish were troubled about their past, and uncertain about the genuinely historical elements in the mass of traditions, myths, and legends that they had inherited. During Carleton's life the question of which writers were entitled to call themselves Irish was never satisfactorily answered on either side of the Irish Sea; all writers drew upon English literary models to a greater or lesser extent. Gaelic was associated vaguely with something the Phoenicians or the Carthaginians might have spoken; it was not analyzed as a member of the Indo-European family of languages until the 1850s, and a systematic study of the available fragments of Old Irish literature could not get under way until the language itself was better understood. Latin, as Carleton's stories indicated, was mangled by hedge-schoolmasters and peasants alike. English was the language of the foreigner, but the superior powers of

1   Portrait of William Carleton by John Slattery

an invading army confused many into thinking that the English
were, in all respects, culturally superior as well. Carleton, who
frequently felt bitter shame for the darker side of Irish life, was
reluctant to draw upon a purely Irish tradition of story-telling, and
perhaps (though this is more debatable) none existed; at any rate,

Carleton's autobiography does not indicate that he spent much time in reading Irish stories written either in Gaelic or English. Very few were available even if he had wanted to seek them out. School-books and pamphlets constituted the bulk of most publishers' stock during the late eighteenth and early nineteenth centuries.

But I should not assume that the details of Carleton's life are familiar to all readers. Because Carleton's background must be appreciated if we are to assess fairly the literary qualities of his narratives, something more must be said about the *Autobiography*. It is indispensable source material. David J. O'Donoghue went to Carleton's widow and children for the manuscript (Carleton had not given it a title), and printed it as the first volume in *The Life of William Carleton: Being His Autobiography and Letters; and an Account of His Life and Writings from the Point at Which the Autobiography Breaks Off* (London: Downey, 2 vols., 1896). Carleton, who lived from 1794 to 1869, began writing it late in life, and his memoir "broke off" in 1820, even before his career as an author began – although references to various short stories and other pieces of writing are scattered throughout the text.

But it is also most unsatisfactory as a source of information for the first quarter-century of his life. Its lacunae are, to say the least, noticeable. A reader can seldom be sure that Carleton's confessions of personal failings are straightforward treatments of what went wrong between Carleton and family relations, or priests, or the world in general. Dates are missing, and those that are supplied are reliable only in a general way. Since Carleton does have something to say about literature, one might hope for a few thoughts on the aesthetics of story-telling in nineteenth-century Ireland (no writer of his time was better qualified); but he does not review the way in which his own tales benefited from the examples of earlier writers, and his primary emphasis is not on literature anyhow. And, of course, he has nothing to say about the Dickensian editors who loomed large in nineteenth-century Dublin, and for whom he wrote his tracts, fiction, and essays: Thomas Davis, James Duffy, and Richard Pigott. They entered his life only after 1828, the year in which he published his first periodical piece, "A Pilgrimage to St. Patrick's Purgatory," in the *Christian Examiner and Church of Ireland Magazine*.

William Carleton was born in County Tyrone. The youngest of fourteen children who lived with their parents on a fourteen-acre farm, he admired his father's phenomenal memory and loved his mother's gentleness. Yet, understandably, his family lacked the financial means to provide an education better than that given by hedge schools, and Pat Frayne, Carleton's first tutor, may be taken as representative of a crudely-lettered, sadistic, and unattractive teacher-class that permanently crippled the interest of bright, imaginative Irish children in serious literature. More important as a tutor was the Reverend Doctor Keenan, who taught a classical school in County Monaghan, and who saw something worthwhile in his pupil (1814–16). But Carleton disappointed his parents; he refused to go further on the road to Munster (he was travelling there as a poor scholar) when a dream warned him of grave problems in his future, and his pilgrimage to Lough-derg shortly thereafter persuaded him that he was not suited to the Church. What, then, might be appropriate for one with so slender a set of resources? He tried a life of a tutor on the farm of Piers Murphy in County Louth, but did not enjoy it; Murphy was an uncongenial taskmaster at best, and more important, a savage in dress and tastes. Carleton's life at this stage borders on farce, though his efforts to make his way in Dublin – entering that city with all of two shillings and ninepence in his pocket – introduced him to a poverty more ferocious than any he had known, and certainly enlarged the range of his subject-matter in future fictions. The story of his volunteering to be an assistant to a taxidermist has become a classic exchange in any retelling of his life. (When asked what he should use for the stuffing of birds, Carleton replied, "Potatoes and meal.") Nor does it take much imagination to perceive that the letter that Carleton wrote in Latin to the colonel of a regiment was more than sufficient grounds for the colonel to reject him as a would-be recruit; Pat Frayne may have "taught" Latin to his young disciple, and Carleton's fellow-townspeople at Prilisk may have admired his show of erudition, but he was woefully ill-prepared for any serious profession.

Hence, his emergence as the first great Irish writer of fiction in the nineteenth century is as mysterious in its genesis as the reasoning that lay behind the decision of Thomas Hardy, later in the century, that his true vocation lay in novel-writing rather than architecture. *Traits and Stories of the Irish Peasantry*, published first in 1830 and subsequently much-revised and expanded, capitalized upon the small sensation created by his essay on his adventures as a religious pilgrim at Lough-derg. Carleton's long string of novels began with *Fardorougha the Miser* (1839). His subject-matter was always topical, his moral position always strongly stated. He treated secret societies, the land question, the vices of a decaying aristocracy, the famine years of the 1840s, emigration, and (in various forms) the need for Protestants and Catholics to work together. Nevertheless, he always had great difficulty in making a living; there is no question that publishers and editors cheated him. Finally, a petition addressed to the government, signed by a large number of well-known writers (including Maria Edgeworth), secured Lord Russell's endorsement; from 1848 on a pension of two hundred pounds a year was paid to Carleton, and prevented him from sinking hopelessly into debt. He died in Sandford, County Dublin, some two decades after the granting of the pension.

So brief a summary scarcely explains the number and severity of the problems Carleton created for himself almost everywhere he turned. His reputation while he lived was not as high as his talents deserved, partly because he treated too candidly the prejudices, superstitions, and crimes of the Irish, and said that he knew he was doing so (as in his preface to *Tales of Ireland*, 1834). For more than a century after he died his name evoked mixed feelings. William Butler Yeats, who reprinted five stories by Carleton in one of his anthologies in the 1890s, was severely censured by the *Nation* for having, in some way, committed an unpatriotic act. Those who have praised Carleton do so frequently in a manner that suggests they are settling old scores with Irish philistines, e.g., Patrick Kavanagh's claim that Carleton is "a universal writer, as good, say, as Cervantes, but with no opening into the world."[1]

In addition to his willingness to describe gloomy and unattractive aspects of Irish life, Carleton emphasized violence (though his descriptions were not excessive in terms of the violence that actually existed). No other Irish writer could, or would, describe the putrefying flesh of hanged conspirators in details as fulsome as Carleton in "Wildgoose Lodge." He entertained controversial political views, and overloaded his fiction with them, particularly in his later years; since they were frequently conservative, and even reactionary, his willingness to trim sails to "sell his pen" became for many critics a dismal black stain on a genuine major talent.

Above all, his equivocating views on Roman Catholicism endangered his posthumous fame. Perhaps his anger at the Catholic hierarchy may be traced back to his days with Father Keenan, when he wanted to apply for a diocesan scholarship at St. Patrick's College, Maynooth, and the Bishop refused to allow him to compete. Robert Lee Wolff has suggested that the Bishop's decision

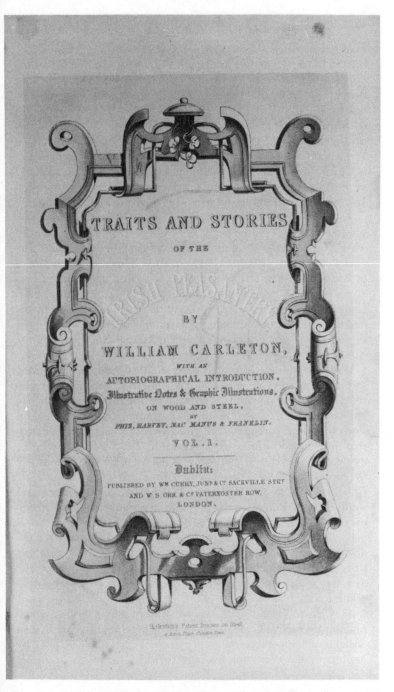

Title page of William Carleton's *Traits and Stories of the Irish Peasantry*, edition of 1843

marked the real moment at which Carleton's gradual disillusionment with the Catholic faith began.[2] Lough-derg provided ample opportunity for reflection on the grimmer aspects of a faith that demanded self-humiliation from its communicants. That pilgrimage took place in 1817, though Carleton probably did not break with the Church for some five years thereafter. At any rate, his attitude toward the Church underwent more than one sea-change, and he cannot be characterized as a *consistently* bigoted Orangeman.

This troubled, and still troubling, figure of a man, for so many years no better than a poor scholar begging his way through Ireland, became a successful writer in the 1830s, an internationally famous one in the 1840s, and (in Thomas Flanagan's words) a written-out "hack whose pen was for hire in Dublin's ugly literary wars"[3] in the 1850s. Late in the twentieth century Carleton's true achievement may be seen as having recorded, more honestly and in greater detail than any of his contemporaries, the world of pre-famine Ireland; he was in his fictions an able historian; and if his historical sketches are viewed, simultaneously, as exercises in the creative imagination, one can understand – and even forgive – the slipperiness of practically every piece of factual information in the *Autobiography*.

With the passage of time, Carleton's problems with imposing suitable structures on his disparate materials, his melodramatic incidents, his sentimentalized characters, and his rhetorical flights, appear to have damaged his novels far more than they spoiled his stories of briefer compass.[4] The glib generalization, often repeated, that his best short stories are contained in *Traits and Stories* must be qualified, however; Carleton wrote at the top of his bent in several of the pieces in *Tales of Ireland* and in *Tales and Sketches, Illustrating the Character ... of the Irish Peasantry* (1845). Most of his editors have shuffled indiscriminately the stories from all three volumes. Moreover, Carleton changed lines, and omitted passages, as his political and religious opinions underwent transformation; an editor is not always to blame for the very different "feel" that a later version of a story provides. Small wonder, then, that the very titles of his stories are often inaccurately transcribed even by those critics who most admire his art.[5]

The *Autobiography* offers a few observations arising from a general philosophy, such as Carleton's conviction that "man's life is divided or separated into a series of small epics; not epics that are closed by happiness, however, but by pain,"[6] which seems to be firmly

grounded in his own experience. Very close to the moment at which
he set down his pen forever, Carleton ruefully admitted that there
was "a good deal of dramatic incident" in his life,[7] and the sentiment
is consonant with his opening sentence: "Alas! it is a melancholy task
which I propose to execute – the narrative of such a continued and
unbroken series of struggle, difficulty, suffering and sorrow as has
seldom fallen to the lot of a literary man."[8] Yet much in Carleton's
upbringing was pleasant enough. At the age of ten he served as both
stage director and prompter to the Catholic and Protestant
amateurs who were acting in a local production of *The Battle of
Aughrim*. (Sympathetic Catholics appear in stories written over the
next half-century.)

On one hand, Carleton condemned the numberless administra-
tions that had "utterly disregarded" the cause of education;[9] the
idiocy of factionalism (intensified by the Rebellion of '98);[10] the
"irresponsible power" of Orange ascendancy in the North of
Ireland;[11] the use of "snakes" (polished, sharpened pieces of sheet
iron set in the ground, and designed to cut deeply into the foot of
anyone who might illegally "liberate" orchard fruit),[12] as well as of
man-traps and spring-guns; Ribbonism, the inevitable bitter
counter-force created to cope with the excesses of Orangeism;[13] the
numerous "rash and unreflecting marriages" of Ireland,[14] though
the usual custom – protracted courtship because the state of a
couple's circumstances did not justify "undertaking the serious
responsibilities of domestic life" – could not have been an attractive
prospect for many young men or women; Irish brutality and
miserliness, as exemplified by the farmer Piers Murphy; the hard-
hearted stinginess of close relatives, who refused to support
Carleton's idle wanderings beyond a brief time-period; the quality
of students at Maynooth; the treatment of beggars in Dublin
(Carleton's description of the cellar in which he was forced to sleep,
along with dozens of similarly indigent vagabonds and "cripples," is
chillingly mordant); the dubious ethics of publishers and owners of
circulating libraries who specialized in works recounting events
marked by "obscenity and profligacy";[15] and the failure of
Dubliners to take advantage of the riches of Marsh's "almost
unknown library in St. Patrick's Close."[16]

On the other hand, Carleton also enjoyed the love of his mother, a
talented singer; the stories told by his father, who knew "all kinds of
charms, old ranns or poems, old prophecies, religious superstitions,
tales of pilgrims, miracles and pilgrimages, anecdotes of blessed

priests and friars, revelations from ghosts and fairies"; a wide circle of friends and the love of more than one good woman; the exultation of sports and the full enjoyment of his good health; and an extraordinary ability to recover from setbacks that would have crushed lesser men.

Carleton's youth and adolescence were not *primarily* years of disappointments, even though the *Autobiography* often enough pauses to lament victimization by his own romantic imagination,[17] as well as by unscrupulous Gaels. Like the splendid eccentric in Boswell's biography of Dr. Johnson who might have been a professional philosopher if cheerfulness had not persisted in breaking in, Carleton could not refrain from celebrating his early years even as the gloomy sentiments of later life persisted in reinterpreting the feelings experienced during those years.

Little enough is said in the pages of the *Autobiography* about attitudes toward fiction, but we do learn that from the beginning Carleton wanted to read for the story. When studying the Fourth Book of Virgil, he found himself "affected almost to tears" by the death of Dido, and he read on oblivious of grammatical difficulties.[18] He read trash with avidity; he has less to say about *Tom Jones*, which opens up vistas of "wonder" and "feeling," than about *Amoranda, or the Reformed Coquette*, which he encountered at approximately the same time.[19] Other books aimed primarily at entertaining included *The Arabian Nights*; *The Life of Edward, Lord Herbert*; Defoe's *History of the Devil*; hundreds of annuals like *The Lady's Almanack*; *Castle Rackrent*; pornographic ephemera like the *History of Mrs. Leeson*, *The History of the Chevalier de Faublas*, and the *Irish Female Jockey Club*; and the novels of Maturin. Above all, there was *Gil Blas*, a picaresque narrative which served as the basis for important moments of decision in Carleton's life. When he first read it, he took for granted that all the adventures were true; the adventures recounted in it were seldom out of his head over a period of several years; he set out for Dublin looking for adventures in the manner of Gil Blas; he reassured himself after disappointments on the ground that "there were worse cases in *Gil Blas*";[20] and he believed that "after struggles and adventures" he might, like Gil Blas, "come to a calm and safe harbour at last."[21]

Carleton believed that fiction and fact were inextricably mixed. He might not have the patience to examine closely the workings of imagination – that which belonged to him or to professional story-tellers – but he knew, and relished, the powers of his own invention.

When he took to devising original narratives (a habit that he thought began in approximately 1818, prior to his visits to the Jesuit College of Clongowes Wood and St. Patrick's College, Maynooth), he composed them while walking about, and recited them "at the fireside in the evening." The oral element was thus crucial from the beginning, and the success of his improvisations exhilarated him: "The number of people who came to hear me in the evening was surprising, as were the distances they came from."[22] The stories he told might well turn out to be thinly-disguised versions of what actually happened to him; what he had seen; what was actually going on in Ireland.

And so, it turns out, whatever references Carleton makes to his short stories are identifications of the historical realities which underlay his fictions. Carleton's narratives are replete with Irish "facts." He uses the terms "sketch," "story," and "essay" interchangeably, as in his first essay, written for the Protestant clergyman Caesar Otway, a visitor to Lough-derg himself. Otway entertained dark suspicions about sexual practices of priests and nuns, but had not seen Station Island during the pilgrim season. Fascinated by Carleton's description of his trip there more than a decade earlier, he invited the younger man to provide a full narrative for the *Christian Examiner*. The *Autobiography*, written in the 1860s, is not to be trusted when it declares: "There is not a fact or incident, or a single penal step of duty – and God knows there is many a penal step to be taken there – which is not detailed with the minuteness of the strictest truth and authenticity. There is not even an exaggeration of any kind in my account of it."[23] But Carleton was mistaken about the impact of the pilgrimage on his Catholicism at the time, as we have already indicated (ten years play tricks on anybody's memory); he was writing for an editor notorious for his anti-Catholic bias, and he badly wanted to be published; and there is no way today, nor was there in 1828, to verify the particulars of Carleton's pilgrimage. The article (can it be called that?) "resembles a coloured photograph more than anything else,"[24] Carleton wrote; in his time, as we know, colors were added to a photograph after it had been printed. Carleton took pride in truth-telling, and insisted on identifying the factual basis of his yarns lest they be mistaken as the inventions of a mere *improvisatore*.

When he alludes to "The Poor Scholar," he insists that his separation from his mother and family is described there "exactly as it happened . . . leaving his father out."[25] He really dreamed about a "mad bull" about to gore him, and awoke in terror on his first night, an event which led him to return home.[26] His description of the battle that took place during the Lammas fair of Clogher, given in magnificent fullness in "The Party Fight and Funeral," is mentioned as being "a full and historical detail of it." Carleton identifies himself as an eye-witness to an event that involved no less "than from three to four thousand men" who fought in "the greatest battle that ever took place in the North of Ireland between the two parties" of Orangemen and Ribbonmen. The primary value of "Dennis O'Shaughnessy," in Carleton's late judgment, is that it accurately depicted its author – Carleton himself – as "one of the finest and best made young men in the parish ... in the very bloom of youth – six feet high – with, it was said, a rather handsome and intelligent set of features," and an unrivalled "early fame at all athletic exercises."[27] In "The Battle of the Factions" Carleton recorded somberly the fate of Frank Farrell, the miller of Clogher: he cracked his spine while trying to lift an enormously heavy set of bells in the cathedral of Clogher.[28] Carleton's brother John, who was married to the tunes of the fiddler Mickey McRory, proved to be the inspiration of "Shane Fadh's Wedding," and the original ceremony, Carleton solemnly assured his reader, was the largest he ever witnessed.[29] To justify the art of "Wildgoose Lodge," Carleton emphasized that it was based on "the facts" with which he had become acquainted during his residence in the parish of Killaney, "where the awful tragedy was enacted."[30] He also expressed some doubt that his recreation of the event could be called a "tale," since he had talked to so many local residents for whom the event remained a vivid memory. (The hanging of Paddy Duvaun, a Ribbonman, and his followers took place on October 29, 1816, little more than a year after they had burned to death eight members of a Catholic family named Lynch.) He had verified his information by reading the newspapers collected by Dr. Stuart, the rector of Lough Swilly. He exploited his experiences with Piers Murphy, "the most overbearing and most brutally tempered man" he had ever met, "in fact, a low-minded, ignorant ruffian," when he described the world of Bodagh Buie O'Brien in *Fardorougha the Miser; or, The Convicts of Lisnamona* (1839).[31] And though others might characterize *The Squanders of Castle Squander* as a novel, Carleton, somewhat uneasily, spoke of it as his "work upon Ireland," and mentioned the fullness with which he had reproduced the curriculum of young men at Maynooth in 1848.[32]

Carleton always emphasizes fact even when his story is written to illustrate a theory or a moral. For example, in his Preface to *The Fawn of Spring-Vale, The Clarionet, and other Tales* (3 vols., 1841), speaking of "The Clarionet," he insists that "The humble hero and heroine of the story were known in every town of any importance in Ireland." He himself had seen "the female" by herself in Dublin, carrying her husband's clarionet – bound in crape – on her arm, "a circumstance which told the story of his death with singular pathos and beauty."[33]

Perhaps Carleton best expressed his determination to raise the frail superstructure of a conventional narrative over well-attested historical events in his Preface to *The Tithe Proctor* (1849), a novel which dealt with the Tithe Rebellion of 1830–7. He admitted the existence of anachronisms in his story, and justified his telescoping of time on the ground that he could not have included all the history essential for an understanding of the context of "the fearful tumults and massacres" taking place during these years. More important, he defended himself against the charge that he had chosen to emphasize only "the worst feelings and the darkest criminals" of Ireland. "This, however, was not my fault," he wrote. "If they had not existed, I could not have painted them; and so long as my country is disgraced by great crimes, and her social state disorganized by men whose hardened vices bring shame upon civilization itself, so long, I add, these crimes and such criminals, shall never be veiled over by me. I endeavour to paint Ireland, sometimes as she was, but always *as she is*, in order that she may see many of those debasing circumstances which prevent her from being what she *ought to be*."[34] Carleton believed himself propelled forward by "the truth," and if it be argued that he never admitted a previous opinion to be wrong even as he pressed the validity of his current, directly opposite, position, he was correct in insisting that critics hostile to his bleak portrait of Irish vice and folly failed to recognize his efforts to draw, at the same time, "the warm, generous, and natural virtues" of his countrymen.[35] He was also right in denouncing the super-patriots of his age who believed that a creative writer had to disguise or distort the truth by suppressing anything that might lessen Ireland "in the eyes of the world," and by giving the public only "the bright and favourable side." "These thin-skinned gentlemen are of opinion," Carleton snorted, "that the crime itself is a matter of trivial importance compared to the fact of its becoming known, and that provided the outside of the platter is kept clean, it matters not how filthy it may be within."[36]

Carleton's use of fictional names, his deliberate clouding of the

identities of localities, his vagueness about dates, and his avoidance
of "that intolerable Scoto-Hibernic jargon which pierces the ear so
unmercifully" should not mislead any reader into believing that he
saw his function as being other than that of a faithful chronicler of
Irish scenes and characters. He was depicting the "genuine Irish,"
as he said in his Preface to the First Series of *Traits and Stories*. He
disclaimed any political purpose, but he endeavoured to render his
portraits "as true to nature as possible,"[37] and he wanted to show his
countrymen not as demons, suffering innocents, or saints, but "as
they really are – warm-hearted, hot-headed, affectionate creatures."[38] In the "Author's Introduction" to a new edition (published in monthly parts in 1842–3 and reissued in two volumes in
Dublin and London in 1843–4), Carleton added to his observations
on fiction two important insights.

The first had to do with the generally poverty-stricken literary
landscape of Ireland in the early years of the nineteenth century.
Carleton, angered by the conventional view of Irish speech as being
"an absurd *congeries* of brogue and blunder," censured even
Sheridan's creation, Sir Lucius O'Trigger, as "*his* Irishman, but not
Ireland's Irishman."[39] Stage Irishmen dominated the English
imagination, and whatever attention the English might pay to John
Bull's other island was focused on Captain O'Cutters, O'Blunders,
and Dennis Bulgrudderies. The Irish had suffered from centuries of
hostility and repression; Gaelic was not as widely spoken or
understood in the 1830s as it had been when Carleton was a child;
but, even so, "where the English *is* vernacular in Ireland it is spoken
with far more purity and grammatical precision than is to be heard
beyond the Channel."[40] In thus taking up the cudgel (as Carleton
would have quickly amended it, the "shillely" or the "homemade"),
he was expressing an attitude toward language of some importance
to his own practice in writing dialogue.

The bull – conjoined with the term "Irish" relatively late when it
is used in this sense – means a self-contradictory proposition. The
O.E.D. defines it as "an expression involving a ludicrous inconsis-
tency unperceived by the speaker."

An Irishman, Carleton maintained, was never as guilty of
perpetrating bulls as those who were prejudiced against him
claimed. It may have been true, at an early stage in the relationship
between Ireland and England, that the "wild English," who
"expressed himself with difficulty," frequently "impressed the
idiom of his own language upon one with which he was not

familiar,"[41] but explaining the origin of a problem did not justify later generations of critics in continuing the "national slander." Much as Carleton admired Maria Edgeworth's talent, he still felt called upon to attack her defence of Irish bulls: ". . . Miss Edgeworth herself, when writing an essay upon the subject, wrote an essay upon that which does not and never did exist."[42] On this matter, Carleton's objection was well-founded. It did not take much trouble to move from an attitude of laughter to one of derision, and even one of despising the perpetrator of a bull; all too swiftly the consequences of this patronizing became political. Ridicule restricted to the stage might have been relatively harmless, "but this was not the case. It passed from the stage into the recesses of private life, wrought itself into the feelings until it became a prejudice, and the Irishman was consequently looked upon and treated as a being made up of absurdity and cunning – a compound of knave and fool, fit only to be punished for his knavery or laughed at for his folly."[43]

Carleton's diagnosis of reasons for the existence of the problem – the relative backwardness of Irish culture, the fact that Irish writers of talent "uniformly carried their talents to the English market, whilst we laboured at home under all the dark privations of a literary famine,"[44] and "the narrow distinctions of creed and party" that disfigured Irish periodicals[45] – is all too easily confirmed by a review of the publishing history of Ireland in the late eighteenth and early nineteenth centuries. In addition, Carleton's argument that increasing familiarity of the populations of both nations with each other would lead to "mutual respect" proved not to be the case; nor did the best productions of John Banim, Gerald Griffin, Samuel Lover, Maria Edgeworth, Lady Morgan, and Anna Hall fully compensate for the draining of the country's intellectual wealth that England's superior marketing possibilities for literary commodities encouraged.

Even so, when Carleton used bulls in his dialogue, he did so to make a point in characterization, and he had no more respect for the mangling of the King's English than any of his contemporaries across the Irish Sea. The outrageousness of metaphor in the schoolmaster's speeches in "The Poor Scholar" was based on Carleton's memories of Pat Frayne and his Findramore hedge school. Carleton was unforgiving. Frayne was ill-educated, and Mat Kavanagh, the fictional re-creation of Frayne, was as droll, low in his humor, and capricious in the administration of punishment, as his original. Kavanagh, like Frayne, came to a miserable end. His language – hyperbolic, crammed with ill-digested tags and scraps of information, and bad Latin – provoked little laughter; rather a sense of dismay mixed with chill; more than once Carleton described his hedge-schoolmaster as a "savage."

In later life Carleton saw the advantage of knowing both Gaelic and English versions of traditions and legends. He was thus better able to "transfer the genius, the idiomatic peculiarity and conversational spirit of the one language into the other," precisely as his countrymen themselves did in their dialogue "whenever the heart of imagination [happened] to be moved by the darker or better passions."[46] His father could speak both languages with equal fluency; his mother sang to him the "old Irish versions" of songs, partly because some had never been translated into English, and partly because she did not enjoy singing English words to Irish melodies. "I remember," he wrote, "on one occasion when she was asked to sing the English version of that touching melody 'The Red-Haired Man's Wife,' she replied, 'I will sing it for you; but the English words and the air are like a quarrelling man and wife: *the Irish melts into the tune, but the English doesn't*' – an expression scarcely less remarkable for its beauty than its truth. She spake the words in Irish."[47] For Carleton music and poetry distinguished the Irish people, attested to their refinement. Even the keener who lamented the death of a relative in her "high but mournful recitative" benefited from "the genius of the language, which possesses the finest and most copious vocabulary in the world for the expression of either sorrow or love."[48] The use of Gaelic in such a state of excitement permitted the extemporizing of sentiments that were "highly figurative and impressive."

Carleton's second insight was related to a developing appreciation that his present condition and future prospects, no less than his past, were tied permanently to those ordinary Irishmen, and that he could never afford to alienate himself from their humble status, or turn his back on their aspirations. True enough that for a while, during his adolescent years, he enjoyed the opportunity to associate with older boys, and, too keenly, enjoyed as well his growing reputation as "a prodigy of knowledge."[49] "Indeed, at this time, I was as great a young literary coxcomb as ever lived, my vanity being high and inflated exactly in proportion to my ignorance, which was also of the purest water."[50] His knowledge of Greek and Latin may have been woefully finite, and he may have exploited the innocence of his auditors, and he may have swaggered about as a "pompous" imposter for much longer than was good for his soul. But something else had been going on simultaneously with his preening. The following passage is of some consequence in understanding Carleton's veering away from a career in the priesthood, and helps us understand the background of his frequent statements about the "truth" of his fictions; it is worth quoting in full.

In the meantime, I was unconsciously but rapidly preparing myself for a position in Irish literature which I little dreamt I should ever occupy. I now mingled in the sports and pastimes of the people, until indulgence in them became the predominant passion of my youth. Throwing the stone, wrestling, leaping, football, and every other description of athletic exercise filled up the measure of my early happiness. I attended every wake, dance, fair, and merrymaking in the neighbourhood, and became so celebrated for dancing horn-pipes, jigs, and reels, that I was soon without rival in the parish.[51]

Such pride in his own physical accomplishments, in his being a roaring boy worth the watching, might be accounted smug if from the beginning Carleton had not evinced a rueful, if only partial, awareness that he was less than he pretended to be, less of a scholar, man of the world, lover, and gentleman than he would have liked the world to believe. But the emphasis on his belonging to the people, and on the strengths of his fiction deriving from the completeness of his identification with the common folk, is worth remembering. He took pride in being accepted by the peasantry because of his accomplishments as an athlete, and because of his romantic appearance. J. J. Slattery's portrait, in the National Gallery, Dublin, provides some proof that Carleton, even in middle years, must have been a handsome boy, just as the *Autobiography* maintained. Slattery shows Carleton as he wanted to appear to the world: solid of appearance, an elbow on a copy of *Traits and Stories of the Irish Peasantry*, and a quill in his right hand poised for future literary productions.

In *Traits and Stories* Carleton's obsession with the need for reassuring his audience that the best fiction had a solid factual basis, and that his fiction in particular could be trusted, did not destroy a reader's interest in the narrative element. Some stories, to be sure, were straightforward reporting, based on first-hand information or a gathering of accounts from those locally based. Indeed, in the Second Series Carleton even included "An Essay on Irish Swearing" as a story before he became embarrassed by its anomalous nature and converted it into an introduction to another story, "The

Geography of an Irish Oath." But he was a genuine story-teller; the impulse which led him to move beyond the strained propaganda of his thirteen *Christian Examiner* tales, published between 1828 and 1831, was one that he shared with all masters of the craft. The first story of *Traits and Stories*, "Ned M'Keown," introduces us to a village circle of friends: Andy Morrow, Bod Gott, Tom M'Roarkin, Bill M'Kinny, Alick M'Kinley, Shane Fadh, and Pat Frayne. Here, as the first story begins, Carleton sets the scene: these personages are sitting around Ned's fire, contented by "their chirping pints of ale or porter" or their mountain dew, while outside "The night was dark, close and misty – so dark, indeed, that, as Nancy said, 'you could hardly see your finger before you.'"[52]

The story concludes with Ned's recognition of the obligation to tell the next story: "Sit down, gintlemen ... sit down, Father Ned, you and Father Pether – we'll have another tumbler ..." It is pouring outside. The priest, unable to return home, urges Ned to go on with his story "and let it be as pleasant as possible." This linking device leads into "The Three Tasks, or, The Little House under the Hill." After that story has concluded, the villagers adjourn until the following evening, when, assembled again about Ned's hearth, Andy Morrow asks for full particulars about Shane Fadh's wedding. This fairly lengthy narrative proves so satisfactory that the next evening Tom M'Roarkin describes Larry McFarland's wake in a "desperately asthmatic" voice. Each story, thus far, begins and ends with a drinking round. Bill M'Kinny urges Tom to "take a pull of the malt now, afther the story, you soul!" – and Tom agrees that he deserves another "thrate."

Carleton evidently found this frame-device too constricting, for he abandoned it before he began his next story, and the reshufflings of the contents of the First Series during the remainder of the century made the chronology of their composition-sequence increasingly difficult to follow. But in these early stories Carleton assumed the presence of an audience. Colloquialisms stressed the oral element. Drink made the occasion truly sociable. A story-teller did not monopolize the floor, but had to endure the remarks of his listeners (some irreverent) as he proceeded.

"Shane Fadh's Wedding" – based, as already noted, on a real ceremony attended by Carleton – is a story told by Shane himself, with the encouragement of a double measure ("For talking's druthy work," as Andy Morrow points out).[53] Carleton could not keep to his original plan of having only one person tell each story. All the characters keep chattering, and commenting on the creative efforts of the yarn-spinner. There is an inter-play between those of the charmed circle (a tale-teller and his auditors) and the world that presses darkling from the outside. "Shane Fadh's Wedding" is the middle story of the group, coming after "Ned M'Keown" and "The Three Tasks," but before "Larry M'Farland's Wake" and "The Battle of the Factions." Carleton, in writing the last of these stories, was to confess his weariness with the framing device. There were better ways to illustrate Irish life, feeling, and manners than through the inventing of a different voice for each narrator; and when Carleton sighed wearily that he might overwork Irish dialogue "and its peculiarities of phraseology," that he felt nervous about overly narrowing the sphere of his work if he continued as he had begun, he really wanted to leave himself more room for "description and observation."

Carleton was increasingly anxious to discover a congenial point of view from which *all* stories might be told; he was working his way toward a greater freedom as an authorial commentator; and even though his circle of story-tellers in the public house of Kilrudden had its venerable roots in Chaucer's band of pilgrims en route from the Tabard Inn at Southwark, the "description and observation" he reserved as a privilege for his own voice allowed for greater versatility and a wider range of sensibility than any single member of Ned M'Keown's circle might legitimately claim. Unfortunately, this interest in editorializing damaged Carleton's later stories more seriously than he appreciated.

The five yarns recounted around Ned's fireplace are rich in characterization and humor. Their defects – loose construction, repetitions of speech idiosyncrasies beyond a point of no return, the notorious Irish sin of non-arrival (the story never reaches its announced destination), weakness in trailing off at the end – are, after all, shared by practically all Irish short-story writers in the nineteenth century.

Later stories are more concerned with current issues, and the moralizing is freer, more ubiquitous. For example, "Tubber Derg, or The Red Wall," was first published under the title "The Landlord and Tenant, an Authentic Story" in 1831. Its complete text did not appear until it was reprinted in *Traits and Stories* (1833). It is one of the better narratives of the Second Series, but its pace is frequently slowed by Carleton's speaking, in his own voice, about the truth of his narrative; "vile and heartless landlords";[54] the capacity of the Irish to bear toil and privation, greater than that possessed by any other people;[55] pauperism and begging, inter-twined phenomena peculiar to a ground-down economy; the burning desire of the Irish to be independent ("Their highest ambition is to hold a farm"[56]); the extreme divisions of Irish society, "the wealthy and the wretched," with no room for a "third grade of decent, substantial yeomen, who might stand as a bond of peace between the highest and the lowest classes";[57] and – finally – about his moral. As the narrator (Carleton) contemplates the "noble character" about whom he has written, he concludes: "The sun, too, in setting, fell upon his broad temples and iron-grey locks with a light solemn and religious. The effect to me, who knew his noble character, and all that he had suffered, was as if the eye of God then rested upon the decline of a virtuous man's life with approbation; as if He had lifted up the glory of His countenance upon him. Would that many of his thoughtless countrymen had been present! They might have blushed for their crimes, and been content to sit and learn wisdom at the feet of Owen M'Carthy."[58]

These digressions and sentimental meditations were to be cleared away, by later Irish writers, as so much undergrowth blocking a clear view of the main narrative-line. Carleton's interest in having the right to express himself whenever he wished, and for however many lines he thought necessary to make a polemical point, was self-indulgent, and dangerously so in terms of craft. He had a wonderful sense of the Irish character, and indeed was one himself, but he saw no connection between the exercise of his privilege as a master of ceremonies to interrupt, hector, and teach, and the difficulties that that exercise imposed on narrative pacing, credibility of character-ization, suspension of reader disbelief in hyperbolic action and dialogue, and a sense of form: on the aesthetics of his story, in brief. But without his example – and his dedication to the art of story-telling, however imperfectly practiced – the more sophisticated and better-shaped short stories of Joseph Sheridan Le Fanu would have had a very different look.

2

Joseph Sheridan Le Fanu: developing the horror tale

Shifting our attention to Joseph Sheridan Le Fanu at this point does not imply that the history of the short-story genre is best illustrated by Irish narratives, or that equally convenient examples of a changing aesthetic may not be obtained from English literature. But Le Fanu's contributions move so rapidly, and with such assurance, from the more verbose, loosely structured, and self-indulgent narratives of William Carleton that the contrast could not be more dramatic. Le Fanu is not *talking* to his reader; the oral tradition has receded into the background; his stories are meant for the study, and for a reader who holds a book in his hand. The emphasis lies on a shaped fiction. Seldom will a reader become impatient with excessive length, or suspect that the narrator lacks a true sense of destination. Le Fanu – no less than Carleton – has designs upon the reader's possible willingness to be persuaded of the validity of an intellectual position, but the didactic element is better controlled, more subtle. Whatever message Le Fanu wants to convey is implicit in the dramatic situation. The narrator does not intrude himself continually upon the reader's consciousness, for between the reader and himself there is another sensibility, a distinct and well-characterized persona.

Le Fanu did not create the horror story or the vampire story, but he identified the ways in which either kind of narrative could become an artistically finished production, one worthy of the time of serious readers.

These, then, constitute his two major achievements: he produced an impressive number of short stories which emphasize form and economy of means, and he mastered the story of terror before any of his contemporaries.

As in the case of Carleton, some words of biographical background may be welcome. He lived between 1814 and 1873, and during the period of his greatest literary productivity he deliberately chose to retreat from polite society in Dublin; indeed, he was known as "the Invisible Prince," and even his contemporaries saw less of him, and knew less about him, than they would have liked.

His Huguenot ancestors included Charles de Cresserons, who
enlisted on the side of William of Orange; merchants, financiers, a
surveyor, and a clergyman from Cork who attempted to persuade
Robert Emmet, shortly before his execution, to renounce heresy and
return to a faith in God; and, on the side of his paternal
grandmother, Richard Brinsley Sheridan, who was her brother. His
father, a conventional clergyman, believed in the long-established
tradition of absentee-landlordism, and did very little for his
parishioners; when the Tithe Wars broke out in 1831, Irish Catholics
withheld their payments from him, and the little-loved Rector of
Abington and Dean of Emly was forced to watch his family income
drop by more than fifty percent. Bitterly poor tenant-farmers called
him names, and there was even an attempt to murder one of his sons,
a brother of Joseph. It is not surprising that Joseph became a
conservative at Trinity College, Dublin, or that he strongly opposed
the Reform Bill of 1832.

Such biographical data help to explain the grimness of much of Le
Fanu's fiction. Called to the bar in 1839, he never practiced law, and
disappointed his family. He became increasingly dedicated to the
writing of fiction, and his stories depicted families over their heads in
debt, insecure, haunted by the spectre of failure, subjected to
humiliations that shattered confidence and any hope in a better
future. During the 1840s – a challenging and unsettling decade for
many Victorians – he underwent a crisis of religious faith, and many
of his stories deal with the inability to sustain faith in God when
worldly circumstances conspire against personal fortune and health.
In 1844 he married Susan Bennett, the third youngest in a family of
nine, and fathered several children whom he could barely support;
his contributions to *The Protestant Guardian, The Dublin Evening
Packet*, and *The Dublin Evening Mail*, and his part-time ownership of
The Warder and the *Statesman*, were not financially lucrative. He was
sued for libel twice, and lost – expensively – on both occasions. He
suffered sieges of ill health, worried about mounting debts, and
exploded in temper-tantrums on several public occasions. Susan
died in 1858, and the husband she left behind doubted the efficacy of
doctors, medicine, and science in general. Though his marriage had
been, for the most part, a happy one, chords of unhappiness about
the married condition sound powerfully in several of the short stories
that, in his increasing isolation from polite society, he now began to
write.

Le Fanu's sensational novels began with *The House by the*

3   Joseph Thomas Sheridan Le Fanu, c. 1843

Churchyard (serialized between October 1861 and February 1863). They are of more than passing interest in any history of the Victorian novel because of the skill with which shocking incidents are depicted, the wealth of information about Anglo-Irish tribal ways that they contain, and the connections that key incidents and intellectual arguments make with Le Fanu's own troubled life. But since my primary concern is with the powerful creative fictions that he wrote in shorter form, I should note immediately that the strongest link between Carleton and Le Fanu was their emphasis on the truthful substratum lying beneath what they had imagined.

Take, as one example, "A Chapter in the History of a Tyrone Family." This extraordinary narrative of a secret first wife and a bigamous second ends with an attempted murder of the second wife, the sudden onset of insanity on the part of the husband, and a gory suicide. (The story served as inspiration for an important strand in the narrative of *Jane Eyre*.) Le Fanu's story concludes: "Thus ends a brief tale whose prominent incidents many will recognize as having marked the history of a distinguished family; and though it refers to a somewhat distant date, we shall be found not to have taken, upon that account, any liberties with the facts, but in our statement of all incidents to have rigorously and faithfully adhered to the truth."[1]

Similar protestations of historical fidelity are made in other stories. The conclusion of "Strange Event in the Life of Schalken the Painter" records the somewhat complacent satisfaction of the storyteller that he has "studiously" omitted the heightening of "many points of the narrative, when a little additional colouring might have added effect to the recital . . ."[2] Francis Purcell, whose collected papers include a number of stories about supernatural visitants and inexplicable occurrences, is presented to the reader (in a prefatory note to Le Fanu's first-published story, "The Ghost and the Bone-Setter") as a real parish priest who for nearly fifty years has resided in the south of Ireland, and who is widely known as an antiquarian with literary tastes.

In a Glass Darkly (1872), perhaps the most popular collection of Le Fanu's stories, is unified by its brief introductions, all of which refer to the narrator's friendship with a fellow-physician, Dr. Martin Hesselius. The stories are, presumably, records of "cases," since the narrator, who acted for twenty years as the German doctor's secretary, finds himself fortuitously in a position where he can recount the more interesting, amusing, or horrifying narratives, those (in other words) which do not possess interest limited to a specialist. The medical jottings which constitute the major text of the prologues to the tales are scientific in their diction; they lend greater credibility to each case. For example, the introduction to "The Familiar"[3] differentiates three kinds of disease on the basis of a subjective-objective dichotomy, with learned allusions to a periodical "vibratory disturbance" which affects the brain-covering. The remarkable precision of nomenclature in these prefaces exhibits a lawyer's delight in mastering the details of a brief. The curtain-raiser for the novella "The Room in the Dragon Volant" alludes to Doctor Hesselius's "extraordinary Essay upon the Drugs of the Dark and the Middle Ages," and to several "infusions and distillations well known to the sages of eight hundred years ago," i.e., the *Vinum letiferum*, the *Beatifica*, the *Somnus Angelorum*, the *Hypnus Sagarum*, and the *Aqua Thessalliae*. To the narrative which recounts "The Fortunes of Sir Robert Ardagh" Le Fanu appends a final note: "The events which I have recorded are not imaginary. They are FACTS; and there lives one whose authority none would venture to question, who could vindicate the accuracy of every statement which I have set down, and that, too, with all the circumstantiality of an eyewitness."[4]

Were there indeed any contemporaries of Le Fanu who needed to be told that the happenings of these incredible stories were founded on "FACT"? Probably not. This story-telling convention, emphasizing the provability or historicity of fictional materials, had been important to Carleton; it went back to Defoe's time, and beyond, to Queen Elizabeth's day.

But it does not do to be cynical about the seeming ingenuousness of these claims. If on the one hand Le Fanu imagined more than he willingly admitted, on the other he was writing more autobiographically than many of his contemporaries appreciated. His financial difficulties in Merrion Square were not all that dissimilar from those suffered by the Wares in *The Tenants of Malory*, a book that he completed after the crash of 1866. W. J. McCormack, a recent biographer, reads *All in the Dark* (1866) and *Haunted Lives* (1868) as "an assault on authority as understood in Le Fanu's generation," on a society which was "patriarchal, hierarchical, and, ultimately, justified by God the Father."[5] Moreover, the "psychic decomposition" in a large number of his stories had its painful roots in the troubled politics of 1842-8, and in his own marital and domestic crises of 1850 and 1858. And always he made the miseries of his life into the materials of his art. Unlike Charles Lever, who stressed both the comic and the happier aspects of Irish character, and whose novels (as a direct consequence) were greatly admired by English readers, Le Fanu saw Irish life as essentially tragic. He was depressed by man's willingness to commit evil; there was something within man that made evil an attractive course of action; and in his world, in Ireland, he identified a number of recurring themes for his fiction.

These themes have political overtones. The first that I want to consider is the conviction that the nineteenth century had inherited, and must pay for, the sins of the eighteenth. The story "The Watcher" (first published in 1847) describes events dated vaguely "somewhere about the year 1794." Its major character is a former frigate commander "during the greatest part of the American war," a baronet named Sir James Barton. He is a free-thinker. Not long after the announcement of his engagement, he disputes, at the home of the dowager aunt of his fiancée, the evidences of revelation. He states firmly his utter disbelief in the supernatural and the marvelous. "French principles," particularly those which profess allegiance to Whiggism – and hence of some concern to the conservative Le Fanu – have so infiltrated fashionable society that "neither the old lady nor her charge were so perfectly free from the taint as to look upon Mr. Barton's views as any serious objection to the proposed union."

Captain Barton sees ghosts, a series of spectral appearances, and gradually loses faith in the universality of natural laws of cause and effect. Visitants keep turning up at inconvenient moments, and his "pride of scepticism" deteriorates. Proofs of the existence of a malevolent watcher multiply. He visits a doctor, who attempts to discover the cause lying behind his "occasional palpitations, and headache." Can these be traceable to something physical, something factual? The medical analysis proves useless; Captain Barton fights against "superstitious tremors," and his mind gradually turns in upon itself. He visits a celebrated preacher, and confesses to him that he is an unbeliever, "and, therefore, incapable of deriving help from religion." But he protests that he holds a very deep interest in the subject despite his rejection of what is ordinarily called revelation, despite his inability to pray. He is becoming convinced that "there does exist beyond this a spiritual world – a system whose workings are generally in mercy hidden from us – a system which may be, and which is sometimes, partially and terribly revealed." The preacher advises the Captain to change his venue, take a few

4 Illustration by "Phiz" of Le Fanu's "The Watcher," from *Ghost Stories and Tales of Mystery* (Dublin: James McGlashan, 1851)

tonics, diet, and exercise. These are the counsels of sense and sensibility. They are what Barton himself, before he became convinced of the close relationship between guilt and retribution, might have prescribed for himself. Long before story's end, however, he knows that he cannot be saved, and, more important, he has become convinced of his own damnation by the evidence supplied by his own rational faculties.

Le Fanu's line of argument may be paraphrased thus: we deny, on the basis of reason but at our peril, the existence of forms and presences that must (for want of a better term) be denominated "supernatural." A man may know, in his mind, that no one else can see what he sees, and that, therefore, what he sees cannot exist. But in this story, as in a number of others, the combined forces of law (an M.P.), medicine, and the military are as helpless as Barton in the presence of a vengeful visitor from the grave. There is something beyond reason, something greater than the principles of the Enlightenment. We have no right to believe that the existence of the real world in any way undermines the fact of the existence of the world of the imagination. The nightmares of the mentally ill cannot be "talked through." Le Fanu's anger against the presumptions of the *philosophes* of the 1790s burns through story after story, and it is no accident that so many of his narratives are set in the past. Human history, he seems to be arguing, took a turn for the worse as a consequence of the doctrines of a generation of rationalists.

That is one point. The second has to do with the lovelessness of marriage arrangements. Miss Montague, the fiancée, attracts admirers, but her matrimonial prospects are dim until the advent of Captain Barton, who is willing to ignore the problem of her family's limited finances. Miss Montague accepts his suit "conditionally upon the consent of her father," and her dowager aunt promptly withdraws her "from all further participation in the gaieties of the town" (Miss Montague regards this as somewhat extreme). Le Fanu provides little or no evidence of genuine affection between the two parties, and at a late stage in the narrative, stresses the "singularly painful" status of the neglected fiancée, who has become "an object of pity scarcely one degree less to be commiserated than himself." She is nowhere near Barton's age; she shares few, if any, of his habits. Le Fanu remarks that she has not enjoyed "anything like very vehement or romantic attachment on her part," and adds: "Though grieved and anxious, therefore, she was very far from being heartbroken; a circumstance which, for the sentimental purposes of our tale, is much to be deplored. But truth must be told, especially in a narrative, whose chief, if not only, pretensions to interest consist in a rigid adherence to facts, or what are so reported to have been." The owl presented by the gardener to Miss Montague as a pet (caught "napping among the ivy of a ruined stable") turns out to be connected, in some inexplicable fashion, with the bloody murder of Captain Barton. The "grim and ill-favoured bird" is much-loved by Miss Montague, who, in her unwitting fashion, by sheltering instead of releasing it, becomes responsible for her lover's death; while Barton, from the first, regards it "with an antipathy as violent as it was uttered unaccountable." Miss Montague is not heartless; rather, Le Fanu suggests, from such stony soil – a marriage contract formalized for financial benefit to one side only – a genuine flower of affection cannot grow. A similar world-weary, even jaundiced attitude toward marriage may be traced in other tales.

A third point is related to Le Fanu's striking view of Dublin as a ruined city. This matter goes beyond the isolation of the hero from friends his own age, from the love of his fiancée, from sympathy that might be extended by older and more experienced members of society. Nor is it related to the stock language of Gothic fiction. On the first of Barton's "solitary" walks homeward, Le Fanu emphasizes the "unfinished dwarf walls tracing the foundations of projected rows of houses on either side"; on the second, the "quite deserted" appearance of the streets; on a later occasion, even as Barton approaches "frequented streets," the foundations of a street, "beyond which extended waste fields, full of rubbish and neglected lime and brick kilns, and all now as utterly silent as though no sound had ever disturbed their dark and unsightly solitude."

"The Watcher" is not the best or most subtle of Le Fanu's stories, but it illustrates several striking themes, and Le Fanu, using slight variations, kept returning to them. "The Watcher," however, possesses an intrinsic interest beyond anything so far discussed. The fact that *others can see the apparition* who haunts Captain Barton is significant. Both Barton's servant and General Montague see "a deep indenture, as if caused by a heavy pressure," in the bed that holds the body of the murdered Captain; as the servant puts it, "There was something else on the bed with him!" Before the reader reaches this point in the story, however, there can be no doubt the M.P. has seen the "singularly evil countenance" of the passer-by who so shocks his companion Barton; or that a real musket-ball whistles close to Barton's head; or that General Montague sees the very person "whose appearance so constantly and dreadfully disturbed the repose of his friend"; or even that Lady Rochdale's maid sees the "singularly ill-looking little man, whose countenance wore the stamp of menace and malignity" and whose appearance signals a return of the persecuting demon to Barton's life; also, the stranger passes on a message to the terrified hand-maiden (never delivered, on the orders of Lady Rochdale); that is to say, he actually speaks, and someone other than Barton hears and understands what he has to say.

Le Fanu began his career as story-teller by emphasizing the possibility of natural causes leading to horrifying effects. It may be that Barton was pursued by someone who never died at all, and that the owl behaved in owl-like fashion without necessarily being the visitant – a reincarnation of a sailor who died of lockjaw in a Lisbon hospital. But Le Fanu was growing dissatisfied with conventional explanations of what was happening, and why.

It is curious, for example, how often some form of suicide becomes the only possible solution to the problems created by abnormal tastes in living. "Mr Justice Harbottle," another of the tales in *In a Glass Darkly*, suggests in its Prologue that "the contagious character" of the intrusion of the spirit-world "upon the proper domain of matter" manifests itself "in certain cases of lunacy, of epilepsy, of catalepsy, and of mania, of a peculiar and painful character, though unattended by incapacity of business." The narrative deals with a judge of the mid-eighteenth century who has "the reputation of being about the wickedest man in England," and whose "great mulberry-coloured face" exhibits "a big carbuncled nose, fierce eyes, and a grim and brutal mouth." Yet he possesses intellectual power (which makes him all the more formidable), and when he learns, from a stranger, that a secret tribunal has been formed to try him for his crimes, he cross-examines his informant in high and zealous style. The judge, profane, sarcastic, and ferocious in his administration of the criminal code of England ("at that time a rather pharisaical, bloody and heinous system of justice"), has every intention of hanging the man whose wife he has converted to his mistress; and does. But the hanged grocer – later – makes an unexpected appearance in court, distracting the judge from his charge to the jury in a case of forgery; Harbottle receives a letter from Caleb Searcher, "Officer of the Crown Solicitor in the Kingdom of Life and Death," announcing that he will be tried for wrongfully executing the grocer. One night, after a play at Drury Lane, he suddenly finds himself pinioned between two "evil-looking fellows, each with a pistol in his hand, and dressed like Bow Street officers." He is driven, in his carriage, to a gigantic gallows, and then to a courtroom where the presiding judge is a Chief Justice Twofold, "a dilated effigy of himself; an image of Mr. Justice Harbottle, at least double his size, and with all his fierce colouring, and his ferocity of eye and visage, enhanced awfully." The not-unexpected verdict of guilty is followed by a sentence of execution – the tenth of the ensuing month is named – and by the forging of iron bands around Harbottle's feet by two blacksmiths ("naked to the waist, with heads like bulls, round shoulders, and the arms of giants"). He wakes from his nightmare and tries to deny its warning to him by complaining to others that he has suffered a sudden seizure of gout. Nevertheless, the passing days find him increasingly gloomy: "I wish I were well purged of my gout. I wish I were as I used to be. 'Tis nothing but vapours, nothing but a maggot." His friends analyze the problem as illness, and his doctor diagnoses his case as hypochondria. On the night before he is scheduled to go to Buxton, "that ancient haunt of crutches and chalk-stones," the hanged grocer reappears, as a vision, to the housekeeper's child and to Harbottle's mistress. A scullery-maid – who does not "vally a ghost not a button" – sees the most frightening ghost of all, "a monstrous figure, over a furnace, beating with a mighty hammer the rings and rivets of a chain." In the morning the Judge is found dead, without the smallest sign of any struggle or resistance, "hanging by the neck from the banister at the top of the great staircase." It may be, as the medical evidence shows, that he has been in a sufficiently atrabilious state to have wanted to do away with himself. But suicide seems pathetically inadequate as an explanation for a death that occurred on the tenth of the month, as predicted. More – Le Fanu strongly implies – is at stake here.

The mind creates its own terrors. Mr. Justice Harbottle (when first we meet him) is described as having features "fixed as a corpse's," so that his violent death is prefigured; but we also remember him as cunning – he does not commit himself even as he cajoles and bamboozles juries to have his own way – and sarcastic for calculated effect. He betrays his best gifts for the sake of mean triumphs over helpless prisoners in the dock; it is impossible to sympathize with him even when the powers which destroy him turn out to be mirror images of his own diabolism, even when Chief

Justice Twofold roars him down "with his tremendous voice"; or when he pants and gloats and nods and grins and gibes as he dismisses contemptuously Harbottle's attempt to defend himself. Le Fanu is telling us that Harbottle has done all this to himself, and has, consequently, defined the parameters of his own hell.

"Green Tea" deals with the problems of the Reverend Mr. Jennings, a well-intentioned and charitable bachelor. His frequent breakdowns of health may be due to a failing heart or brain; Dr. Hesselius does not presume to say which. But the narrator, who, in almost every Le Fanu tale, expresses a reasoned view of what transpires, has a Swedenborgian view of materiality: "I believe the entire natural world is but the ultimate expression of that spiritual world from which, in which alone, it has its life. I believe that the essential man is a spirit, that the spirit is an organized substance, but as different in point of material from what we ordinarily understand by matter, as light or electricity is; that the material body is, in the most literal sense, a vesture, and death consequently no interruption of the living man's existence, but simply his extrication from the natural body – a process which commences at the moment of what we term death, and the completion of which, at furthest a few days later, is the resurrection 'in power.'" The argument has implications for medical science, as Dr. Hesselius rightly points out; it suggests further thoughts relevant to the meaning of Captain Barton's persecution; and it characterizes the spiritual continuum which ultimately destroys Jennings. Dr. Hesselius has conducted explorations in metaphysical medicine that remain untranslated from the German, but he can speak with some scientific authority on the ties between the visible and the invisible worlds. He guesses – on the basis of a relatively brief acquaintance with Jennings – that his father had seen a ghost; Lady Mary Heyduke confirms his intuition by adding that his father had, in addition, talked to it. There follows a remarkable chapter, "Dr. Hesselius Picks Up Something in Latin Books." The doctor, visiting Jennings's home on "Blank Street," must wait for a few moments in the library; he is particularly taken by a complete set of Swedenborg's *Arcana Caelestia*, in the original Latin. These volumes have been carefully read, with paper markers in several places. Dr. Hesselius transcribes a number of passages which speak of "the evil spirits associated with man," spirits neither in heaven or hell but rather in their own world. Their enmity is undying: "If evil spirits could perceive that they were associated with man, and yet that they were spirits separate from him, and if

they could flow in into the things of his body, they would attempt by
a thousand means to destroy him; for they hate man with a deadly
hatred ..." The passage of greatest interest to Dr. Hesselius, which
he is reading at the very moment that Jennings's entrance interrupts
his absorption with the text, announces that "evil spirits, when seen
by other eyes than those of their infernal associates, present
themselves, by 'correspondence,' in the shape of the beast (*fera*)
which represents their particular lust and life, in aspect direful and
atrocious."

It is possible to read Le Fanu's story as basically a narrative of a
clergyman whose addiction to strong green tea leads to over-
stimulation of the nervous system and the conjuring-up of a spectral
monkey that seems increasingly real and diabolically dedicated to
driving him out of his mind. But the connection between Jennings's
intellectual pride and his spiritual undoing is crucial. When Dr.
Hesselius finishes reading this note about the *fera*, he is drawn into a
conversation with Jennings, the first topic of which is their mutual
interest in Swedenborg, and the second is Dr. Harley, "one of the
most eminent who had ever practised in England." Presumably this
is George Harley (1829–96), whose investigations of the nervous
system, among other pioneering research projects, led to high
honors and distinguished appointments. Jennings denounces him
as "one of the very greatest fools" he had ever met, "a *mere*
materialist," one whose mind is "paralytic" and "half dead." He
has consulted him about his own nervous disorder – in vain. He has,
in other words, no faith in modern medicine, because scientists like
Dr. Harley refuse to credit the possibility of the existence of powers
beyond their ken.

On a later occasion Jennings reveals that he has spent some four
years of his life on "the religious metaphysics of the ancients." This
topic is of great interest to Dr. Hesselius, who himself has published a
book on metaphysical medicine. He responds to Jennings's revelation: "I know ... the actual religion of educated and thinking
paganism, quite apart from symbolic worship? A wide and very
interesting field." Jennings responds that his labors have not been
good for the Christian mind. "Paganism," he continues, "is all
bound together in essential unity, and, with evil sympathy, their
religion involves their art, and both their manners ..." He has
become obsessed with his studies: "I wrote a great deal; I wrote late
at night. I was always thinking on the subject, walking about,
wherever I was, everywhere. It thoroughly infected me." The

infection derives from his investigation of a forbidden past, from free-thinking: "God forgive me!" The first time he encounters his "small black monkey," he is on his way to visit, in a very out-of-the-way section of the city, a collector of "some odd old books, German editions of mediaeval Latin," to indulge still further his taste for a subject which he knows to be "a degrading fascination and the Nemesis sure." He is, unmistakably, collaborating in his own destruction; his pride will bring him down. It does him no good to argue that his "bestial companion" can be explained (Dr. Harley must have thus diagnosed the problem) as "purely disease, a well-known physical affection, as distinctively as small-pox or neural-gia," or to turn to empirical knowledge for solace: "Doctors are all agreed on that, philosophy demonstrates it. I must not be a fool. I've been sitting up too late and I daresay my digestion is quite wrong, and, with God's help, I shall be all right, and this is but a symptom of nervous dyspepsia." But Jennings does not believe a word of this.

The Faustian compact – knowledge of God's design purchased at the expense of man's right to Heaven – has been variously interpreted in Western cultures, but two major versions dictate the direction of most dramatizations of the last four centuries. The first is the strongly orthodox retelling, by Christopher Marlowe, of Faustus's damnation. Faustus has renounced theology for human knowledge; he deserves the eternal damnation that awaits him at play's end, and he knows it; hence the failure of his efforts to call on the living Christ to save him before the final stroke of midnight. The second major version is Goethe's ringing affirmation of the right of man to investigate the laws which govern the universe ("*Es irrt der Mensch so lang er strebt*"); Goethe's Faust can be, and will be, saved; and by the eighteenth century it was well understood that God could forgive the sinner if his primary sin consisted of aspiration toward a higher state of *knowledge*.

Since Goethe's version has been more congenial to modern assumptions, it is striking that Le Fanu's curate takes us back to the older, more dogmatic reading of the symbolic values inherent in the Faust legend. Jennings despairs because Harley's materialism fails to give spirit its proper rank (Dr. Hesselius, whom he meets too late for any real change in his destiny to take place, is the man he should have consulted in the first place), and because Harley is himself writ large. Jennings cannot believe in God as his "comfort and reliance" – these are the terms in Dr. Hesselius's prescription – or in the inability of the "brute" monkey to hurt him. He is beyond medicine, beyond dietary recommendations. After Jennings cuts his throat with his razor, Dr. Hesselius concludes his narrative with the melancholy observation, "My memory rejects the picture with incredulity and horror. Yet I know it is true. It is the story of the process of a poison, a poison which excites the reciprocal action of spirit and nerve, and paralyses the tissue that separates those cognate functions of the senses, the external and the interior. Thus we find strange bed-fellows, and the mortal and immortal prematurely make acquaintance." The echo of Swedenborgian doctrine, allied with a sternly doctrinaire denial of the possibility of Faust's redemption, bestows upon Le Fanu's version a peculiar power.

This particular story has a postscript of some importance to our understanding of the characterization of Dr. Hesselius. After all, Dr. Hesselius's proposed treatment of Mr. Jennings had not even begun before the tragic suicide occurred, and the narrator, for understandable reasons, did not want to accept responsibility for a failed cure. There had been no medical treatment, no laying-on of hands. Dr. Hesselius, a believer in some kind of arterial and venous circulation of fluid through the nerves, can accommodate his understanding of Powers beyond those which a Dr. Harley can accept, and argue that this fluid is material, spiritual, and changeable as a consequence of various abuses (drugs in general, green tea more specifically). The eye is the seat of exterior vision, the nervous tissue and brain of interior vision, of an "inner eye." That eye may be opened by delirium tremens; Jennings opened it by pursuit of the truth underlying religious mysteries in the pagan world; and, Dr. Hesselius informs us somberly, the case of Jennings was complicated by a totally different malady, "hereditary suicidal mania." It may be, as the narrator says, that Jennings had not yet bestowed upon him "his full and unreserved confidence." If he had, Dr. Hesselius is convinced that a treatment extending to a period of possibly two years would have sufficed to cure him ("I have not any doubt ..."). Patience, "a rational confidence in the physician": these are the "simple conditions" that will lead to an "absolutely certain" cure.

But Dr. Hesselius's confidence that a spectral illusion can be "no less simply curable than a cold in the head or a trifling dyspepsia" is not Le Fanu's, and the evidence supplied in all the stories of *In a Glass Darkly* denies the treatability of mental problems that originate in *hubris*, in ignorance of the proper limits that circumscribe human ambition. *We are too complacent in our conviction that we are situated upon the brink of an understanding of this universe.* Nor is the doctrine simply a commonplace of stories that seek to dignify their treatment of supernatural possibilities: it seems to be as deeply imbedded in 'The Room in the Dragon Volant," a novella which emphasizes rational explanations for seemingly eerie events, as in "Carmilla," that notorious progenitor of Bram Stoker's *Dracula*.

Mortis Imago is the name of the drug that the narrator of "The Room in the Dragon Volant" takes, unknowingly, in his wine (the Countess, whom he loves passionately, has entered into a conspiracy to murder him). The name also denotes a death of the illusion which has sustained the youth in his adventures during "the eventful year, 1815," when Englishmen, for the first time in a long while, are able to travel without fear on Continental roads. What is this illusion? It has to do with the right to fall in love with a mysterious and lovely lady; with a conviction that one's own pleasing appearance is talismanic; with a faith that God will protect the innocent. In one sense, the story is an attack on sentimental fiction that propagates the myth of love at first sight; Le Fanu makes clear, early in the narrative, that his hero is an ass to be so trusting, on so little proof, that those he encounters are what they say, or that his own wealth is a matter of indifference to others. The number of foolish, even dangerous pledges to which the hero (a Mr. R. Beckett of Berkeley Square) unthinkingly commits himself becomes rather staggering by story's end, and it is not necessary here to recapitulate the problems created by his naive behavior. A few matters may be cited, however, by which Le Fanu's assessment of his major character may be, in turn, judged: the fact that Mr. Beckett travels long distances with "two or three idle books," i.e., novels of dubious literary worth; his complacency ("'Alas! what a life it is!' I moralized, wisely," he remarks at one point); his dreaminess about "the wonderful eyes, the thrilling voice, the exquisite figure of the beautiful lady who had taken possession of my imagination," which prevents him from suspecting her husband's villainy, or her own conspiratorial role; his casual dismissal of advice warning him against rogues of Paris, and his all-too-ready admission of being in possession of a purse of thirty thousand pounds sterling; his over-indulgence in wines (which leads, at a later moment, to his being drugged by a not particularly subtle stratagem); his willingness to enter a quarrel between Colonel Gaillarde and the host of the *Belle Étoile* that does not concern him at all; his extraordinary series of misinterpretations of motives, characters, and relationships throughout. His heroics, as he admits to himself just before he takes the paralyzing cup of noyau, a fruit-flavored brandy liqueur, from the hand of the Countess de St. Alyre, were "unconsciously" founded upon the French school of love-making, and his behavior has, alas, been imitative of vile models in other ways. He has been deceived by others, but, first and foremost, he has deceived himself. Finally in possession of the knowledge that he should have acquired days, weeks earlier, he perceives how truly he has deserved being placed, prematurely, in a coffin designed for a "St. Amand": "I had myself been at the utmost pains to mystify inquiry, should my disappearance excite surmises, and had even written to my few correspondents in England to tell them that they were not to look for a letter from me for three weeks at least." If Monsieur Carmaignac, a detective, did not suddenly materialize as the Victorian version of a *deus ex machina*, armed with a search warrant, the coffin-lid would not have been unscrewed, and the hero would have enjoyed an early, terrible, and fatal lesson in the ways of sin. Le Fanu spares him nothing, even so: Mr. Beckett, who serves the prosecution as principal witness, hopes, in his largely uncorrupted innocence, that he might become, as a consequence of the role he plays in the trial that brings to justice the conspirators, "an object of considerable interest to Parisian society." Instead, to his mortification, he discovers that he has turned into the object of "a good-natured but contemptuous merriment," a *balourd*, a *benêt*, *un âne*, and that he figures "even in caricatures." He flees from Paris, and travels to Switzerland and Italy. "As the well-worn phrase goes, I was a sadder if not a wiser man."

The implication here is that Mr. Beckett may yet fall prey to new confidence-men and -women, because he knows, at story's end, that he does not have the self-assurance, and the knowledge of self, that might render superfluous the assistance of a Carmaignac. In a world of shadows and masks, where a hero can bamboozle himself and misjudge everything and everyone, love is treacherous, and the price exacted for it excessive. Le Fanu presents the story dispassionately; part of its skill lies in the hero's failure to understand fully the ways in which he has personally been responsible for the macabre climax to his infatuation for the Countess; a reader will learn more than Mr. Beckett about the symbolic relationship between sin and judgment.

The last story of *In a Glass Darkly*, "Carmilla," deals with vampirism. Le Fanu makes no attempt to explain, in realistic terms, the gloomy and affecting legends that he exploits. Dr. Hesselius's "rather elaborate note," attached to the manuscript, is not reproduced by his medical secretary, who promises, rather, that "It will form but one volume of the series of that extraordinary man's collected papers." Dr. Hesselius, however, has described the subject as "involving, not improbably, some of the profoundest arcana of our dual existence, and its intermediates."

Nevertheless, the story concludes with a learned disquisition on the nature of vampires. "The vampire," we are somberly told, "is, apparently, subject, in certain situations, to special conditions," and Baron Vordenburg confirms this view: "It is the nature of vampires to increase and multiply, but according to an ascertained and ghostly law ..." Superstitions about the vampire are widespread, but their acceptance or universality does not prove them true, and the narrator, a nineteen-year-old girl, does not presume to explain what she has personally witnessed and experienced save in terms of "the ancient and well-attested belief of the country." Legends have been investigated: "If human testimony, taken with every care and solemnity, judicially, before commissions innumerable, each consisting of many members, all chosen for integrity and intelligence, and constituting reports more voluminous perhaps than exist upon any one other class of cases, is worth anything, it is difficult to deny, or even to doubt, the existence of such a phenomenon as the vampire." Even so, the emphasis falls on human corruptibility; Le Fanu no more believes in vampires as *fact* than he does in spectral monkeys or lockjaw victims returned from the grave; and his allusions to the relevant "scholarship" (Baron Vordenburg owns copies of *Magia Posthua*, Phlegon's *de Mirabilibus*, Augustine's *de Curâ pro Mortuis*, and John Christofer Herenberg's *Philosophicae et Christianae Cogitationes de Vampiris*) should not distract a reader from the true subject matter of "Carmilla." Le Fanu's concern, as in all his narratives, is with the continuity between natural and supernatural modes of existence, and the strong emanations of corruption in human society.

To suggest that the victim of a vampire invites the attack is to say no more than that Le Fanu extends to human behavior a sense of its inherent potential for sexual perversion. "Carmilla" is a deeply disturbing story not because its central character sucks blood, but because the innocent eye ("I") of the story is drawn, almost without resistance, into a lesbian relationship with her. The stereotyped language of romantic love is used by Carmilla in ways never contemplated by Le Fanu's contemporary story-tellers: "You do not know how dear you are to me, or you could not think any confidence too great to look for ... You will think me cruel, very selfish, but love is always selfish; the more ardent the more selfish. How jealous I am you cannot know. You must come with me, loving me, to death; or else hate me, and still come with me, and *hating* me through death and after." Carmilla is "devoted" to her victim; and she has "strange paroxysms of languid adoration"; she gloats "with increasing ardour" the more the strength and spirits of the narrator wane. In the earliest period of Carmilla's relationship with her, she whispers rhapsodically, "In the rapture of my enormous humiliation I live in your warm life, and you shall die – die, sweetly die – into mine. I cannot help it; as I draw near to you, you, in your turn, will draw near to others, and learn the rapture of that cruelty, which yet is love ..." She embraces her beloved, and her lips "in soft kisses gently glow" upon the cheek of the young heroine. Carmilla holds her hand "with a fond pressure, renewed again and again," and blushes softly, gazing in her face "with languid and burning eyes, and breathing so fast that her dress rose and fell with the tumultuous respiration. It was like the ardour of a lover ..." This is not necessarily the language of soft-core pornography, despite its emphasis on "hot lips" and gentle caresses along the throat and neck. Le Fanu is dramatizing the heroine's partial willingness to be involved, despite her ill-defined feelings of suspicion: "In these mysterious moods," she writes from the vantage point of a full decade later, "I did not like her. I experienced a strange tumultuous excitement that was pleasurable, ever and anon mingled with a vague sense of fear and disgust. I had no distinct thoughts about her while such scenes lasted, but I was conscious of a love growing into adoration, and also of abhorrence. This I know is paradox, but I can make no other attempt to explain the feeling."

In this confession of emotional confusion there is more than the ingenuousness of a fictional heroine or the disingenuousness of a writer of fiction. Peter Penzoldt's belief that Le Fanu could not have recognized the lesbian love he was describing for what it was need not detain us, any more than the patronizing remarks made by other critics about scenes in Thomas Hardy's novels in which two women are sexually responsive to each other; Le Fanu, no less than Hardy, appreciated the perversity of this kind of relationship, and sought to make his moral point, at some risk because of the situation he was defining and the language he was employing; that point – consistent with earlier points made in the collection *In a Glass Darkly*, and in several stories in *Chronicles of Golden Friars* (1871) and *The Purcell*

Papers (1880) – has to do with the evil, nascent or flowering, within each man's soul.

Le Fanu's intention was certainly not to offend moral proprieties. A conventional way to treat "Carmilla" would be to discuss, yet one more time, its ties to other tales of vampirism written during the nineteenth century. But it is not perverse to think of "Carmilla" as a study in sexual abnormality rather than as another variant of Le Fanu's *revenants*, all of whom make the flesh creep. The story has been deliberately placed at the end of *In a Glass Darkly*. Its emphasis on erotic detail is deliberate, disturbing. Its familiarity with a wide range of vampire lore indicates that Le Fanu could well appreciate the novelty of his addition of a lesbian motif; no reference work in Baron Vordenburg's extensive library had even hinted at the victim's willingness to comply with the masturbatory fingerings of the vampire. The last chapter is also important because it demonstrates that the heroine – even after a sharp stake has been driven through Carmilla's heart, Carmilla's head has been struck off, Carmilla's body and head have been cremated, and the ashes have been "thrown upon a river and borne away" – cannot exorcise the demon, which is now (as in a sense it has always been) mentally conjured: "It was long before the terror of recent events subsided; and to this hour the image of Carmilla returns to memory with ambiguous alternations – sometimes the playful, languid, beautiful girl; sometimes the writhing fiend I saw in the ruined church; and often from a reverie I have started, fancying I heard the light step of Carmilla at the drawing-room door."

Le Fanu provides for his *revenants* a local habitation and a name. By means of framing devices – the collection of Francis Purcell, the parish priest of Drumcoolagh; the medical papers of Dr. Hesselius; the idyllic community of Golden Friars, which is carefully described before we move into the horrors of "The Haunted Baronet" – he suggests the plausibility of the environment, and identifies the motives of the narrator, as necessary preliminaries to the fiction itself. Above all, he traces connections between mind and matter, justifying their existence on Swedenborgian grounds. The disorder of the world may manifest itself in the life of a tormented curate, a retired sea-captain, or a young woman unaware of the strength of her own sexual needs; and the natural world is a dark, sinister complement to the mentally – and even morally – aberrant behavior of human beings.

For all the reasons thus far cited, Le Fanu's short stories are

superior to most stories written by his contemporaries and successors. Their high quality becomes more evident when they are
contrasted with the writings of other tellers of ghost tales.[6] The first
thing to be noted is the ordinariness of the individuals to whom
remarkable things happen in stories written by Le Fanu's rivals.
Dickens, in "The Story of the Bagman's Uncle," one of the semi-
detachable narratives of *The Posthumous Papers of the Pickwick Club*,
describes the uncle who passes through incredible and romantic
adventures: "I am particular in describing how my uncle walked up
the middle of the street, with his thumbs in his waistcoat pockets,
gentlemen," says the bagman, "because, as he often used to say (and
with great reason too) there is nothing at all extraordinary in this
story, unless as you distinctly understand at the beginning that he
was not by any means of a marvellous or romantic turn." Mrs.
Oliphant, in "The Open Door" (one of her *Stories of the Seen and the
Unseen*) introduces us to a father who loves his son; because his son is
terrified by voices in the avenue leading to Brentwood, a home near
Edinburgh, everything – including the father's willingness to
undergo strange and terrible adventures – derives from the basic fact
of his affection for the child. The "hero" of Bulwer Lytton's "The
Haunters and the Haunted" is not driven by a sense of destiny, nor
do the weird events recounted seem to have much bearing on the
kind of life he has already led. He becomes involved simply because
(as he puts it) there is nothing that he should like better than to sleep
in a haunted house.

The divorce of a writer's sense of the importance of character from
the events which befall the leading figure of the story has enormous
implications for the capacity of imagined events to challenge a
reader's imagination *after* the reading has been completed. Malcolm
Malcolmson, the student of "Harmonical Progression, Permuta-
tions and Combinations, and Elliptic Functions" in Bram Stoker's
"The Judge's House," has no connection with the events that took
place years before in the room where he is finally to die. He has led
(so far as we can tell) a blameless life. Why he should have been
selected for this horrifying fate is not only unclear, the question
seems not to have interested Stoker at all. Le Fanu would have
suggested the inevitability of the young man's coming to the house;
something in his past, in himself, in Le Fanu's philosophy of life,
would have stressed connections between his earlier behavior and
his final punishment. And, we may rest assured, the house, which
Stoker describes as being desolate, isolated, old, rambling, heavy-

built, and fortified in its appearance, would have become a convenient symbol of the larger ruin surrounding it, the city of London itself.

"The Trial for Murder," a story written in the main by Charles Allston Collins and reworked by Charles Dickens for the Christmas Number of *All the Year Round*, 1865 (subsequently printed in *Dr. Marigold's Prescriptions*), may be taken as a reasonably successful example of a Victorian ghost story. A bachelor who heads a bank department feels "slightly dyspeptic" (his "renowned" doctor assures him that his real state of health justifies no stronger description), and cannot explain why he takes an extraordinary interest in the newspaper account of a brutal murder. The discovery of the body

had been made in a bedroom, and, when I laid down the paper, I was aware of a flash – rush – flow – I do not know what to call it, – no word I can find is satisfactorily descriptive, – in which I seemed to see that bedroom passing through my room, like a picture impossibly painted on a running river. Though almost instantaneous in its passing, it was perfectly clear; so clear that I distinctly, and with a sense of relief, observed the absence of the dead body from the bed.

The bank manager subsequently sees from his chamber window two men walking. Their faces (though unremarkable) are distinct and unforgettable. Some time later he, along with his servant, sees again one of the two men; his "face was the colour of impure wax," and both know that this is the murdered man described in the newspaper account. The long arm of coincidence reaches out: the banker is called to serve upon a jury at a session of the Central Criminal Court at the Old Bailey, and (almost needless to say) he serves as foreman of the jury that tries, and ultimately finds guilty, the man charged of murder, the second of the two men whom he has seen from his window. The prisoner, who unsuccessfully attempted to have his lawyer challenge the banker's right to sit on the jury, knows from the beginning that he will be found guilty. When the Judge asks him whether he has anything to say before sentence of death should be passed upon him, he responds: "*My Lord, I knew I was a doomed man, when the Foreman of my Jury came into the box. My Lord, I knew he would never let me off, before I was taken, he somehow got to my bedside in the night, woke me, and put a rope round my neck.*"

Collins and Dickens have sought to chill the reader's blood, and no doubt for most readers the story succeeds. The astonishing events of the trial – during which the ghost of the murdered man addresses itself to whoever is speaking, and saws "frightfully ... at its severed throat" in a way that demoralizes jurors, lawyers, and judge – are described in the most matter-of-fact, naturalistic diction. But the story never moves beyond the level of sensation and shock. The authors provide no clue as to why the banker should have been afforded his remarkable vision. There is no lucid or even imaginable connection between the banker and the murderer – save that glimpse from the window, and the appearance of a ghost in the banker's sitting-room – before the trial begins. Le Fanu would have told us more, and most likely would have suggested the involvement of the banker in the guilt of the murderer.

For, ultimately, Le Fanu's stories are about the sharing of guilt, and the need for our recognizing responsibility for the doom which overtakes us (and which, for the most part, we may not evade). Le Fanu dreamed again and again of the fall of a house, and of the death of the dreamer. In this sense we may see something of England's responsibility – more precisely, that of the Ascendancy class – for having ruined Ireland. Such an interpretation is too narrow, even if it enjoys a certain vogue among Irish literary historians. As I have suggested earlier, Le Fanu's anger at the over-optimistic assumptions of the Enlightenment counts for a great deal. But the primary distinction of his subject-matter is that it involves us all, and it refuses to release us from a shared responsibility for sin.

3

Charles Dickens: establishing rapport with the public

Although some of Dickens's short stories have achieved the sort of popularity that normally is reserved for tales told in a nursery – we cannot remember becoming first acquainted with Ebenezer Scrooge, he has *always* been there – the reputation of Dickens has not benefited greatly from the shorter fictions of his crowded career. Many of these stories were introduced by elaborate prologues, and included characters who did not appear in the main body of the narratives. These characters might or might not reappear in the coda that Dickens occasionally – not always – supplied. He often constructed elaborate linkages between stories in Christmas issues of *Household Words* and *All the Year Round*. Yet, when the stories were anthologized, these linkages often disappeared, and elements of the stories promptly became mysterious, even inscrutable.

Dickens himself worked without a clear definition of the genre. Deborah A. Thomas, author of a fine critical study, *Dickens and the Short Story* (1982), believes that she can identify approximately seventy-five distinct pieces written wholly by Dickens (not counting embryonic stories such as those in "Nurse's Stories") which fall into the category of the short story as he conceived it;[1] but honesty compels her to admit that he changed his mind, more than once, about what a short story was.

Dickens seems to have carried over from the eighteenth century a concept of the short story as a marketable commodity that filled space in magazines and newspapers. In the latter part of that century, the practice of printing a short story in such media had proved less expensive than providing hard covers for collections of stories. As already noted, publishers, editors, and printers were exploiting a weakness in the law governing the stamp tax: a sheet and a half of letterpress was better than a sheet, because it minimized the tax. Moreover, fiction (whatever its length) attracted readers.

Stories printed in this mode did not have high literary status, nor could their authors aspire to immortality. As Robert L. Patten has observed, the newspaper that printed fiction may have been discrete bibliographically, but the stories were not. "They were considered fillers and stopped at any point necessary to fill the issue, even in mid sentence."[2]

Dickens made no clear statement as to what constituted a suitable length for a short story, but left behind a few clues. Rather than allow an editor to trim a contribution to the needed dimensions, he wrote to fill the vacant space, and did so in terms of a number of pages for which he had contracted well in advance. He wrote sixteen pages for every monthly issue of *Bentley's Miscellany* in 1837 and 1838. Most of these pages were installments of *Oliver Twist*. If occasionally an installment fell short, a "stray chapter" by Boz took up the slack. *Nicholas Nickleby*, serially published, included one story that digressed from the main narrative. Dickens, working under pressure, had to supply five "slips" for this tale. (A slip was a long piece of paper, normally used for proofs that would be revised before being made up into pages.)

A brief review of his short-story interests will clarify the question of when he wrote the major number of such stories. Between 1833 and 1835 Dickens wrote eight tales that he was later to collect in *Sketches by Boz*; additional short selections, written in the autumn of 1835, were grouped under the general, and perhaps not very illuminating, heading of "Characters" for the same volume. In 1836 he wrote four pieces – two farcical situations ("The Great Winglebury Duel" and "The Tuggses at Ramsgate") and two melodramatic exercises ("The Black Veil" and "The Drunkard's Death"), and these were added to *Sketches by Boz*. The nine tales of *Pickwick Papers* had been written and published independently (most of them in 1836) before they were incorporated into the novel. In the two years 1837 and 1838 Dickens wrote a large number of difficult-to-classify short pieces for *Bentley's Miscellany*, and in 1840 he attempted to establish *Master Humphrey's Clock* as his own miscellany. Despite his valiant efforts to provide a suitable matrix for short pieces, the public soon let Dickens know of its displeasure, and only three short tales, plus a number of shapeless and meandering ruminations that stressed the right of an author to indulge in flights of fancy, were written for *Master Humphrey's Clock*; most of the space in the miscellany was given over to *The Old Curiosity Shop* and *Barnaby Rudge*.

Dickens wrote very few short stories for almost a decade (between 1841 and 1849, to be specific) after *Master Humphrey's Clock* collapsed. His concentration on novels, and on satisfying his public,

5   Portrait of Charles Dickens by D. Maclise, frontispiece to the first edition of
Nicholas Nickleby, 1839

paid off in spectacular successes, one after another. But these are also the years in which one characteristic by-product of his longer narratives appealed to a very large audience indeed: the *Christmas Books* that came out in 1843, 1844, 1845, 1846, and 1848. (I think of these as long short stories, or novellas.) A shift of some significance occurred when, in 1850, Dickens contributed to *Household Words* the first of his holiday pieces (later to be collected as *Christmas Stories*, though the name is misleading inasmuch as many of these stories are remote from that particular season of the year). These contributions appeared regularly until 1860, overlapping, in 1859, the first of a series of contributions to *All the Year Round*. The intricacies of Dickens's collaboration with Wilkie Collins – a team-writing operation that contributed to the huge success of the Christmas numbers of both periodicals between 1856 and 1860 – have been ably delineated by more than one biographer and need not be reviewed here. Nevertheless, the exact extent of Dickens's contributions to anonymously printed stories is not known, and it is quite likely that, over the years, he has been given credit for selections in *Household Words* and *All the Year Round* that he had very little to do with. Add to this problem the fact that some contributors deliberately imitated his mannerisms – George Augustus Sala was notorious for his skill in doing so – and the number of genuine Dickens stories becomes even more indeterminate.

Dickens did not keep a consistent attitude toward his short stories from first to last. He regarded (for example) the seventeen tales in *Sketches by Boz* as being no better than "sketches," "little pictures of life and manners as they really are"; they were an "experiment" at best. In his Preface to the first edition of the First Series (February 1836), he said that they constituted a "pilot balloon," and even though several of the sketches had already received a favorable reception, he begged the indulgence of his audience. The second edition (August 1836) carried a prefatory note belittling the sketches as "little outlines," though he did add that they necessarily preceded the production of "fresh sketches," and of fiction of a higher grade. When the first Collected Edition appeared, Dickens added a note, dated May 15, 1839, which began, "The following pages contain the earliest productions of their Author, written from time to time to meet the exigencies of a newspaper or a magazine." Dickens honestly believed that these sketches were too minor to claim the permanent affections of his public. In October 1850, he wrote, as part of his preface to the first Cheap Edition:

The whole of these sketches were written and published, one by one, when I was a very young man. They were collected and re-published while I was still a very young man; and sent into the world with all their imperfections (a good many) on their heads.

They comprise my first attempts at authorship – with the exception of certain tragedies achieved at the mature age of eight or ten, and represented with great applause to overflowing nurseries. I am conscious of their often being extremely crude and ill-considered, and bearing obvious marks of haste and inexperience; particularly in that section of the present volume which is comprised under the general head of Tales.[3]

More widely read than the "tales" by Boz were the nine stories contained in *Pickwick Papers*, a novel written in monthly parts. At first the installments were intended for a twenty-four-page periodical, to which would be added four plates. After the suicide of Robert Seymour, the well-known illustrator, publication of additional numbers seemed like a high risk. Of the thousand copies of Part I ordered for an initial press run, only four hundred copies were bound; the rate of sales did not seem to justify binding more. Not until the fourth number, with the appearance of Sam Weller, did public interest ignite; and success was assured on a very large scale thereafter. Dickens himself had never faltered in his enthusiasm for continuing the venture. The writing of two sheets each month not only guaranteed him financial solvency, but introduced a new mode of presenting novels to the public: serial parts, each part consisting of thirty-two pages and two illustrations. These elements were to become standard in the publishing trade from the 1830s on.

Dickens's relationship with the publisher Richard Bentley was to prove unhappy, though it lasted for two years (1837–8). (Dickens resigned his editorship of *Bentley's Miscellany* as of January 31, 1839.) Only one of the five original pieces that he published here may be considered a true short story: "Public Life of Mr. Tulrumble Once Mayor of Mudfog," printed in the issue of January 1837. Dickens, incredibly busy during this period, was absorbed not only by the details of reading, judging, and preparing manuscripts for the press, but by the novels *Oliver Twist* and *Nicholas Nickleby*; his editing of an autobiography of Grimaldi the clown; and the writing (anonymously) of *Sketches of Young Gentlemen* (1838).

The launching of *Master Humphrey's Clock* in 1840 signaled a strong desire on Dickens's part to turn away from novels issued in twenty numbers, as well as to earn more money from weekly parts sold for three pence and monthly parts sold for a shilling. The weekly part was designed to contain twelve pages of original material, while another four pages would be given over to the title and to advertisements. But the first number, with a printing of 70,000 copies, was over-optimistically budgeted. Sales fell immediately by one-third. Dickens knew that readers wanted more illustrations, but these cost dearly, and – in addition – he was becoming over-extended with miscellaneous financial obligations. His contractual arrangements with Chapman and Hall, the publishers, were rapidly becoming over-complicated. Between April 4, 1840, and December 4, 1841, eighty-eight weekly numbers appeared. When he made his crucial decision to discontinue *Master Humphrey's Clock*, its circulation was hovering around 30,000 copies per week. But it had served its purpose; here Dickens first printed three tales, "A Confession Found in a Prison in the Times of Charles the Second," "First Night of the Giant Chronicles," and "Mr. Pickwick's Tale."

Dickens plunged into the writing of *American Notes* and *Martin Chuzzlewit*. He was disappointed by a visit to the United States, which did not live up to the expectations he had cherished. His *Notes* irritated more than a few Americans, who believed that he had imposed upon their hospitality and betrayed it immediately upon his return to England.

His next forays into short-story territory were the *Christmas Books*. These small volumes were similar to the story-books that he had read during his childhood: fairy-tales, condensed versions of plays, and miniaturized novels (many of them eighteenth century). Dickens remembered them, and to some extent imitated them, as he wrote *A Christmas Carol*, *The Chimes*, *The Cricket on the Hearth*, *The Battle of Life*, and *The Haunted Man and the Ghost's Bargain*. Christmas invited thoughts of love and good cheer; it also justified stories of reformed human nature. The first, *A Christmas Carol*, was written on commission; Chapman and Hall, like Dickens, thought of its publication as a means of recouping expenses incurred by the disappointing sales record of *Martin Chuzzlewit*. The idea of a *Christmas Book* did not originate with Dickens, though *Pickwick*, some six years earlier, had included a song in verse called the "Christmas Carol" (sung by Mr. Wardle) in the episode recounting the adventures of the Pickwickians at Dingley Dell. Other authors had written especially for the Christmas trade. Publishers were keenly aware of the advantages to be derived from marketing stories aimed at the special audience frequenting bookstores just before the holiday. But Dickens knew that he was writing something special – his emotional paroxysms during the process of composition foreshadowed equally intense fits of laughter and crying in the writing of later works – and he was pleased by the number of copies sold. Sales of *A Christmas Carol* continued for seven editions, well into May of the following year (1844). *The Chimes* came out next, in a handsome format like its predecessor, and sold in generous numbers; as a result, the concept of still another *Christmas Book* came early to him. In May 1844, he was thinking of starting a weekly that would be called *The Cricket*, after the "cheerful creature that chirrups on the Hearth." Even though John Forster, who thought it chancy, soon discouraged him, the name became part of the title of his next occasional publication designed for Christmas book-buyers. *The Cricket on the Hearth* sold even better than its two predecessors. A commentary on both the parlous condition of copyright and the lively interest in plays based on popular works may be derived from the fact that seventeen dramatized versions – by divers hands – reached the theatres within one month after release of the book.

The literary quality of the *Christmas Books* deteriorated even as sales increased. *The Battle of Life* – which Dickens had had enormous difficulty in writing, partly because he needed the bustle of London to stimulate his imagination (he was living on the Continent at the time), partly because he was going through fits of moodiness over a number of disappointments and rebuffs – outsold all that had gone before in the way of *Christmas Books*. The final volume in the series, *The Haunted Man and the Ghost's Bargain | A Fancy for Christmas Time*, appeared after a year's hiatus. Many book-buyers had turned to authors of other *Christmas Books* during the holiday season of 1847; as a result, the book published in 1848 was popular and profitable, but less successful than *The Battle of Life*. Dickens, about to begin the serialization of *David Copperfield*, perhaps his most autobiographical novel, and of a certainty one that meant much to him over and beyond its potential economic return, gave up, for some time, the writing of short stories. He believed that the idea of the *Christmas Book*, at least in his case, had worn itself out.[4] In his preface to the first Cheap Edition (September 1852), he commented dryly, without pushing the point, that "The narrow space within which it was necessary to confine these Christmas Stories when they were originally published, rendered their construction a matter of some difficulty, and almost necessitated what is peculiar in their machinery." He added that he had not attempted to work out detailed characterizations "within such limits, believing that it could not succeed." Each story, then, was "a whimsical kind of masque which the good humour of the season justified ...."[5]

Most of Dickens's short stories from the 1850s on appeared in *Household Words* and its successor, *All the Year Round*. To be more precise, Dickens assumed full responsibility for the major periodical *Household Words* on March 30, 1850, saw it through nineteen volumes, and began publication of *All the Year Round* in 1859. He was not the first editor to make a success of a weekly, retailing at twopence, that printed original work: the *London Journal, Eliza Cook's Journal*, and the *Family Herald* predated *Household Words*; sold for a sum so small that almost anyone could afford copies; and printed fiction of a quality comparable to most of what appeared in Dickens's periodical. But Dickens, along with his assistant editor W. H. Wills, was remarkably successful in his insistence on a high moral tone, literary merit, and an awareness of contemporary social problems in the fiction of his contributors. He achieved – all things considered – considerable distinction as an editor. These were the periodicals, after all, which first published *Hard Times, North and South, A Tale of Two Cities, Great Expectations, The Woman in White*, and *A Strange Story*; their importance in the history of the Victorian novel has long been recognized. Novels and short stories benefited from Dickens's desire to bring technical skills to the description of "all familiar things, but especially those repellant on the surface," as John Forster put it, connecting them with "the sympathies and graces of the imagination."[6] Dickens could count on the appearance of his short stories in a journal with an assured circulation of 40,000 copies a week. He wrote a series of Christmas stories (later to be collected under that title) for the Christmas numbers of *Household Words* between 1850 and 1859, and for the Christmas numbers of *All the Year Round* between 1859 and 1867. Some of these stories were written in collaboration with Wilkie Collins (1856–60), though it is useful to remember, when reading the claims of those who over-stress the extent of Collins's contributions, that Dickens edited a full eighteen years of Christmas numbers, most of them without Collins's assistance; that Collins was responsible primarily for sections of the framework used by Dickens rather than for the narratives themselves; and that Collins made his most important contribution, *No Thoroughfare*, to the Christmas number of 1867. There was no Christmas number in 1868. Dickens, weary of having his own writing "swamped by that of other people,"[7] had come to the end of one of the longer roads in his career; but before he did, he had written twenty-two stories. Only two of them – "The Lazy Tour of Two Idle Apprentices" and *No Thoroughfare* – benefited from the imaginative contribution of Collins.

Stories contributed to the Christmas numbers did not necessarily deal with the holiday season. Between 1862 and 1866 Dickens wrote a number of narratives that seemed designed primarily for platform performance; they have often been collected under the heading "Dramatic Monologues." They include "Somebody's Luggage," "Mrs. Lirriper's Lodgings," "Mrs. Lirriper's Legacy," "Doctor Marigold's Prescriptions," and "Mugby Junction."

By the time Dickens died in 1870, he had written fourteen major novels, and a major fraction of *Edwin Drood*; led a strenuous private life; and given a series of dramatic readings that (more than any other single factor) ruined his health. His short stories, though they would have sufficed for lesser talents, were evidently by-products, and on occasions only filler materials, as in *Bentley's Miscellany*. Dickens did not regard them as embryonic novels; what he set out to accomplish in each case, he usually achieved. The space allowed him permitted neither rounded characterization nor complicated plotting. No Victorian author was more conscious of the precise number of printed lines that a manuscript converted into. It affected his pay. If he exceeded the length contracted for, he incurred extra type-setting costs. Moreover, he might upset the rhythmically scheduled climaxes of serially published narratives.

Dickens probably learned most from the difficulties that he encountered with the installments of *Nicholas Nickleby*. These were much more severe than anything he had encountered in preparing his earlier publications for the press. They dramatized the dangers of falling behind, of re-writing manuscripts at the galley-stage, and of interfering with the plans of printers as well as publishers. He also noted the penalties his tardiness cost him so far as American publishers were concerned.

The relationship of length to available space was underscored every day that he worked as an editor. Dickens's skill in subdividing Mrs. Gaskell's *North and South* into suitable lengths for serialized installments in *Household Words* was a significant element in the instantaneous success of that novel. He improved Bulwer Lytton's *A Strange Story* by persuading its author not to attach a "supplementary chapter" to it. (In a more famous turn-around, Bulwer Lytton persuaded Dickens to alter the ending of *Great Expectations*.) Even so, he occasionally encountered problems that he did not solve satisfactorily. The length of Wilkie Collins's *The Woman in White* proved excessive when the novel was printed in *All the Year Round*, and Dickens, somewhat embarrassed, was obliged to print its last installment in the same issue (August 18, 1860) as the first installment of Charles Lever's *A Day's Ride: A Life's Romance*, an act which unbalanced the contents unduly in favor of fiction.

What, then, may serve as useful generalizations for Dickens's short stories? Their lengths varied remarkably over the years. Dickens had no ideal length, or average length, in mind. The *Christmas Books* averaged 35,000 words. Other "short" stories were fairly lengthy; some sketches, as in "The Uncommercial Traveller," filled only a few pages. Dickens incorporated several short stories within longer works, preparing for their inclusion by elaborate prologues, commenting on their meaning in only slightly less elaborate epilogues. (This generalization is as true of *Master Humphrey's Clock* and the narratives prepared for the Christmas issues of *Household Words* and *All the Year Round* as it is of *Pickwick Papers*.) Dickens, who lavished energy on ways and means of connecting a short story with the personality of the story-teller, considered the Christmas issues of his periodicals to be integrated wholes; the contributions of many different authors were designed to be read together, to be thought of as book-length *units*.

A corollary observation, not so obvious that it should be passed over, is that Dickens wrote as many short stories as he did because he was fascinated by the Christmas season, a time of year when short-story collections were popular items in bookstores and on railway stalls. A large proportion of his stories – fully half – deal with the month of December. Dickens saw in the Christmas season an opportunity to dramatize the replacement of true values for false, a symbolism of regeneration. Because Christ had once come to earth, character reformation was now possible. The *Christmas Books* exhibit a stronger sense of structure because, as allegories, they show us in vivid detail human beings rising from the depths. Chapter headings indicate, from the start, a sense of direction, as when the Three Spirits are named one by one before a final section entitled "The End of It" (*A Christmas Carol*), or when "The Gift Bestowed" precedes "The Gift Diffused" and "The Gift Reversed" (*The Haunted Man*).

Dickens did not write short stories primarily as a means of changing pace from working on full-length novels that might take years to complete. He wrote short stories when he thought his public wanted them; he stopped writing them when he believed they preferred novels; he began again when he found a suitable format in the *Christmas Books*. My most important generalization stresses the conviction, on Dickens's part, that his readers' wishes had to be respected.

Sketches by Boz, as the title announced, consisted of a series of sketches of young gentlemen and of young couples that were "illustrative of every-day life and every-day people." (In actual practice, however, such sketches were less than half of the collected pieces.) Even in his first book Dickens begged the indulgence of his public:

If any further excuse be wanted for adding this book to the hundreds which every season produces, the Author may be permitted to plead the favourable reception, which several of the following sketches received, on their original appearance in different periodicals. In behalf of the remainder he can only entreat the kindness and favour of the public: his object has been to present little pictures of life and manners as they really are, and should they be approved of, he hopes to repeat his experiment with increased confidence, and on a more extensive scale.[8]

Doffing one's cap was common enough in notes attached to works presented to the public. Nevertheless, Dickens's sincerity was patent. He felt himself obligated to his public, which encouraged him by "patronage and approval"; which "stimulated him to fresh efforts, by ... liberality and praise"; and which deserved all the credit if indeed he produced new works of fiction of "a higher grade." Hungering for approval, he would not willingly offend. Such an attitude, of course, circumscribed his subject-matter, since his stories were to be published in periodicals read by well-defined constituencies; furthermore, it concentrated his attention on the entertainment value of his shorter fiction to the exclusion of almost every other value. When the public expressed displeasure at the direction his art was taking (the stories of *Master Humphrey's Clock* seemed to be replacing his interest in the production of more novels like *Pickwick* and *Nickleby*) and turned away from his new periodical, Dickens wasted little time in stopping the pendulum: "My task is done ..." He meant that never again would he misinterpret, by choice or inadvertence, the preferences of his readers.

A closer look at "The Stroller's Tale," one of the interpolated narratives of *Pickwick Papers*, may help to underscore the value that Dickens placed on maintaining the best of relationships with his public. It is, in one obvious sense, the story of the final moments of a clown, too fond of alcohol, whose career as a pantomime actor ends in a back room of a one-storey house built above a coal-shed. His death agonies are those of a man suffering from delirium tremens.

He accuses his wife of harboring an intention of murdering him; he remembers happier days as he recites doggerel verse; he recoils from imagined spectres. In a final paroxysm he rises up, to seat himself in bed; clutches the Stroller (the narrator) by the shoulder; tries unavailingly to speak; and falls back dead. No more than a sketch, really, to which a modest amount of detail has been added. Yet Dickens thought highly of it, and quoted the judgment of some of his literary friends, that it would create "considerable sensation." This was the story that led to a quarrel with Seymour (who was angered by the new direction taken by the longer story of Pickwick), and finally to Seymour's suicide; it was also the story which led to Dickens's assumption of responsibility for the details of publication. Never again was he to be thought of as a handy man with serial installments cut to the proper length, and flowing sedately round the accompanying plates.

Few readers – and even fewer critics – share Dickens's high estimate of the story's merits. The previous history of the dying man has not been hinted at, much less developed. A reader has difficulty in determining how much sympathy he is supposed to feel for an actor who has voluntarily drunk himself to death. Even the Stroller does not pretend that his tale has anything marvelous to commend it to anyone else's attention. As he announces in his prologue, "Want and sickness are too common in many stations of life to deserve more notice than is usually bestowed on the most ordinary vicissitudes of human nature."

Why, then, did Dickens write it? To be sure, drunkenness is a recurring theme in his fiction. "The Drunkard's Death" was written not many months away from the time of composition of "The Stroller's Tale." It appeared in the second series of *Sketches by Boz*, and bears remarkable similarities in theme and tone. An inability to control one's life – to make rational choices – may have been feared by Dickens more than even the prospect of financial failure. Distortions of autobiographical data may be marked in all the tales of *Pickwick*. Edgar Johnson (who does not think highly of any of them) has assessed their importance as lying not in their being "exercises in a conventional form," but rather in the fact that "they spring from emotional experience [that Dickens] has been unable either to dismiss or to get into perspective."[9]

The story is about an artist who fails, and has peculiar interest. "Dismal Jemmy," the Stroller, has reminded Mr. Pickwick, Mr. Winkle, Mr. Snodgrass, Mr. Jingle, and Mr. Tupman that lights and music are illusions that make the stage so wonderful; without them, there is little real "to live or care for." There is the old terrifying chasm between appearance and reality: "To be before the footlights is like sitting at a grand court show, and admiring the silken dresses of the gaudy throng – to be behind them is to be the people who make that finery, uncared for and unknown, and left to sink or swim, to starve or live, as fortune wills it." Dickens supplies us with some information about the brief engagements of actors who are taken on for spectacles with limited runs; these engagements are not enough to constitute a living; not enough, at any rate, to finance an appetite for drinking that has already ruined the actor's constitution. The protagonist of Dickens's tale was sufficiently talented, in his prime, to earn a good salary; but those days have long since gone. When the Stroller meets him, after having lost sight of him for some time, he is startled to see the actor dressed for the pantomime: his face besmeared with thick white paint, the head grotesquely ornamented, the "long skinny hands, rubbed with white chalk." Much of his deathbed raving has to do with his obligation to the theatre and the public house. "It was evening, he fancied; he had a part to play that night; it was late, and he must leave home instantly. Why did they hold him, and prevent his going? – he should lose the money – he must go." Tossing and turning on the bed from which he will never depart alive, he begins to act: "He rose in bed, drew up his withered limbs, and rolled about in uncouth positions; he was acting – he was at the theatre. A minute's silence, and he murmured the burden of some roaring song. He had reached the old house at last ..."

Dickens is haunted by the image of an entertainer who, lacking self-control, loses his audience; the pantomime actor's skills have no longer a commercial market; he is disoriented, lonely, loveless, and perhaps unlovable; the poignance of his final moments is related to the discovery that his occupation is gone. The tale deals with a fear, never wholly absent in Dickens, that his public might turn away from him.

It ends, as we have seen, with melodrama: a choked death-rattle in the throat. Mr. Pickwick does not even enjoy the opportunity to react, with an opinion, to what Dickens – rather slightingly – calls an "anecdote." Three officers enter the room and interrupt Pickwick at the very moment that he opens his mouth. The major narrative-line resumes, and his remarks, "which would have enlightened the world, if not the Thames," are never uttered.

Dickens's short stories – when first they appear – are brief but suggestive, rich in social sympathies, and marvelously fresh in detail. However, most of the *Sketches by Boz* look like preliminary drafts for something more substantial that will be worked up at a later time. "The Pawnbroker's Shop," collected in the First Series, may be taken as typical of approximately fifty such efforts. We first see a "low, dirty-looking, dusty" shop near Drury Lane; Dickens generalizes about its function, differentiates between kinds of similar-looking shops, lists the contents of this specific shop, and moves in closer to examine the human beings he is about to set in motion. These include a pawnbroker, who has "curly black hair, diamond ring, and double silver watchguard"; "an unshaven, dirty, sottish-looking fellow" who strikes an urchin for accidentally stepping on his toe; and "a slipshod woman, with two flat-irons in a little basket," who condemns him for beating his wife in drunken rages, and "his own child too, to make her more miserable." Periodically Dickens inserts stage directions to indicate the manner of speaking "(loud) ... (rather louder.) ... (louder still; women of this class are always sympathetic, and work themselves into a tremendous passion on the shortest notice.)" Four more women complete the cast: a mother and daughter who lack money and suffer from "the coldness of old friends – the stern refusal of some, and the still more galling compassion of others"; and two prostitutes who find themselves increasingly attracted to the mother and daughter's painful case. "There are strange chords in the human heart, which will lie dormant through years of depravity and wickedness, but which will vibrate at last ..."

The sketch breaks off when one of the prostitutes bursts into tears. Dickens poses a number of rhetorical questions that wonder about the probable (or certain) fate of the mother, daughter, and prostitutes. A moment in time, no more. A straightforward account of what a hovel devoted to commercial transactions looks like. The seven characters fulfill representative functions. There is little development of theme, and the sketch wanders amiably – readably – to a final sentence that suggests Dickens is uncertain as to what his main plot should be. (None of the rhetorical questions has been anticipated by earlier sections of the sketch.)

With the *Christmas Books*, however, Dickens took giant steps forward, because these stories are fully developed within a pre-determined space. We can take one of them – *The Chimes* – as typical

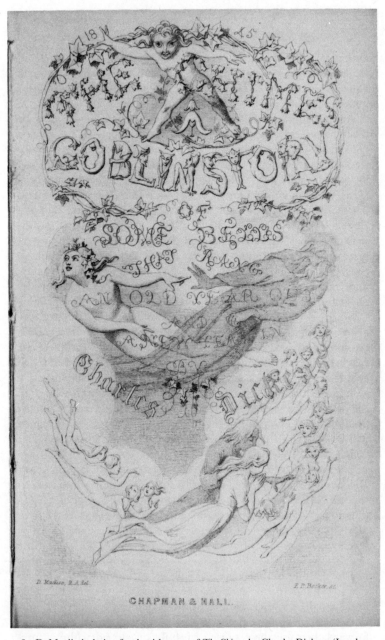

6   D. Maclise's design for the title page of *The Chimes* by Charles Dickens (London: Chapman & Hall, 1845, 9th edition)

of all the others. Dickens read it on December 3, 1844, to ten friends at Lincoln's Inn (the drawing by Daniel Maclise, commemorating the occasion, shows Dickens with light radiating from his head). The occasion acquainted Dickens with the full power of his own dramatic talents; the admiration of his auditors at this reading became the justification, in later years, for his undertaking a series of readings that eventually destroyed his health. *The Chimes* was a more ambitious story than *A Christmas Carol*, which had preceded it. Still it was not short; it contained a number of bathetic elements that were noted even by Dickens's contemporaries; and its use of the dream convention to suggest that the real world was somehow more benevolent than the one in which Alderman Cute, Sir Joseph Bowley, and Mr. Filey operate unhindered by any consideration of compassion for the poor suggested, perhaps a little ominously, that Dickens had become complacent about his particular means of solving narrative difficulties.

One may not speak of set scenes as if Dickens had in mind, from the beginning, a clear sense of where the adventures of Trotty Veck, the ticket-porter, might lead. But as an indictment of social attitudes rather than of hard-hearted individuals, *The Chimes* marks a crucial point in the evolution of Dickens's understanding of what had gone wrong in nineteenth-century life. Sir Peter Laurie, the original inspiration of Alderman Cute, is only slightly less outrageous in his language about putting suicide "down" than Dickens's character. Dickens is taking aim at elements of society, at the Laurie class, at the grim economists of the John Ramsey McCulloch variety (McCulloch was notorious for restating the views of Ricardo and Adam Smith in unqualified language), at the cold and unimaginative businessmen who presume to speak for England; and is doing so with more energy and passion than that with which he had attacked any of his earlier villains – whom he had treated fairly consistently as individuals.

Trotty Veck, because he serves as the hero of a *Christmas Book*, has to be saved from erroneous opinions: e.g., poor people "seem to be dreadful things," "to give a deal of trouble," and to be always "complained of and guarded against." Perhaps, Toby muses even before he eats his meal of hot potato and tripe, the poor are not entitled to a New Year at all. Unable to cope with the "Facts and Figures" of Alderman Cute and Mr. Filer, Toby, more than sixty years old, is hopelessly depressed: "Let me die!" His visit to Sir Joseph Bowley, to deliver the Justice's letter, does nothing to reassure him of his own right to exist, because Sir Joseph informs him, "You needn't trouble yourself to think about anything. I will think for you; I am your perpetual parent. Such is the dispensation of an all-wise Providence!" When Toby returns to his home, a newspaper account of "a woman who had laid her desperate hands not only on her own life but on that of her young child" – a crime that appalls him as "unnatural and cruel" – leads him to the conclusion that all poor people are "bad." He, being poor himself, belongs to that vast company.

This low valuation of self and of the common people cannot, does not, last. "The stern realities from which these shadows come" have not disappeared simply because Trotty Veck wakes from his nightmare, or because, as he rises from his chair, the newspaper (with its dreary recitation of Facts) falls on the hearth, and becomes entangled with his feet, thus assuming its proper place in the order of things (a good heart, love, and the season of the year being so much more important than printed stories of unhappiness and death). Dickens warns the reader, at story's end, that the bleak attitudes of men in power toward those who lack the amenities of life surround us even to this day:

"and in your sphere – none is too wide, and none too limited for such an end – endeavour to correct, improve, and soften them. So may the New Year be a happy one to you, happy to many more whose happiness depends on you! So may each year be happier than the last, and not the meanest of our brethren or sisterhood debarred their rightful share, in what our Great Creator formed them to enjoy."

Dickens's life-long concern with social justice produced remarkably little in the way of legislation. Exhortations to readers to elevate and expand their sense of Christian charity were taken in good grace, because they were perceived as irrelevant by those whom Dickens was censuring. It is not the propaganda of the *Christmas Books* that damages their art as short stories (though whether the Reverend W. H. Brookfield, Thackeray's friend, was complaining about the propaganda or the sentimentality when he condemned *The Chimes* as "utter trash" remains debatable).[10] In the case of *The Chimes*, transitions between dream state and reality are not as sharply marked as they might be. Trotty Veck is, from the beginning, inconsistent in his breast-beating about the unworthiness of the lower orders. He knows that his daughter Meg is lovely and good-hearted; he ignores that evidence. He warns Will Fern against going to Alderman Cute in an effort to procure justice for himself (Will has been caught sleeping in a shed); Toby knows instinctively that justice will not be found in the rulings of the Alderman. Unable to bear the thought of Will Fern and his daughter Lilian sleeping out of doors, he invites them to his home: "The New Year never can be happy for me," Toby tells Will, "if I see a child and you, go wandering away, you don't know where, without a shelter for your heads. Come home with me! I'm a poor man, living in a poor place; but I can give you lodging for one night and never miss it. Come home with me!" Why he should have allowed the browbeating of his "superiors" to convince him that he and his kind have no worth is never plausibly explained, inasmuch as everything Toby does, every instinct he possesses, and every fellow-member of the poorer classes with whom he associates, are portrayed as absolutely first-rate; moreover, Toby knows that they are fine human beings.

The story of a poor man distrusting the poor has its emotional unity, however, if only because Dickens wrote with his "steam very much up"[11] and "in a regular, ferocious excitement . . . wrathful and red-hot." When he completed it, he wrote to Forster that he had had "what women call 'a real good cry.'"[12] Revision was relatively minor; at Forster's suggestion he knocked out a Young England gentleman who praised feudal doctrine, and replaced him with a gentleman who praised "the good old times, the grand old times, the great old times" at the expense of the very age that had produced himself. "This gentleman had a very red face, as if an undue proportion of the blood in his body were squeezed up into his head; which perhaps accounted for his having also the appearance of being rather cold about the heart." Dickens knew that Filers and Cutes and Sir Josephs really existed. He changed very little else before *The Chimes* appeared in print; in a characteristic attack on unfeeling reviewers, he invented a writer (for the *Westminster Review*) who had attacked Scrooge's gift of a turkey to Bob Cratchit as an act "grossly inconsistent with political economy."[13]

Formulaic, and in some respects baffled by the implausibility inherent in the effort to make ringing bells (the chimes) speak a sinister and accusatory language, the story offers a fascinating version of the condition-of-England question, and a recommendation for how it may be answered (a change of heart). We are probably mistaken in wanting to find, within the confines of even a long short story, a more subtle kind of characterization than *The Chimes* provides. But the fact that Dickens concentrated on the conversion of *only* Toby, a man who was recognizably good to begin with, and who was dearly loved by all who shared his social status, foreshadowed the triumph of matter over art.

The question of taxonomy in Dickens's case is not easily resolved. "The Pawnbroker's Shop" appears in *Sketches by Boz* under the heading "Scenes," and lacks a plot. "The Stroller's Tale" is part of a very long novel, and considerable ink has been spent on whether it – and the other brief narratives that swell the bulk of *Pickwick Papers* – were intended to fit exactly where they were put, or whether *Pickwick*, not long after it began rolling along, served as a convenient depository for all kinds of prose scraps, and turned into "a vast scrapbook," as a recent biography remarks, of "memories of Dickens's journeys about England, odd stories, references to current events, and fragments of public gossip."[14] A Christmas Book like *The Chimes* should not be called a short story at all (some critics argue) because of its length, and because of the specialized market that it served. Nor are matters simplified when we come to some of Dickens's final short stories: those published in his periodicals.

For example, if we take "Mugby Junction," written for the extra Christmas number of *All the Year Round* for 1866, it is not easy to determine whether the over-all title should apply to one unit, the four stories that Dickens personally composed; or only to the first two stories, "Barbox Brothers" and "Barbox Brothers and Co.," which use the same characters; or to all eight stories which were "seen, heard, or otherwise picked up, by the Gentleman from Nowhere, in his careful study of the Junction." Four of these stories were written by Andrew Halliday, Charles Collins, Hesba Stretton, and Amelia B. Edwards. Dickens was within a year of abandoning the Christmas numbers forever; he was weary of imitations impinging upon his sales; and the effort involved in creating a unified whole from the contributions of other writers was so severe that even the autobiographical touches in "Somebody's Luggage," written for the Christmas issue of *All the Year Round* of 1862, some four years earlier, are not consistently good-natured. "Mugby Junction" is very close to Dickens's final effort in this genre.

The protagonist of the first two tales, a young man named Jackson, enters whole-heartedly into the mercenary calculations of a financial house, and even adopts its name: Barbox. We are still recognizably within the territory of the *Christmas Books* – a man in need of rescue from his own base instincts can be converted if he is brought closer to sufferers who are pure in heart. "Barbox," a suitably grim name, identifies the nature of the firm which has made

MUGBY JUNCTION,

THE EXTRA CHRISTMAS NUMBER

OF

ALL THE YEAR ROUND,

CONDUCTED BY

CHARLES DICKENS,

FOR CHRISTMAS, 1866.

CONTENTS:

BARBOX BROTHERS . . . . By CHARLES DICKENS.
BARBOX BROTHERS AND Co. . . . . By CHARLES DICKENS.
MAIN LINE. . . . . . THE BOY AT MUGBY . . . . By CHARLES DICKENS.
No. 1 BRANCH LINE. THE SIGNALMAN . . . . . . By CHARLES DICKENS.
No. 2 BRANCH LINE. THE ENGINE DRIVER . . . . By ANDREW HALLIDAY.
No. 3 BRANCH LINE. THE COMPENSATION HOUSE. By CHARLES COLLINS.
No. 4 BRANCH LINE. THE TRAVELLING POST-
OFFICE . . . . } By HESBA STRETTON.
No. 5 BRANCH LINE. THE ENGINEER . . . . By AMELIA B. EDWARDS.

LONDON: 26, WELLINGTON STREET, STRAND, W.C.;

CHAPMAN & HALL, 193, PICCADILLY, W.

AND ALL BOOKSELLERS AND NEWSMEN.

7   Cover of *Mugby Junction*, the Christmas number of *All the Year Round*, by Charles Dickens (1866)

the young man "hard-lined, thin-lipped, repressive, changeless ... with a wax mask on." During a stop-over at Mugby Junction he meets an invalid woman who teaches little children, and her father (Lamps). These two selfless, compassionate, and understanding spirits teach Jackson how to return to his best self.

Mugby Junction, of course, is Rugby Junction, familiar to Dickens because he had passed through it more than a hundred times on his way to various speaking engagements. The young man has come to a crossroads in his life. The seven lines which radiate from the Junction resemble "a great Industrial Exhibition of the works of extraordinary ground spiders that spun iron." All the lines look equally tempting, or equally unpromising (he cannot decide which). It is easier to take no train at all, and to linger at Mugby Junction. He acquires the title of "the gentleman from Nowhere," nor, in his acedia, does he care. "It's as good a name for me as any other you could call me by," he tells Lamps. "I am, to myself, an unintelligible book with the earlier chapters all torn out, and thrown away." He regards himself as being on a journey, traveling from his birthday. "My childhood had no grace of childhood, my youth had no charm of youth, and what can be expected from such a lost beginning?"

Once the mystery surrounding the past of Barbox is cleared up – an event that takes place not long after the narrative begins – Jackson's conversion and final happiness become assured. But the symbolic richness of the Junction appealed sufficiently to Dickens to inspire him to write a dramatic monologue, "Main Line: The Boy at Mugby," and a well-shaped story, "No. 1 Branch Line: The Signal Man."

The monologue is not a true short story. Though the Boy is a compulsive talker, and assumes our presence, he talks past us; obsessed with his own concerns, he is created – in large measure – by his own language. He is a voice, not a character. The sketch develops a lovely conceit, one that Dickens enjoyed developing to an outrageous length. Refreshment Rooms in English railway stations exist only to discomfit or poison their patrons (as opposed to Refreshment Rooms in French railway stations). Their staffs are organized expressly for such purposes. "Look here," the Boy tells us. "I am the boy at what is called The Refreshment Room at Mugby Junction, and what's proudest boast is, that it never yet refreshed a moral being." The details that follow – stale sponge-cakes, sawdust "sangwiches," inferior sherry, tea served without milk to those who want it with (and "tea with milk given to people as wanted it without") – are appropriate furnishings for an establishment proudly displaying signs such as "May Albion Never Learn" and "Keep the Public Down," and for a Missis who consistently refers to her customers as "The Beast."

In "No. 1 Branch Line: The Signal Man," Dickens set out to make the flesh creep. Even though the question of whether the Signal-Man saw a genuine spectre remains unresolved at story's end, Dickens's delineation of the Signal-Man's over-wrought condition is particularly well done. This is, after all, the narrative of an impending emotional breakdown as well as a ghost story, and Dickens has learned, since the days of "The Stroller's Tale," how to dramatize convincingly the problems created by excessive "expectation and watchfulness."

There are two main characters here: one, a Signal-Man who has been deeply disturbed on two occasions by a spectre that holds its left arm across the face, and violently waves its right arm (though it can be seen by no one else); and a sympathetic man who, happening to be in the vicinity, falls into conversation with him. The first suspects that he has been receiving messages from the other world. The other is curious about the incursion of the supernatural on an otherwise peaceful landscape. A rational man, he has a limited imagination. He attempts to account for the spectre by reminding the Signal-Man that the "delicate nerves that minister to the functions of the eye" sometimes become diseased. Moreover, an imaginary cry might be ascribed "to the wind in this wild unnatural valley ... and to the wild harp it makes of the telegraph wires." Even a remarkable series of coincidences (he continues) should not be taken too seriously by "men of common sense," or too radically alter "the ordinary calculations of life." Rather than attempt to communicate what the Signal-Man has told him to the Signal-Man's superiors in the Company, the narrator prefers to take him "to the wisest medical practitioner" known in the area, and get an informed opinion.

As in Le Fanu's stories, there is no reason to trust men of science to solve such problems, and the reader senses early rather than late that the catastrophe in store for the Signal-Man is inevitable. It is a brilliant story, really very close to the best effort made by Dickens in the genre (if not the best). But it is understandable why Dickens became wary of further efforts to unify Christmas numbers periodicals – despite the selling-out of the entire press-run of 265,000 copies of this particular issue within a month. He perceived that the Mugby Boy knew nothing of the Signal-Man, and the Signal-Man knew nothing about the boy. Jackson, the Gentleman from Nowhere, may have collected the stories during his stay at the Junction, but he did not attempt to identify any relationship between them. When, in the reading tour that began in 1867, Dickens discovered that audiences in London, Birmingham, and Leeds cared less for his two selections from "Mugby Junction" than for other, more tried pieces in his repertory, he dropped "Barbox Brothers" and "The Mugby Boy" from the evening's entertainment; though he prepared a reading-version of "The Signal-Man," he never used it. In brief, wearying of attempts to unify further the contents of his Christmas issues, he also learned that his most recent stories, written for this individualized context and market, could not be exploited for the lecture circuit. It turned into a double disappointment of major proportions.

A short story by Dickens may resemble short stories by his contemporaries much less strikingly than it does longer stories by himself. In this genre, as in so much else that he wrote, Dickens created his own universe. He left behind dozens of sketches, tales, morality plays, *Christmas Books* and Christmas stories, dramatic monologues, and shorter stories – all written as a direct result of his efforts to understand, and satisfy, his public's roaring appetite for fiction.

4

Anthony Trollope: baking tarts for readers of periodicals

Trollope, like Dickens, earned his bread and butter from his novels, and thought his short stories commercially viable, but on the whole marginal material for the making of a reputation. It is precisely this ordinariness, or casualness about the genre, which makes Trollope's case at mid-century so useful as an index to attitudes widely shared by professional authors. What Trollope wanted to do – and what he wanted every author to do – was observe the world around him, and record, in fiction, what he had seen and heard. He believed that he had done as much in his novels. In his brief comment on *An Editor's Tales* (1870) he insisted that every story had been founded on "the remembrance of some fact."[1] (He may have been a little ingenuous in arguing that no single incident "could bring back to any one concerned the memory of the past event.") He believed, in brief, that story-telling was related to the real world in exactly the sense that Thackeray once declared was essential to the good health of the *Cornhill*: it draws its inspiration from the behavior of men and women, who provide more than enough material for the sharply observant. (Children are not important in Trollope's short stories.)

"The Panjandrum," a short story first published in *St. Paul's Magazine* (January-February 1870), makes a point about Trollope's personal philosophy perhaps more sharply than it does about the fictional characters involved. A group of parlor intellectuals want to start a review that will be the best ever conceived, a nonpareil in a great city given over unthinkingly to mere pleasure in its reading tastes. The contents of the magazine will be divided by a given number of pages; twenty-one printed pages will be assigned to each writer. Trollope does not stress the editorial function of deciding which contributions shall be accepted, which rejected. His concern is with the problem of identifying an appropriate source of inspiration for fiction. The second section of the story, labeled "Despair," deals with the "very great mental distress" of the narrator, whose eagerness to complete his assignment is frustrated by the fact that he does not have a story to tell; nobody will assign him a subject, or even advise him on what sort of subject might appeal to the public. He swiftly rejects "the ballot" as potential subject-matter because he knows so little about it. "The twenty-one pages loomed before me as a wilderness, which, with such a staff, I could never traverse."[2] Days pass: "My mind had absolutely fled from me . . . The paper was there, and the pen and ink; – but beyond that there was nothing ready. I had thought to rack my brain, but I began to doubt whether I had a brain to rack."[3] A full week elapses: "There still lay on the little table in the corner of the room the square single sheet of paper, with its margin doubled down, all fitted for the printer, – only that the sheet was still blank."[4] On a drizzling November morning, terrified by his awesome responsibility, he ventures forth into a park, where he sees a stout woman, her back toward him, leading a ten-year-old girl; a scrap of conversation ("Oh, Anne, I do so wonder what he's like!" "You'll see, miss") sets off his imagination. The "he," perhaps, is her brother – nay, must certainly be her brother. The girl becomes the writer's sister, and older, too, in his mind's eye: "a sister whom I had never seen till she was thus brought to me for protection and love . . ."[5] Possessed by the tale that must be told, he begins to write his tale, "The New Inmate." Because he has been in touch with life, his musings have proved superior to the incident which coaxed them forth. "What need is there of a sister or a friend in the flesh, – a sister or a friend with probably so many faults, – when by a little exercise of the mind they may be there, at your elbow, faultless?"[6]

The editorial board (alas!) votes against the inclusion of a short story in the first issue of the magazine. But then, the magazine itself founders when still another manuscript – a lengthy and tedious review of Bishop Berkeley's philosophy – is rejected. "The New Inmate" may not have won a vote of approval, but the narrator – the would-be writer – has found his métier. Having taken from life the inspiration of his first fiction, he will know how to proceed in the future.

In his *Autobiography*, Trollope had very little to say about his short stories, but he did mention that somehow or other each story that he wrote had been based on an actual incident. He quoted at length Thackeray's response to a letter of inquiry that he had sent (October 23, 1859), offering several stories for possible printing in the *Cornhill*; Trollope enjoyed Thackeray's praise (perhaps heightened by the fact that Thackeray was rapidly wearying of his duties as editor, and enjoyed the thought that Trollope might in some fashion lighten his

8   Portrait of Anthony Trollope by S. Laurence, 1865

burden), but did not miss the import of Thackeray's advice: to write more about "life and its doings." "When events occur," Thackeray wrote, "and you have a good lively tale, bear us in mind. One of our chief objects in this magazine is the getting out of novel spinning, and back into the world. Don't understand me to disparage our craft, especially *your* wares. I often say I am like the pastry cook, and don't care for tarts, but prefer bread and cheese; but the public love the tarts (unluckily for us), and we must bake and sell them."[7]

The kitchen view of literature as so many edible wares is, to be sure, shared by all editors, and the metaphor must not be censured severely. Still, Trollope's short stories were written for an audience that devoured tarts and turned the page to see what else might be offered in the same issue. Trollope had little to say about any single story once it had served its purpose, and, as with his novels, he did not "quarrel with public judgment in affairs of literature."[8] He dismayed more than one generation of younger writers with his stout opinion, "The writer of stories must please, or he will be nothing."[9] He sought in his stories to make virtue alluring and vice ugly, and of the six great English novelists he found it possible to say that Miss Edgeworth, Miss Austen, Walter Scott, Thackeray, Dickens, and George Eliot had never published "a scene, a passage, or a word that would teach a girl to be immodest, or a man to be dishonest."[10] He refused to allow the division between sensational and realistic modes of story-telling, i.e., the easy differentiation between Wilkie Collins and himself. "A good novel" (he often used the bland term "good" to denote a characteristic that pleased his own sense of the fitness of things) should be both sensational and realistic; should emphasize both character and plot.[11]

To some extent these truisms do not take us far. Indeed, Trollope begged off from his original intention of recording a series of rules for the writing of novels; he used as his double excuse the required length for such a discussion, and his uncertainty as to the nature of the rules. But the congruence of his casual asides in the *Autobiography* and the dramatized situations in his stories about writers and editors is sufficiently striking that we may infer the existence of a view of writing that stands for something more than a pastry-cook's adventures in the kitchen. "The Panjandrum" illustrates beautifully his notion that an artist has to write from a conviction that he has something to tell, and that his story has been based on something which has tickled his fancy or moved his pathos. If, however, he continues to write without inspiration, "not because he has something which he burns to tell, but because he feels it to be incumbent on him to be telling something,"[12] he will have fallen into that most terrible trap of all, writing because he has to tell a story, not because he has a story to tell, and his character will move woodenly, and the course of the tale will become a "stiff mechanism."[13]

Trollope, it must be remembered, had earned many times over his right to make such observations. Before he became an established novelist, he had assembled the elements of a successful career in the General Post Office, rising from a salary of 90 pounds a year in 1834 to 400 pounds a year in 1844 (when he married Rose Heseltine), and his promotion to Surveyor in 1845. When he turned his mind to the profession of writing, he assumed a similarly brisk, no-nonsense manner as a prerequisite for getting on. He did not think it beneath his dignity to call upon his mother after he had completed his first novel, *The Macdermots of Ballycloran*, in order to use her good offices in placing the manuscript. Still, it was no easy task, winning either fame or fortune. For a full eight years, during the period when he wrote *The Kellys and the O'Kellys* and *La Vendée*, he was lured into a number of half-profits schemes of publishers that never seemed to pay him a single sovereign. Perhaps (he wondered) he was pursuing the wrong vocation. We cannot tell today whether he was swindled by his earliest publishers (the sharpness of the dealing may remind some readers of Thomas Hardy's experiences, only two decades later, with William Tinsley). Trollope gradually came to see that novels with Irish subject-matter, or historical novels with French titles, appealed neither to publishers nor to the lending-library audience, mostly female, who largely subsidized the publishing trade. He also felt keenly his limitation in being cut off from any society of literary men, and his ignorance of how to negotiate with editors and publishers. There were all kinds of false starts: letters on Irish poverty in the *Examiner*, for which he received no payment; a dramatization of *The Noble Jilt*, which was never produced, but which he later cannibalized for his novel *Can You Forgive Her?*; and a handbook for Ireland, prepared for Mr. John Murray but apparently not read before being returned (nine months after submission). The energy invested in all these works, for little or no return, can only make us marvel at Trollope's determination to persevere.

Early in his literary career, however, Trollope had to make a decision about the usefulness of criticism. The sensitivity of a writer at the beginning of a career noted more for false starts and outright failures than for even modest successes made the issue critical to him during the 1840s. He decided that he hated log-rolling, and would not depend on "the friendship of a friend" (an awkward phrase) for a notice in a respectable journal. "And I made up my mind then," he added, "that, should I continue with this trade of authorship, I would have no dealings with any critic on my own behalf. I would neither ask for nor deplore criticism, nor would I ever thank a critic for praise, nor quarrel with him, even in my own heart, for censure."[14] This indifference toward the printed opinions of critics had significant consequences, as we shall see; it rendered him immune to even the friendliest advice; and it minimized any need to debate the aesthetics of his views on fiction.

Most of Trollope's forty-seven novels – over forty, in fact – were written after 1855, along with a large number of articles and essays for periodicals, five travel books, and forty-two short stories. *The Warden*, though not a commercial success, convinced him, on several scores, that he had been correct in aiming at a literary career. He had felt instinctively that his apprenticeship was over by the time he concluded *The Warden*; he was satisfied with his characterizations; and the gap between intention and achievement in this novel was narrower than in any previous fiction he had undertaken.

Late in life (the 1870s) Trollope liked to say that he did not revise or re-read much of what he had written, though examination of his manuscripts in recent years confirms the impression that he did more editing of first drafts than was long assumed to be the case. Since it is not our intention to review novel by novel the development of Trollope's career over the next twenty-seven years, some general statements about the triumphant phase of his writing career (1855–82) seem in order, if only because Trollope's emphasis upon orderliness, regularity of output, and sums of money earned rapidly became, for younger writers, the essence of sordid commercialism in Victorian novel-writing. There is no question that Trollope invited such a reaction. His self-satisfaction is recorded in a series of complacent and even fatuous evaluations. Though his comments about *Orley Farm* are perhaps more hyperbolic than those about other novels that he admired as well done, they may serve as representative of the class:

The plot of *Orley Farm* is probably the best I have ever made; but it has the fault of declaring itself, and thus coming to an end too early in the book. When Lady Mason tells her ancient lover that she did not forge the will, the plot of *Orley Farm* has unravelled itself; – and this she does in the middle of the tale. Independently, however, of this the novel is good. Sir Peregrine Orme, his grandson, Madeline Stavely, Mr. Furnival, Mr. Chaffanbrass, and the commercial gentlemen, are all good. The hunting is good. The lawyer's talk is good. Mr. Moulder carves his turkey admirably, and Mr. Kantwise sells his tables and chairs with spirit. I do not know that there is a dull page in the book. I am fond of *Orley Farm*; – and am especially fond of its illustrations by Millais, which are the best I have seen in any novel in any language.[15]

The *Autobiography*, posthumously published, did a great deal of harm to Trollope's reputation for several decades. Many agree with George Eliot that Trollope's emphasis on "a sheer matter of industry"[16] left little room for imagination; the word went forth that Trollope had been a writing-machine rather than a genius. It is true that Trollope never claimed that he was a genius; indeed, repudiated the notion. He wrote for lengths,[17] and it was a trick, as he told his son, who had embarked upon the writing of a book; but Trollope knew it was a mechanical trick, and to accomplish what he needed, more than one such trick had to be mastered. The duties of his work for the Post Office, which continued until 1867, the year in which he resigned and left the Civil Service, required him to rise early, to begin writing by five-thirty, and to use fully whatever irregular hours were available to him. He wrote "so many pages a week" because he had allotted such a number to himself. Each page contained 250 words, and Trollope candidly confessed that he counted them. He developed a "diary" or "working-table" for the efficient utilization of time from 1856 on, when he was writing *Barchester Towers*. He wrote for three hours a day, and the record for *The Claverings* shows that he planned to write 35 pages a week for 22 weeks, for a total of 770 pages. When he concluded his working-table with the triumphant single word, "Finis," he had written 768 pages – despite the loss of two weeks, marked, in each case, by the melancholy exclamation, "Alas!"[18]

In the chapter of his *Autobiography* entitled "Conclusion," and hence a convenient place for a reader to hope to discover Trollope's reflections on what a career of writing several extraordinary sequences of novels meant to him, pride of place is given to a table that records not only the titles of the books he had written, but the sums that he had received for them. The total came to more than £68,000; Trollope identifies the number of shillings and pence as well.

Trollope did not boast of his rightful claim to the attention of posterity, nor did he, in his *Autobiography*, record much of interest having to do with his inner life, mostly because he believed that doing so was impossible for any writer; but also, he thought that revelations of hitherto unsuspected scandals or secrets were unwanted by the intelligent reader, and of minor consequence so far as his own life was concerned. He did praise his own "preserving diligence" in his profession, and held up the fact that nine-tenths of his literary work had been accomplished within two decades (twelve of those years having been spent in Post Office employment) as encouragement to younger writers. He had been constant, he repeated, "and constancy in labour will conquer all difficulties."[19]

We will not find a theory of fiction in these pages. But if Trollope treated writing as a trade with a number of learnable techniques that any serious apprentice might acquire, he was nonetheless serious about the obligations that accompanied the privileges of authorship, and he treated them in several short stories written late in the 1860s. By then he had published more than two dozen novels. Short stories were, at any rate, not high on his agenda; he wrote his first in 1859, and published a delightful collection, *Tales of All Countries*, in 1861, followed by a second series in 1863. These stories appeared originally in *Harper's New Monthly Magazine*, *Cassell's Illustrated Family Paper*, *Public Opinion*, the *London Review*, and the Christmas Supplement to *The Illustrated London News*. Neither *Hunting Sketches* (1865) nor *Travelling Sketches* (1866) is to be considered fictional in its treatment, and , of course, *Clergymen of the Church of England* (1866) was intended to be regarded as a companion volume to these collections of sketches. *Lotta Schmidt and Other Stories* (1867) gathered stories from two anthologies (Emily Faithfull's *A Welcome* and A. A. Proctor's *Victoria Regia*), *The Argosy*, and *Good Words*. All of Trollope's stories about the profession of writing, first published in *St. Paul's Magazine*, were collected in *An Editor's Tales*. A final volume, *Why Frau Frohmann Raised Her Prices and Other Stories* (1882) gathered short stories from *Good Words*, *The Graphic*, and *Light*.

Trollope's interest in Christmas stories, printed in special supplements and editions intended to be sold and read during the Christmas season, led to the writing of a number of stories not collected during his lifetime, such as "The Two Heroines of Plumplington" (appearing in *Good Cheer*, the Christmas number of *Good Words*), and "Not If I Know It" (appearing in the Christmas Annual of *Life*).

The clustering of Trollope's short stories in a single decade is due, as might be expected, to the availability of ready markets, not only those created by the growing popularity of several periodicals intended for middle-class tastes, but to Trollope's own work as an editor, first for the *Fortnightly Review* from 1865 on, and then for *St. Paul's* from 1867 on. Trollope thought his own stories better than most of those submitted to *St. Paul's*, but suffered no embarrassment from the frequency of his appearances in the pages of that magazine. The writing of stories for special Christmas issues also paid well,

though. His stint of duty at *St. Paul's* ended because the circulation of
the magazine seldom reached 10,000, and the periodical "never
paid its way." Trollope added, mordantly, "Literary merit will
hardly set a magazine afloat, though, when afloat, it will sustain it.
Time is wanted – or the hubbub, and flurry, and excitement created
by ubiquitous sesquipedalian advertisement."[20] He then returned
full-time to the writing of novels, which, whatever may be said about
their "literary merit," or lack of it, paid more substantial sums than
short stories.

It is not surprising that Trollope preferred Thackeray to Dickens.
The former always had a story to tell; the latter, dispensing with
human nature, concentrated on a "stagey and melodramatic
pathos." Thackeray's language was pure; Dickens's language was
"jerky, ungrammatical, and created by himself in defiance of rules –
almost as completely as that created by Carlyle."[21] Thackeray's
attitude toward the reality on which any fiction must be based
proved more congenial to Trollope, and more useful to his own
story-telling, than anything Dickens had to teach him. Perhaps most
significant in his high praise of Thackeray ("I do not hesitate to
name Thackeray the first. His knowledge of human nature was
supreme, and his characters stand out as human beings, with a force
and a truth which has not, I think, been within the reach of any
other English novelist in any period")[22] was his admiration of
Thackeray's astringency. Like his chosen model, Trollope wanted
to be honest and dry-eyed in his examination of human problems
that, all too easily, might have been treated sentimentally.

Trollope, for reasons that are worth examining, believed that
"The Spotted Dog" (1870) was his best short story. To begin with, it
was based upon a *fact*, or "the tragedy of a poor drunkard, who with
infinite learning at his command made one sad final effort to reclaim
himself, and perished while he was making it ..." Also, as a story
about the relationships between authors and editors, it deals with
subject-matter that Trollope knew intimately, and enjoyed discuss-
ing with his family and friends. But above all, there is its coolness of
manner, a trick of distancing that Trollope had learned from
Thackeray.

The narrative tells of a man of intellect who has been reduced to
the writing of filler-material for the "Penny Dreadfuls." Married,
the father of four children, desperately poor and unhappy, Julius
Mackenzie sketches a self-portrait of desolation – in a letter to a
publishing firm – that, for its fullness of horror in the awareness of

talents gone to seed, can scarcely be surpassed in Victorian fiction. He knows that his character is not attractive to others, if only because he has separated from his family, his tutor at Cambridge (a quarrel has forced him to leave the university without a degree), and his own social class (he has married his wife because of a determination "to take refuge from the conventional thraldom of so-called 'gentlemen' amidst the liberty of the lower orders"). Immersed in dirt, a confessed habitual drinker, insolvent, and a man who has dallied with the thought of suicide, he begs for the chance to reduce his income – from forty-five shillings a week to thirty – in order to undertake work more dignified than the "blood and nastiness" he is compelled to record, week after week, in his work for debased periodicals. He has passed the age of forty, and even as he struggles to make one more effort to clear himself from the "filth" of his present position, he entertains "no hope of any success." Indeed he expects no answer to his cry for help, but if one were to be sent, it should be addressed to "Mr. Grimes, the Spotted Dog, Liquorpond Street."

The rest of the story charts the progress of a major, sustained effort by the recipient of the letter – an editor at the publishing firm – to save Mackenzie from his own weaknesses. Mackenzie's seriousness in beginning his assignment – improving an index for "a certain learned manuscript in three volumes," a two-month project suitable to someone who possesses "a scholar's acquirements" – is matched by the kindly concern of his new employer. If Mackenzie succeeds, the editor's confidence in the possibility of his regeneration will prove to have been justified. If Mackenzie fails to complete the index, the language of excess in his original letter will be matched by a hyperbolic emotional line in everything the narrator has yet to tell us.

What the reader does not expect is an austere tone as the subsequent narrative unfolds. Trollope never once asks us to weep for Mackenzie, a man who has sinned fully as much as he has been sinned against. The full working-out of Mackenzie's destiny, painful and sometimes surprising as it is, is followed from start to finish without a single appeal to an easy emotion of either pity or contempt.

Trollope, imagining himself as an editor, cast himself in a congenial position: he could observe a varied cast of characters with sympathy and understanding. It was not always essential that he render judgment. We discover in Trollope's short stories more self-

revelation than in his novels. Michael Sadleir notes that in several of
these stories Trollope himself appears.[23] Sadleir concentrates on
Tales of All Countries: he identifies Archibald Green in "The
O'Conors of Castle Conor" and "Father Giles of Ballymoy," John
Pomfret of "John Bull on the Guadalquivir," and Jones of "A Ride
Across Palestine" as all Trollopian in manner, "massive, apprecia-
tive, inquisitive and amazingly English."[24] But the editor of "The
Spotted Dog," who takes "infinite trouble" only to reach a point of
total frustration when everything falls apart, is how Trollope often
saw his own endeavors. (*St. Paul's* collapsed because its finances were
shaky from the beginning, not because of bad editing. "Perhaps too
much editing might have been the fault," Trollope wrote
bemusedly. "I was too anxious to be good, and did not enough think
of what might be lucrative.")[25] In "The Panjandrum" the lack of a
true center of consciousness – the firm hand of an editor in control –
was the real cause of the downfall of the periodical projected by *les
jeunes*. A review might have survived an overlong and arid distillation
of Bishop Berkeley's wisdom, and even outlast the unfortunate
impression made by a short story entitled "The New Inmate." It
could not make the next issue if it lacked an editor's guidance. (In
Trollope's short story, the review did not even make its first issue.)

Trollope's experiences as an editor were not all that dissimilar
from those of Dickens, though Dickens made a greater commercial
success from his periodicals than Trollope was able to do. An editor's
situation, Trollope believed, was always insecure. Most of what a
varied lot of contributors submitted was unprintable, and some
contributors – for example, the "most hateful and the most hated" of
them all, Mrs. Brumby – were impossible human beings to deal
with. An editor had to be polite, but firm. Occasionally he had to
deliver his rejection in person (as in "The Turkish Bath"); and if he
did accept a story that needed re-shaping, or re-thinking, it
benefited nobody if he obscured his editorial advice by a desire not to
offend. But he enjoyed the savor of small victories along the way; he
met women to whom he willingly gave his heart ("Mary Gresley"
and "Josephine de Monmorenci"); and he might, on occasion, even
find something worth printing.

Trollope's interest in writing short stories coincided with his stints
as editor of several general-interest periodicals, which is understandable enough. When he wrote about editors, he consistently
portrayed them as kind and helpful to contributors (save always the
Mrs. Brumby type, which he detested). He thought himself to be an

expert in bureaucratic in-fighting, and boasted that no writer of his time possessed more experience in dealing with publishers of all varieties. As a consequence, he believed that he had the right to give advice to his younger contemporaries.

This advice was given both by preachment and by example. Trollope believed, and wrote in the beginning pages of the history of English fiction that he proposed to undertake, in his lecture on "English Prose Fiction as a Rational Amusement," in his correspondence with fellow-authors and would-be contributors to his periodicals, and in his *Autobiography*, that fiction should avoid indecency. He judged a large number of authors on this basis.[26] Much of what he said about Defoe, Smollett, Fielding, and Sterne, and about contemporaries like Ainsworth and Disraeli,[27] was curiously ill-tempered for a man who invariably portrayed editors as tolerant and humane. But he wrote too frequently on this subject to be misunderstood. Even though he argued that Victorian novelists owned higher standards of taste than their predecessors, he insisted on vigilance against lapses from grace, which might occur at any time.

Trollope's case illustrates what might (and often did) happen to a writer who insisted that the novel and the short story were intended to serve as vehicles of moral edification. One grouping of his stories – those dealing with Christmas – are especially uninteresting to modern readers precisely because they fulfill Trollope's exhortation to do good.

They seem bloodless. "The Mistletoe Bough" insists that misunderstandings between lovers cannot be cleared away by sympathetic parents or guardians, but must be made right by those directly involved. Mrs. Garrow tells Bessy that a note to her sweetheart must be written: "I will write the words for you if you like, but it is you who must resolve that they shall be written. I cannot bid my darling go away and leave me for another home. I can only say that in my heart I do believe that home would be a happy one."[28] If Maurice Archer, in "Christmas Day at Kirkby Cottage," announces that Christmas is a bore,[29] he must be shown that it is the right season of the year for moral regeneration. "The Widow's Mite" concludes with the unexceptionable message, delivered by Mrs. Granger, that "It is my belief that all that is given in a right spirit comes back instantly, in this world, with interest."[30] And even the carnage of the American Civil War yields up its appropriate sermon in "The Two Generals," which bears the appropriate subtitle, "A Christmas

Story of the War in Kentucky," for it describes a conflict between brothers who choose opposing sides, and who are finally reconciled. Trollope's admiration of Thackeray as a novelist who marvelously conveyed to the mind "a feeling of distress that women should ever be immodest or men dishonest" is, implicitly, a pledge to do likewise in his own stories; to do good for and to young men and women; to preach through example, subtly if possible, but not so subtly that the message can be missed altogether.

Trollope's emphasis on providing in his fiction a picture of common life enlivened by humor and sweetened by pathos is formulaic, but – rather surprisingly – we cannot judge Trollope by the formula. As Bradford A. Booth notes, Trollope made only sparing use of both humor and pathos.[31] A judgment of Trollope's art must be made on the basis of how accurately it depicts common life. This is a large issue. Nathaniel Hawthorne wrote to an actor friend in St. Louis, "Have you ever read the novels of Anthony Trollope? They precisely suit my taste, – solid and substantial, written on the strength of beef and through the inspiration of ale, and just as real as if some giant had hewn a great lump out of the earth and put it under a glass case, with all its inhabitants going about their daily business, and not suspecting that they were being made a show of."[32] Trollope quoted these words of Hawthorne with gratification (he regarded the American as a "very much greater" author than himself); but common life to Trollope meant the life of members of the upper end of the middle class, and "all" the inhabitants of Victorian England are not to be found in Trollope's fiction. His concern with romantic love – with the question of who should marry whom – is so closely bound up with a moral view of what may safely be brought to the attention of magazine-readers that his short stories suffer from a monotony of subject-matter. And, apart from the repeated allusions to the chores of editing, many of them animated by the wondrous variety of character types who haunt the offices of editors, Trollope has surprisingly little time for a description of how members of the middle class spend their working days. (His novels are far more detailed in their treatment of bankers and merchants.)

In any history of the short story, therefore, Trollope's contributions must be summarized as relatively unadventurous, shrewdly observant but disinclined to venture on experimental ground so far as narrative technique is concerned, and wholesomely moral. Trollope's claim to our interest, even our gratitude, is that he does

well what needs to be done for his audience – bakes so many tarts at
so many pence – and cheerfully provides a money-back guarantee if
the wares prove unsatisfactory for any reason. None of his stories
patronize a reader's intelligence; all offer full value. They cannot be
compared advantageously to the short stories of several French and
Russian contemporaries, but they are representative of much that is
Victorian in the best sense.

Two additional aspects of Trollope's work in this genre must be
marked: his treatment of the problem of who tells the story (at a time
when story-telling perspective failed consistently to engage the
attention of critics), and his steady sense of decorum. The perspective of *An Editor's Tales* – that of an editor – does not change from one
tale to the next. But what about such a story as "The Two Heroines
of Plumplington"? From whose vantage point are the events in two
different households recounted? As a characteristic narrative of
young love that wins its way despite obstacles (the opposition of
parents who want wealthier suitors for their daughters' hands), the
story is worth looking at for its handling of a point of view. I do not
want to suggest that Trollope was innovative in this technical
matter; even that he thought much about it; or that "The Two
Heroines of Plumplington" indicated a changing attitude toward
technique. (Trollope's story-telling mannerisms remained remarkably consistent over three and a half decades.)

Trollope was writing here about Barsetshire's second town, with a
population of over "20,000 souls, and three separate banks."[33] The
teller of the tale, an observer, seems to hear a great many rumors.
For instance, Mr. Greenmantle, the manager of one bank, "is
reputed to have shares" in it. His daughter Emily "is supposed to be
the heiress of all he possesses." After Mr. Philip Hughes, a cashier in
her father's bank, turns out to be the man she prefers (over a richer
Harry Gresham), "it became known at once" that her father was
very angry.

It may be supposed that the story-teller knows what everyone else
knows, and no more. Since this is the story of young love
triumphant, he will have a slightly wry, optimistic view about
whatever obstacles Emily Greenmantle and Polly Peppercorn (the
other heroine) may encounter; the obstacles will invariably prove to
be temporary. His value judgments will be those of the community,
which means in turn that he cannot be sarcastic in any heavy way
about the limitations of understanding shared by the two fathers.
His mission is to record what "all Plumplington knew" and what
"all Plumplington said."

Just the same, the narrator knows more than they do, for he can eavesdrop on private conversations; if he chooses not to listen at keyholes, he can disclaim special knowledge; the quarrel between Polly and her father takes place behind closed doors, and "no one" hears the exchange; but Plumplington can guess reasonably well what went on because it observes social behavior afterwards; and not infrequently the narrator will speak for himself, in the first person, as in the remark, "With the affairs of Miss Greenmantle much more ceremony was observed, though I doubt whether there was much earnestness felt in the matter."[34] Trollope analyzes the thinking of both young ladies from the angle of vision of an older man who has fallen in love with their charm and naiveté; as Henry James said, when reviewing Trollope's career in 1888, Trollope bestowed upon his "girls" a patient, tender, and copious consideration; and there is really nothing in Victorian fiction quite like it. The heroines of Plumplington have distinct personalities, and are quite different from each other, even though they are in no way extraordinary in intelligence. We are privileged to witness the full range of their manoeuverings to win their lovers despite the disapproval of their fathers, and it is a tribute to the narrator's amused and sympathetic reporting that we never once sympathize with their fathers' natural, and understandable, passion to provide for the future welfare of their daughters.

But how is this trick accomplished? We return, inevitably, to Trollope's choice of a point of view. In this story, as in practically all his others, Trollope adopts – in rapid alternation, as the events of the story render necessary or desirable – the special knowledge of either an older observer who approves of those whose behavior is approvable, or of a character whose movement is, despite possible moments of self-doubt, even failure, consistently toward the light. It would never do to tell the story from the point of view of either Mr. Peppercorn or Mr. Greenmantle, or for that matter of Harry Gresham. Trollope can enter, if he wishes to do so, the mind of a fool or villain, and (to take only one novel as an example) *The Claverings*, which is particularly rich in knavery, allows us to appreciate the inner windings of the reprehensible Sir Hugh Clavering, his brother Archibald, Sophie Gordeloup, and her brother Count Pateroff. But in the short stories, he practically never does so. "Mrs. Grumby" is not narrated in the first person by Mrs. Grumby. "The Spotted Dog" is not given to us from the pen of Julius Mackenzie, the doomed drunkard.

Finally, we come to the matter of decorum. It is not necessary to relate the stories to events in Trollope's life, although, as already noted, *Tales of All Countries* in three series (*Lotta Schmidt* constituting the third series) presents Trollope himself under fewer disguises than do the other stories. Trollope's lack of sympathy with Dickens's free-wheeling imagination, with the "episodes" distracting from the "story" that mar the novels of Cervantes and Fielding, with Bulwer Lytton's determination "to give his readers the benefit of what he knew" (i.e., to preach),[35] with Disraeli's imagination ("The wit has been the wit of hairdressers, and the enterprise has been the enterprise of mountebanks")[36] meant that he preferred to work with a palette of more subdued colors. His short stories invariably posit the existence of absolute values, or a code of ethics that can be discovered, and must be, if one is to live at peace within oneself. The right way to do things requires the exercise of intelligent choice.

Too much has been made of Trollope's occasional fits of bad temper, his unwillingness to forget snubs, his too-ready dismissal of the first third of his life as nothing but miseries, his recurring melancholia. Michael Sadleir, in a stout defence of Trollope's character, a final chapter entitled "The Portrait of Anthony" in *Trollope: A Commentary*, reminds us that these failings even taken as a whole are less significant than his coherent, considered philosophy: "Put shortly, that philosophy was one of honest commonsense, tempered with generosity and deriving sanction from the achievement of a definite standard of personal behaviour. There are wisdoms and there are follies; but there is something higher either than prudence or recklessness – the duty that a man owes to his own sense of what is right."[37] The manner in which a character responds to such a duty affects, in turn, our response to him and to the short story. This is as true of tales dealing with courtship and marriage – vital issues to Trollope's audience no more than to Trollope himself – as of stories concerned with the behavior of Englishmen and Englishwomen in foreign lands, or with the relationships between editors and contributors. Decorum has to do with the propriety of a moral choice made *after* a review of the available alternatives. We are fully and fairly informed of the nature of those alternatives: what leads up to "the cruel marriage" in "La Mère Bauche," for example, and why suicide is the inevitable result of a choice wrongly made; or why Mrs. Thompson, a widow, makes "a wise decision" when she accepts the marriage offer of M. Lacordaire after a visit to "The Château of Prince Polignac." Perhaps Trollope's insistence that a choice is right or improper is too plain for modern tastes, but it was reassuring to his audience, and it provided an anchor in the turbulent waters of human relationships. More than a century later one may not find it easy to reject the propriety – the decorum – of the moral decisions that Trollope approved; only the occasional failure of the art to integrate the proposition sufficiently smoothly within the fiction disturbs a modern reader. Pascal believed that an audience, listening to a sermon, should be so illuminated by the preacher's exposition of the word of God that it would be excited to the practice of virtue. Trollope's stories, in a more modest sense, seek to do much the same, and at their best – as in "The Spotted Dog," "The Two Heroines of Plumplington," and "The Château of Prince Polignac" – succeed with grace and authority.

5

Thomas Hardy: an older tradition of narrative

For Thomas Hardy the oral element was no less significant than it had been for William Carleton; many of his stories were told to an expectant audience already familiar with similar unusual, even horrifying, narratives told by generations of story-tellers. "Originality" as such was not considered to be a virtue, and Hardy would have been surprised at censorious criticism on this account. At the same time, Hardy's attitude toward magazine editors was far from complaisant, and he bitterly resented the way in which the taste of a largely feminine audience for periodical fiction determined content and affected an author's creative prerogatives.

Hence, even at the beginning of a consideration of Hardy's work in this genre, we must understand that although Hardy – like Dickens and Trollope – wrote stories for minor sums of money, and without any serious expectation that they could support his standard of living, he nursed grudges against the philistinism and the grundyism of his audience that Dickens and Trollope never shared. Hardy's relationship to the reading public, in some respects, is more ambivalent than theirs. His experiences in writing for serial publication were seldom happy (the history of changes made in successive versions of the text of a novel is so difficult to trace that even Hardy's revisions for the Wessex Edition of 1912–31, in twenty-four volumes, must not be considered final). Moreover, he came rather late to the writing of short stories, and a number of his attitudes had hardened as a consequence of the treatment of his novels.

Hardy's first short story, however, was an amiable trifle entitled "How I Built Myself a House," which was printed in *Chambers's Journal* for March 18, 1865, at the very beginning of his career as a professional author. He thought of it as a sketch. (Indeed, he never clearly differentiated a sketch from a tale, or a tale from a short story.) He wrote it as an educational device for younger pupils of Arthur Blomfield, the architect for whom he was working, and it was the first time he earned money from the sale of a piece of writing. It is not clearly fiction, however; the description of a young man's problems in building a house for a specified sum, complicated by his wife's desire to add "extras" that inevitably add to the cost, is innocent of either plot or characterization. Hardy was correct in describing it – in later years – as a "trifle" and "unrepresentative." Even so, its date of publication preceded by two years the writing of *The Poor Man and the Lady,* Hardy's first attempt at a novel, and its success was probably an element in his decision to attempt to make a living from professional authorship. The last of Hardy's short stories, "Enter a Dragoon" and "A Changed Man," were not published until 1900. This thirty-five year period is longer than the quarter-century Hardy devoted to his novels, and rivals the time-period (1895–1928) given over to his concentration on poems, a consequence to some extent of his disgust with a number of harsh reviews of *Jude the Obscure.* Hardy kept touching up several of the short stories as they were reprinted in new editions after the turn of the century. Novels, as Trollope knew, and as Hardy was to learn, made the money. Once a short story had found its market in a periodical, it was unlikely that a collection of short stories would find enough buyers to justify its publication. But Hardy liked the shape of a short story; it was sufficiently baggy to accommodate almost any kind of complication; it could be as brief as the fifteen pages of "The Duke's Reappearance," or as long as the hundred pages of "The Romantic Adventures of a Milkmaid."

With a few minor exceptions of uncollected tales, Hardy's short stories were gathered in four volumes by the author himself: *Wessex Tales* (1888), *A Group of Noble Dames* (1891), *Life's Little Ironies* (1894), and *A Changed Man and Other Tales* (1913). There were some shiftings of stories in subsequent printings – for example, in 1912, for Macmillan's Wessex Edition, Hardy removed from *Life's Little Ironies* "A Tradition of Eighteen Hundred and Four" and "The Melancholy Hussar," and put them into *Wessex Tales*; while from *Wessex Tales* he removed "An Imaginative Woman," and placed it in *Life's Little Ironies*, because it turned "upon a trick of Nature, so to speak." An odd production is the twenty-thousand-word short story, "Our Exploits at West Poley," which first appeared in the Boston-based periodical *The Household* (November 1892 to April 1893); it is the only story that Hardy wrote expressly for a juvenile audience. *The Household*, "Devoted to the Interests of the American

9   Portrait of Thomas Hardy by Augustus John

Housewife," had a limited circulation, and Hardy's story – a treatment of rustic life in the Mendip Hills – was not reprinted until 1952.

By the time he wrote "The Distracted Preacher" (1879) Hardy was, of course, a well-established novelist. It took him a decade, publishing in journals as diverse as *New Quarterly Magazine*, *The English Illustrated Magazine*, *Longman's Magazine*, and *Blackwood's Edinburgh Magazine*, to accumulate enough stories for his first collection, *Wessex Tales*. Unfortunately, the volume sold fewer than 650 copies on its first printing, and unbound sheets for 116 additional copies had to be remaindered.

A new collection, *A Group of Noble Dames*, required thirteen years (1878–91) to assemble. Hardy based half the stories on bits and pieces of information about pedigrees recorded in John Hutchins's *The History and Antiquities of the County of Dorset*, a work that, throughout his life, he enjoyed consulting. Linked with the eighteenth century and with old mansions and castles in southwestern England, these narratives dealt with "exclusively persons of title." Six of the ten stories – "Barbara of the House of Grebe," "The Marchioness of Stonehenge," "Anna, Lady Baxby," and "The Lady Icenway," "Squire Petrick's Lady" and "Lady Mattisfont" – were written for the Christmas Number of the *Graphic* (1890). William Algernon Locker, the assistant editor, and the Directors objected to a number of fictional details. In particular, Locker thought that the first four stories needed revision "to suit our taste," and regarded the fifth and sixth as "hopeless." "Frankly," he wrote to Hardy, "do you think it advisable to put into the hands of a Young Person stories, one of which turns upon the hysterical confession by a wife of an imaginary adultery, and the other upon the manner in which a husband foists upon his wife the offspring of a former illicit connection?"[1]

Hardy recorded a note in his journal to the effect that he had talked with Arthur Locker (William's father). Apparently he learned from him more specifically what the objections were. "Here's a pretty job!" he added, with some disgust. "Must smooth down these Directors somehow I suppose."[2] He never admitted that writing stories about family genealogical records – when living descendants had a right to be curious about his treatment – was a risky proposition; he never conceded that his subject-matter was potentially offensive, inasmuch as almost every story dealt with childbirth and (in William's phrase), "those relations between the sexes over which conventionality is accustomed (wisely or unwisely) to draw a veil." On the blue-pencilled manuscript of "Squire Petrick's Lady" Hardy wrote, "[N.B. The above lines were deleted against author's wish, by compulsion of Mrs. Grundy: as were all other passages marked blue.]."[3]

Perhaps Hardy yielded to the Lockers' advice on what needed to be done to placate the Directors because he foresaw the problems he would soon confront in the preparation of *Tess* for its serial form.

The argument about his "noble dames," when compared to what was next bound to irritate his publisher or elements of his reading public, hardly seemed worth the candle. Hardy might well have wanted to include "The Doctor's Legend" as part of *A Group of Noble Dames*, and the ending of this story – published in the American periodical *The Independent* (March 26, 1891) – is suggestive of a relationship to a cycle of stories; but Hardy worried that he might offend a local family, and did not submit it to the Lockers. At any rate, he took the opportunity of the American reprinting, in *Harper's Weekly* (four installments between November 29 and December 20, 1890), to return the manuscripts of his six stories to their original form.

The third gathering, *Life's Little Ironies*, contained nine stories, mostly written late in 1890 and early 1891. By now *Tess* had been published, and many readers, eager for more of Hardy's fiction, bought up five good-sized editions in less than two months.

Hardy did not write short stories because he preferred them to the novels which had made his reputation. In every case the story was published first in a periodical, and only then did he consider it as possibly suitable for a collection. As in the case of over half his novels, he undid the damage wrought by censorship to a periodical form when he moved over to book-covers. (For the book-edition of *A Group of Noble Dames*, he added appropriate links between stories.) He published his stories in a surprisingly wide cross-section of periodicals, identifying more markets for his short fiction than either Dickens or Trollope had chosen to do (but, of course, Hardy never worked as an editor, and hence never enjoyed the advantage of an ever-available market for his short stories). In addition to periodicals already mentioned, he published his tales in *Harper's New Monthly Magazine*, *Harper's Weekly*, *Light: A Journal of Criticism and Belles Lettres*, the *Bolton Weekly Journal* (one of the pioneers of syndication), *The Illustrated London News*, the *Fortnightly Review*, *The Universal Review*, *The English Illustrated Magazine*, *Black and White*, the *Bristol Times and Mirror*, *Scribner's Magazine* in New York, *The Sphere*, *Murray's Magazine*, *The Manchester Weekly Times*, *St. James's Budget*, and *The Saturday Review*. He published, in brief, wherever a market existed, and wrote stories in response to specific inquiries about the availability of short pieces of fiction. As a canny self-made man who had triumphed over all kinds of difficulties – he belonged to no novelists' school; he enjoyed only a limited knowledge of fashionable society; his sphere of authority was Dorset, which during his lifetime was very remote from London (for much of the twentieth century it remained the least-populated county of England); and he knew that use of the Dorset dialect had severely limited the potential audience of William Barnes, the poet and linguist whom he admired so greatly – he took an understandable pleasure in naming the sum of money that he considered suitable for payment even before he submitted his story for editorial judgment. Examples may be cited: his letter to Tillotson and Son, dated August 10, 1881, in which he specified £7 per 2,000 words for a story to be published in the Christmas Leaves supplement of *Bolton Weekly Journal*, "provided you send me proofs of the same early enough for publishing simultaneously in America";[4] and a letter to Arthur Locker, dated April 1, 1889, in which he briskly set the price of £125 for a *Graphic* Christmas story (of a specified length) that he had not yet written.[5]

For his first three volumes of short stories Hardy supplied transitional links and prefaces, unifying each collection for the first time. Hamlet's advice to Gertrude may be remembered: "Assume a virtue if you have it not." But his fourth collection, *A Changed Man and Other Tales*, was not put together with comparable meticulousness. Hardy regarded the twelve stories of this gathering as minor efforts (though he referred to them, somewhat casually, as "Novels"). They covered roughly two decades of intermittent effort, the first going back to 1881, the latest being completed in 1899. They were brought together primarily because Hardy's readers had asked for them, not because Hardy himself admired the accomplishment of any single narrative; he acknowledged, however, that they had been scattered in diverse, not always easy-to-get periodicals. He was pleased, however, to be able to reassert his author's rights by reprinting "The Romantic Adventures of a Milkmaid," a story originally printed in 1883, in the Summer Number of the *Graphic*, which had been pirated in several American editions.

Hardy, like Carleton, Le Fanu, Dickens, and Trollope, insisted on the factual base underlying his fictions, but may have gone beyond them in believing that fiction was truer than history anyhow. He defended himself against the charge of narrowness of subject-matter in *Wessex Tales* – in a small collection he had included "two stories of hangmen and one of a military execution" – by arguing that "hanging matters" were important in county-towns and local traditions. In 1896 he explained as a matter of "forgetfulness" whatever divergences from the data of the original event might be traced in "The Withered Arm," and added, "Our imperfect memories insensibly formalize the fresh originality of living fact – from whose shape they slowly depart, as machine-made castings depart by degrees from the sharp hand-work of the mould."⁶ But fiction could never forget its factual substratum. In a suggestive note published in the Wessex Edition of 1912, Hardy wrote that his tale, "A Tradition in Eighteen Hundred and Four," became the basis of "a real tradition" some years after 1882, the date of its first printing. He had invented an incident – Napoleon's visit to the southern coast of England to assess the likelihood of a successful invasion – and was mildly surprised to learn that his invention had been rapidly assimilated into the folklore of Wessex, and its truth sworn to by numberless greybeards. In his preface to *Life's Little Ironies* when it was printed as volume XIV of the Osgood, McIlvaine & Co. edition of the Wessex Novels (1895–6), Hardy again emphasized the closeness of the nexus between fact and fiction; he confessed that "something real" in the history behind each short story accounted for the interest he himself entertained for the story, and was "usually independent of any merits or demerits" such stories "may show as specimens of narrative art." He identified the historical basis of "The Melancholy Hussar of the German Legion," and spoke of the old people for whom the incidents of the story had, at one time, been contemporary truth. "Several of the other stories are true in their main facts," Hardy added, "if there should be anybody who cares to know it."⁷

Hardy's pride in his craft did not derive from invention, but from the sense that he had given life to reworkings of historical figures, and dignity to their motivations. Since relatively few of his stories deal with the modern world, this pride was related to his desire to render justice to the complexity of human behavior in ages past; despite the outcries of those who sought to censor his tales in *A Group of Noble Dames*, he was delighted by "the courtesy and kindness of several bright-eyed Noble Dames yet in the flesh," who, far from being offended by their recognition of the historical realities underlying his narratives, demonstrated "a truly philosophic absence of prejudice in their regard of those incidents whose relation has tended more distinctly to dramatize than to eulogize their ancestors." Hardy, with understandable amusement, alluded to additional materials for a second "Group of Noble Dames" that they had eagerly supplied him.⁸

What he said about novels in his two key essays, "The Profitable Reading of Fiction" (1888) and "Candour in English Fiction"

(1890) applied equally well to shorter fiction: it was a matter for melancholy reflection that the magazine and the circulating library had become, in Hardy's time, the primary media of fiction, because their object was "lateral advance; to suit themselves to what is called household reading ... The number of adults, even in a large household, being normally two, and these being the members which, as a rule, have least time on their hands to bestow on current literature, the taste of the majority can hardly be, and seldom is, tempered by the ripe judgment which desires fidelity."[9] Fiction could not reflect and reveal life under such circumstances, and Hardy, dismayed by the reception of *Tess*, saw little chance for sincere authors to use the subjects that had served as "the bases of the finest imaginative compostions" in previous centuries; "the censorship of prudery," which had become awesome in its power during the last quarter of the nineteenth century, prevented them from perfecting their art. Hardy knew that the system which prevented him from treating serious topics in a mature fashion was unlikely to change in the near future. Even so, he believed that magazines were likely to become more candid in the assumption of their role as "a purveyor of tales for the youth of both sexes," so that "the present lording of nonage over maturity" would at least come out into the open. Hardy hoped that in the future books might be bought rather than borrowed; that newspapers or magazines aimed primarily at adults – and taking the contemporary scene as their subject-matter – might come into existence ("as in France"); and that fiction might incorporate "adult opinion on conduct and theology," and dramatically appeal to readers with a sincere interest in the welfare of such fiction. (He added that "Nothing in such literature should for a moment exhibit lax views of that purity of life upon which the well-being of society depends; but the position of man and woman in nature, and the position of belief in the minds of man and woman – things which everybody is thinking but nobody is saying – might be taken up and treated frankly.")[10]

In important ways Hardy's attack on the "indescribably unreal and meretricious" dénouements which writers of fiction were obliged to arrange for their longer fictions was an indictment of conventional prose narrative as practiced by his fellow-writers. It was certainly acerbic about the conditions of the market-place, despite one superficially soothing sentence: "That the magazine and library have arrogated to themselves the dispensation of fiction is not the fault of the authors, but of circumstances over which they, as

representatives of Grub Street, have no control."[11] Hardy harbored
a life-long resentment against the novel itself as a distraction from
the poetry he preferred to write; in his mind the increasingly old-
fashioned hierarchy of genres placed poetry at the top, and the novel
– or extended prose fiction – well down the list. He preferred Scott's
Marmion ("the most Homeric poem in the English language") to all
of Scott's novels; he even went so far as to say that Scott "declined on
prose fiction." Implicit in this theory, which attacked those who
wrote and those who read novels, and which made clear statements
about the inadequacy of French naturalism and the whole doctrine
of the representational norm, was Hardy's own belief in a special
kind of narrative, a non-Jamesian chronicle of extraordinary
possibilities. Unlike Zola, he distrusted scientific processes.[12] Narrative had to be absorbing, and the best kind of fiction was that kind of
imaginative writing which lay nearest to the epic, dramatic or
narrative masterpieces of the past. "One fact is certain: in fiction
there can be no intrinsically new thing at this stage of the world's
history."[13] For Hardy the art of novel-writing was as yet in its
"tentative stage only." Fiction written in the form of prose
narratives was more true than history or nature could hope to be,
because "In history occur from time to time monstrosities of human
action and character explicable by no known law which appertains
to sane beings; hitches in the machinery of existence, wherein we
have not yet discovered a principle, which the artist is therefore
bound to regard as accidents, hinderances to clearness of presentation, and, hence, weakeners of the effect."[14]

Hardy's low opinion of nineteenth-century standards of taste in
fiction was thus a very broad argument against the novel as a genre,
the conditions whereby it was published and disseminated, the
prurience which governed the moral code of the times, and the
decline in imaginative powers of the reading public. The reader of
fiction, Hardy maintained, should not be "too critical. In other
words, his author should be swallowed whole, like any other
medicinal pill. He should be believed in slavishly, implicitly.
However profusely he may pour out his coincidences, his marvelous
juxtapositions, his catastrophes, his conversions of bad people into
good people at a stroke, and *vice versa*, let him never be doubted for a
moment ... The aim should be the exercise of a generous
imaginativeness, which shall find in a tale not only all that was put
there by the author, put he it never so awkwardly, but which shall
find there what was never inserted by him, never foreseen, never

contemplated. Sometimes these additions which are woven around a work of fiction by the intensitive power of the reader's own imagination are the finest parts of the scenery."[15] Hardy, who had had a number of very unpleasant experiences with readers who were determined to "so twist plain and obvious meanings as to see in an honest picture of human nature an attack on religion, morals, or institutions," concluded "The Profitable Reading of Fiction" with a favored quotation from Carlyle, "The eye sees that which it brings with it the means of seeing."[16]

The inevitability of an author's defending his preferred kind of fiction whenever he attempts to formulate a general theory of fiction is understandable. Whatever else may be said about the limitations of Hardy's somewhat bleak characterization of the achievements and inherent limitations of the novel as a literary form, his assessment of what a writer of fiction might accomplish in the late Victorian Age was firmly grounded on experience. In addition, Hardy remained remarkably consistent from decade to decade; his views underwent no dramatic transformation in 1895, when he renounced novel-writing; he was simply recognizing the hopelessness of the match between his kind of fiction and the kind of commercial market for which he was writing; but signs of unhappiness had shown up in his journal-entries, his correspondence, and his conversations with friends and fellow-authors, for many years before 1895.

It is not accidental that Hardy supplies as subtitle to the first edition of *Wessex Tales* the three words "Strange, Lively, and Commonplace." Kristin Brady, who has written the fullest critical treatment of Hardy's short stories, thinks of these terms as "a possible description for the kinds of information passed down from generation to generation in rural communities," and goes on to emphasize the oral tradition in Hardy's first collection of short stories, a tradition which preserves for the reader "the mood and the substance of a rural community's belief in the improbable."[17] This is an important way of viewing Hardy's reliance on bizarre events as a means of stimulating reader interest. Hardy, as we have seen, took pride in his personal interviews with those who remembered the original happenings that he fictionalized; but facts were not, ultimately, his main interest, even those transmitted by oral tradition, and in every case the story itself had to be worth telling. "A story must be exceptional enough to justify its telling," he wrote on February 23, 1893. "We tale-tellers are all Ancient Mariners, and none of us is warranted in stopping Wedding Guests (in other words, the hurrying public) unless he has something more unusual to relate than the ordinary experience of every average man and woman."[18] Making magic out of the familiar, and learning how to adjust "things unusual to things eternal and universal": the fiction-writer who knew how to do these things possessed the key to Art.

Hardy's impatience with the social realism of Zola, and others who believed that the minutiae of a day's activities were worth recording for their own sake, meant that he recognized much earlier than his friends and supporters the diminishing market for his own favorite subjects, and the growing appeal of greyer, more sociological, more heavily documented accounts of "ordinary" lives. Hardy believed (even if the word "believe" had to be enclosed within quotation marks) in "spectres, mysterious voices, intuitions, omens, dreams, haunted places, etc., etc."[19] He hearkened back to those who had built the great earthwork Maiden Castle, the unknown beings who had constructed Stonehenge, the Roman soldiers who had walked at Maumbury Ring; his imagination encompassed centuries; these figures lived for him, they were not dead; he was not weighed down by the pressure to be up-to-date either in his choice of subject-matter or his method of telling a tale.

Wessex Tales stresses the violent and the extraordinary more than any of the subsequent three collections. It dramatizes Hardy's long-held theory that "Art is a changing of the actual proportions and order of things, so as to bring out more forcibly than might otherwise be done that feature in them which appeals most strongly to the idiosyncrasy of the artist." This note, recorded on August 5, 1890, continues: "Art is a disproportioning – (*i.e.* distorting, throwing out of proportion) – of realities, to show more clearly the features that matter in those realities, which if merely copied or reported inventorially, might possibly be observed but would more probably be overlooked. Hence 'realism' is not Art."[20] Hardy might well have chosen to define his version of reality as the *best* version for all other writers. But he speaks of "the idiosyncrasy of the artist," and implies that every writer is entitled to disproportion reality as he sees fit – at any rate, will do so whenever he sees fit.

The fugitive sheep-stealer who coolly hob-nobs with the hang-man in "The Three Strangers," and the brother who discovers the very man he had expected to see in the condemned cell at Casterbridge, must not be tested by conventional criteria of what is likely to happen at a place like Higher Crowstairs. In "A Tradition of Eighteen Hundred and Four," the improbability of Napoleon's examining a chart of the Channel on English soil must not be looked at too closely. Hardy has no interest in explaining in natural terms the extraordinary events of "A Withered Arm": the dream suffered by Rhoda Brook in which Gertrude – in the form of a hag – sits on her chest; the seizing of the apparition; Gertrude's discovery, some miles away, that bruises (resembling finger-marks) appear on her arm; the terrible "remedy" proposed by Conjurer Trendle; the discovery that the hanged man is the son of Rhoda Brook and Farmer Lodge; the death of Gertrude. A large number of ironic coincidences mark the turnings of the plot in "Fellow-Townsmen," and their concatenation beats down disbelief far more effectively than the use of a single coincidence. The role of superstition in "Interlopers at the Knap" is crucial; when Darton sees the woman he once loved in a dress that he has purchased for his new love, he is overwhelmed by the strange workings of a destiny he is ill-equipped to understand. "He seemed to feel that fate had impishly changed his *vis-à-vis* in the lover's jig he was about to foot; that while the gown had been expected to enclose a Sally, a Helena's face looked out from the bodice; that some long-lost hand met his own from the sleeves."[21] A reader may call Darton's reaction a surrender to superstition; but he must accept Darton's reaction as natural if he is to enjoy the tale. "The Distracted Preacher," last of the *Wessex Tales*, describes a series of events associated with smuggling during the 1830s. Hardy's intense interest in this history was far more than that of an antiquarian reviewing the decade preceding that of his own birth. Some of his relatives had been involved, and he had often heard about the techniques for handling contraband liquor. But Hardy's choice of an outsider, Mr. Stockdale, a Wesleyan minister, as the chosen point of view transforms these events into mysterious, exotic, and indescribably romantic "happenings" at Nether-Moynton. Mr. Stockdale understands very little of what he sees. At the end of the story Lizzy decides to give up smuggling, and marries him; Victorian conventionality has won out; but we know from Hardy's footnote, added to the Wessex Edition, that he would have preferred another ending, one in which Lizzy married (instead of the minister) Jim the smuggler, and both emigrated to Wisconsin. This outcome would have corresponded "more closely with the true incidents of which the tale is a vague and flickering shadow." But the tamer version, in which marriage serves as the "proper" resolution of Lizzy's moral and ethical dilemma, was "almost *de rigueur* in an English magazine at the time of writing."[22]

We can, if we choose, trace similar ironies and coincidences which disproportion reality in later short stories, but it is more important to see that Hardy shrugged off adverse criticism if it concentrated on the degree of believability of his narratives. Indeed, part of Hardy's importance to the history of the Victorian short story is that he clearly perceived how sharply his preferred subject-matter, and his heavy reliance on oral tradition, contravened currently fashionable doctrine about documentation of fictional setting, the need for verifiable detail in the depiction of manners and social behavior, and analogies between the technique of a story-teller and that of a scientist.

For example, "The Romantic Adventures of a Milkmaid," which deals with the same social milieu as *Tess*, could hardly be more resolute in its refusal to depict the Valley of the Exe in the same fashion as the Vale of the Great Dairies, in which Tess worked as a milkmaid. Hardy's description of a fog ("Nature had laid a white hand over the creatures ensconced within the vale, as a hand might be laid over a nest of chirping birds") is of a piece with his sketching of Margery's demon lover (when his expression changes, the effect is "almost phantasmagorical"). Her ball-dress is a "heavenly cob-web," and she herself turns into "a lovely white apparition." The Baron conjures up a carriage: "There stood the brougham, the horses, the coachman, all as still as if they were growing on the spot, like the trees." Other-world metaphors abound. Margery's request to save a scrap of the lace (after the ball has ended) is refused by the Baron, who becomes "as immovable as Rhadamanthus." She had fallen under the spell of "some great enchanter. Indeed, the Baron's power over [the] innocent girl was curiously like enchantment, or mesmeric influence . . . It was that of Prospero over the gentle Ariel." When the story comes to its conventional close Margery marries Jim Hayward, whose feet are planted firmly on Wessex soil – we can be sure that this is not the ending Hardy wanted to use. Indeed, such an ending was forced upon him. As he confessed later, the story at first printed in the *Graphic* carried an ending "adopted to suit the requirements" of that periodical.[23]

The fairy-tale elements are everywhere. Imbedded in a story with a number of intractably ordinary, homely details about the way life is lived by prosaically minded people, such elements disturbed many of the original readers. "It is not altogether necessary," Hardy wrote in "The Profitable Reading of Fiction," ". . . that the stories chosen should be 'of most disastrous chances, of moving accidents by flood and field',"[24] and this quotation from *Othello* was intended to remind readers that Hardy had always specialized in mixing story-telling traditions; that he had never written an unadulterated Gothic story, or a completely realistic one; a reader's indulgence was being implored; a reader's willingness to suspend judgment and follow whither the story-teller led was essential for the fullness of the story's effect. A good story is to be known by its emphasis on story first, on artistic development second.[25]

Closely allied with this doctrine is Hardy's emphasis on Wessex as the country of his imagination. Biographers and critics have identified Wessex as a convenient Other Place when, for Hardy, the charms of London faded, or when, more precisely speaking, his future career as an architect in London became impossible because of failing health. (Dorset friends were alarmed at his pallor by the summer of 1867; his employer Blomfield recommended that he return to the country "to regain vigour"; and Hardy himself was thinking of a permanent move. "He constitutionally shrank from the business of social advancement, caring for life as an emotion rather than for life as a science of climbing, in which respect he was quizzed by his acquaintance for his lack of ambition.")[26] Hardy first used the term "Wessex" while writing *Far From the Madding Crowd* in 1874; it was a deliberate resurrection of the name of an extinct kingdom, as he explained in a preface added in February 1895, to the Osgood, McIlvaine edition of the Wessex Novels. He took some pride in the immediate popularity of the term, which, for purposes of copyright, he guarded jealously thereafter; as he solemnly avowed in the preface, the term "Wessex," until its appearance in the pages of the *Cornhill*, had referred to "nothing later in date than the Norman Conquest."[27] Now, quite apart from the two obvious consequences of this coinage – he could cross county boundaries freely in his fiction, and he could rename villages, houses, and topographical features with impunity[28] – Hardy learned, over a period of years, that his technique of disguising the West Country provided a powerful means of unifying the varied localities of his fictitious universe.

The hundred thousand acres of heathland west of the Avon valley known to the eighteenth century are now diminished by urban development, new land-uses (forestry and agriculture), a tank training-ground (Bovington), and the Atomic Energy Establishment at Winfrith. Today only fifteen thousand acres remain in anything resembling their original condition. In countless ways the Wessex of Hardy's fictions has turned into something else, and on the whole something less attractive, in the century and a half since his birth (1840). But even to the members of the Wessex Field and Antiquarian Club who recount to each other the stories that constitute *A Group of Noble Dames* – as a substitute, in Hardy's ironic phrase, "for the regulation papers on deformed butterflies, fossil ox-horns, prehistoric dung-mixens, and such like"[29] – Wessex is a realm of romantic possibilities. The members are much obliged to the local historian, whose narrative of the First Countess of Wessex has begun the two-day meeting, "for such a curious chapter from the domestic histories of the county,"[30] and they agree with the rural dean that "there was no lack of materials. Many, indeed, were the legends and traditions of gentle and noble dames, renowned in times past in that part of England, whose actions and passions were now, but for men's memories, buried under the brief inscription on a tomb or an entry of dates in a dry pedigree."[31] The members of the Club share male prejudices, and their reactions to the tales are notably lacking in sympathy toward the unhappy fates of the noble dames. Hardy is saying something about their resemblance to the curious specimens which populate their meeting-place when he concludes *A Group of Noble Dames*: "The last member at length departed, the attendant at the museum lowered the fire, the curator locked up the rooms, and soon there was only a single pirouetting flame on the top of a single coal to make the bones of the ichthyosaurus seem to leap, the stuffed birds to wink, and to draw a smile from the varnished skulls of Vespasian's soldiery."[32] Only two of the tales they have heard have happy endings ("The First Countess of Wessex" and "The Honourable Laura"); these are placed by Hardy at the beginning and ending of his cycle of tales; and the names of only these two stories lack ironical implications.[33]

The use of the word "ironical" reminds us of the long and respectable critical tradition which persists in seeing all of Hardy's short stories as miniaturized statements of human helplessness in a universe dominated by the Immanent Will; as a succession of life's little ironies. Yet only a few of Hardy's stories – among others, "An Imaginative Woman," "For Conscience' Sake," "A Tragedy of Two Ambitions," and "The Fiddler of the Reels," – illustrate the doctrine that is most fully worked out in *The Dynasts*. Hardy himself emphasized this point. "It may seem something of a paradox to assert that the novels which most conduce to moral profit are likely to be among those written without a moral purpose," he wrote in "The Profitable Reading of Fiction." "But the truth of the statement may be realized if we consider that the didactic novel is so generally devoid of *vraisemblance* as to teach nothing but the impossibility of tampering with natural truth to advance dogmatic opinions."[34] In "The Science of Fiction" he insisted that "A sight for the finer qualities of existence, an ear for the 'still sad music of humanity,' are not to be acquired by the outer senses alone, close as their powers in photography may be."[35]

Hardy chose Wessex as the stage for his dramas because he entertained some suspicion of the ambitious novel which covered "large extents of country," moved easily between towns and cities, and even wandered "over the four quarters of the globe." He refused to concede that stories with a limited geography narrowed the range of human nature that might be exhibited therein. "I consider that our magnificent heritage from the Greeks in dramatic literature," he wrote in the General Preface to the novels and poems that he added to the Wessex Edition of 1912, "found sufficient room for a large proportion of its action in an extent of their country not much larger than the half-dozen counties here reunited under the old name of Wessex, that the domestic emotions have throbbed in Wessex nooks with as much intensity as in the palaces of Europe, and that, anyhow, there was quite enough human nature in Wessex for one man's literary purpose."[36]

Hardy's art may be defined, on the basis of these criteria, as an attempt to render, against a Wessex background, the emotions ("passions") known to every human being. "Our true object is a lesson in life, mental enlargement from elements essential to the narratives themselves and from the reflections they engender."[37] A representation of life, shaped by the imagination, is not the same as a view *about* life; the story-teller is not a philosopher, essayist, or shaper of epigrams.

Hardy must be considered the best judge of how to group his stories. Though his irony is stronger in the handling of some stories than in others, and though occasionally the artlessness of the telling (when a story seems to tell itself) seems strikingly different from the tale which is consciously, artistically "told," grouping the stories by subject-matter or dominant image irrespective of the volumes in which they first appeared seems distinctly unsatisfactory. Norman Page identifies four categories: "humorous," "romantic or super-natural," "realistic and often ironic or tragic," and "historical,"[38] while Kristin Brady, seeing some inherent dangers in this arrange-ment, labels the first three volumes, *Wessex Tales, A Group of Noble*

Dames, and *Life's Little Ironies*, as "pastoral histories," "ambivalent exempla," and "tragedies of circumstance."[39] Yet even as we reject D. H. Lawrence's sneer that Hardy wrote a number of "little tales of widows and widowers," or regard with due caution Evelyn Hardy's judgment that "Hardy regarded his short stories as novels in miniature,"[40] we sense that attempts to disregard the patternings provided by Hardy in three of his four collections – his unifying links; his efforts (however sketchy) to characterize the tellers of the tales; his emphasis on oral tradition in one volume, genealogical records in another, and the oddity of marriage relationships in still another – are unfair both to Hardy and to the unified impact of each gathering of tales.

Although short stories were not as profitable as novels, Hardy drew from this observation a conclusion different from that which had governed Trollope's practice. A short story was not an isolated performance, written when other pressures were off, and gathered along with a number of other tales and sketches when sufficient bulk might entitle an author to bring out a new "title." Rather, a short story dealt with human nature and circumstances, and, Ancient Mariner-like, was worth stopping the reader for.

In the four years (1888–91) when Hardy wrote the largest number of short stories for any comparable time period, he became proprietary about the use of the term "Wessex" for his fictional world; turned quietly but with determination from historical settings of the previous two centuries to more modern themes, as in "A Tragedy of Two Ambitions," which embodied "present day aspiration,"[41] and "For Conscience' Sake," "On the Western Circuit," and "The Son's Veto"; and though he had a rather somber view of the quality of most short stories published in the periodicals of the last quarter of the century ("many are written, but few worth reading"),[42] he preferred to write short stories rather than novels, at least for a brief period in the 1890s.[43]

Almost as many readers choose unexpectedly when asked to name their favorite short story by Hardy as they do when forced to select one of his poems as "his best." Hardy told Rebekah Owen that "The Son's Veto" was his best short story; the reasons why he should think so are worth exploring. For it is, all things considered, a remarkable drama of deep feelings held by ordinary Wessex folk, and what goes wrong in their lives could not be solved by any rearrangement of laws or social institutions; it documents Hardy's conviction that his "imperfect dramas of country life and passions"[44] succeeded best when their moral was implicit in the events recounted. Its art is ripe; we are a long way from *The Poor Man and the Lady* of 1867–8, with its "unmitigated utterances of strong feeling" against the upper classes of society; but Hardy's thesis in "The Son's Veto," his "lesson in life," bears strong resemblances to views held a full quarter-century earlier.

The heroine, a parlour-maid named Sophie, marries a vicar because she hardly dares "refuse a personage so reverend and august in her eyes," but she really loves Sam Hobson, a young gardener. Sam is characterized as kindly, eager to have her even after the passage of years and the death of the vicar; but her son, Randolph, for whom everything has been sacrificed, and whose education has "completely ousted his humanity," is an insufferable prig who not only forbids her remarriage, but forces her to swear to this effect "before a little cross and altar that he had erected in his bedroom for his private devotions." She pines away, dies, and is carried to her grave; in the mourning coach "a young smooth-shaven priest in a high waistcoat [Randolph] looked black as a cloud at the shop-keeper standing there [Sam]."

An anecdote, but told with great art. Hardy does not attempt to make uncomplicated Wessex types into enigmas, but he suggests – by means of a provocative image early on – that there is more to Sophie's character than can readily be appreciated. "To the eyes of a man viewing it from behind, the nut-brown hair was a wonder and a mystery." Sophie's hair has "weavings and coilings," it represents "ingenious art." Those who admire her head from the rear expect greater handsomeness and piquancy in her features than Sophy's face actually possesses. The world expects to find in Wessex something different from what it does find, and does not recognize the worth of what it actually sees.

Interlocking images enrich the telling of "The Son's Veto," such as those which suggest immobility and stasis. These accompany the descriptions of Sophie, a "chaired lady" listening to the bandstand concert; her London home, "a narrow, dusty house in a long, straight street"; her restrained activities after her husband's death ("she really had nothing to occupy her in the world but to eat and drink, and make a business of indolence, and go on weaving and coiling the nut-brown hair ...");[45] her despair after the vow not to marry Sam Hobson ("Her lameness became more confirmed as time went on ...").[46]

Hardy – whose sleep at 5 Upper Phillimore Place, London, had been disturbed more than once in 1888 by wagons such as the one used by Sam to bring his vegetable produce to market – made Sam into a messenger of a life principle, bringing to the center of the great metropolis "green bastions of cabbages nodding to their fall, yet never falling, walls of baskets enclosing masses of beans and peas, pyramids of snow-white turnips, swaying howdahs of mixed produce."

The differences between country and city multiply as the story progresses; and London, for Sophie, leads inevitably to death of the spirit. The fine peal of bells in the village has been exchanged "for the wretchedest one-tongued clangour that ever tortured mortal ears."[47] Lest a reader underestimate the full force of Hardy's dislike of the environment in which Randolph grows to his unlovely and unlovable manhood, Hardy describes in fulsome detail the "great coaches" at Lord's, "the *débris* of luxurious luncheons; bones, piecrusts, champagne-bottles, glasses, plates, napkins, and the family silver," and "the proud fathers and mothers" of the boys who, like Randolph, wear "broad white collars and dwarf hats."[48] Progress in the modern world, looked at closely, consists of "rhythm and racket";[49] and it is difficult to keep in time with such movements.

This story is more than a review of the unsatisfactory relationship of a loving mother to her ungrateful, even monstrous son; more, indeed, than a caricature of London as a city offering vistas of "sooty trees, hazy air, and drab house-facades,"[50] and from which Sophie can escape only by being borne back to her village in a coffin. The narrator is in complete control, and his genuine concern with the inter-workings of character and circumstance, his distribution of image and detail, are telling. "The Son's Veto" shows Hardy at his best; his anger toward the smug and hypocritical clergy, though unmistakable, is only one reason for writing the story; and the complexity of his reasons for shaping the story in this particular way leads the reader here, as in a number of other tales, to a fuller knowledge of the Wessex that Hardy knew better than any other Victorian.

6

Robert Louis Stevenson: many problems, some successes

Let us assume that the outline of Robert Louis Stevenson's eventful, and not always happy, life is familiar to most readers. Let us also assume that it will not change dramatically because of the discovery of hitherto unsuspected biographical material. Two critical questions are our major concern here: why Stevenson thought of a large number of his short stories as being deficient in form or content, and why (despite his reservations) a particular category of his short stories – that of the horror tales – retains the affection of general readers and most literary critics.

Stevenson's reputation declined precipitously after the turn of the century, partly because the reading public became uneasily aware that more had been promised than delivered. Andrew Lang's enthusiasm – so important in establishing Stevenson's fame while he lived – was, in important respects, an excuse for attacks on naturalistic fiction, which Lang, like Stevenson, regarded as a dreary dead end; looked at more closely, Lang's analyses of Stevenson seemed to say less about the man whom Henley had described as

> Most vain, most generous, sternly critical,
> Buffoon and poet, lover and sensualist:
> A deal of Ariel, just a streak of Puck,
> Much Antony, of Hamlet most of all,
> And something of the Shorter-Catechist,

or about his writings, than about Lang's restless need to find still another culture-hero who opposed Zola's teachings and example.

Stevenson wrote approximately thirty short stories. Their unevenness makes them both exciting and exasperating. He wrote freely when inspiration flourished, and labored mightily over both first- and fifth-rate pieces of fiction in what sometimes seems to have been equal measure. He often began with brio, wandered through wildernesses of increasingly wild situation and characterization, and wound up hastily, and in great confusion, when the ground gave from under him. His manuscripts were littered with false starts;

10   Portrait of Robert Louis Stevenson by W. B. Richmond, 1887

there were uncounted unfinished drafts. These, if completed, would
have swelled the number of volumes in the Edinburgh Edition (26),
the Vailima (26), or the South Seas (32); no edition can be
accounted complete even for the materials that Stevenson did finish.
    Should we lament lost possibilities, fragments of masterpieces not

written? Stevenson occasionally talked in exactly such a way, as when he referred to the printed version of his novella *The Beach of Falesa* as "the slashed and gaping ruins" of his art. (He was blaming the corrupted text on printers, proofreaders, publishers, editors, and friends; much more often than Victorian readers appreciated, he found himself opposed to moral and ethical positions held by those exercising editorial decisions on periodical fiction. Not until 1984 did Stevenson's original version of *The Beach of Falesa*, edited by Barry Menikoff for Stanford University Press, come into print.)

Nevertheless, Stevenson believed that much of the blame for his failed art rested with himself. He enjoyed writing horror stories, or "crawlers," because Fanny liked them, and encouraged him to write them; but he was sensitive about their limitations – perhaps on occasion over-estimating the seriousness of these limitations – and wrote candidly to his correspondents that most of them were sub-literary. He frequently confessed that he had failed to think out the implications of his narrative-line.

What was the source of Stevenson's diffidence? We may begin with his rather odd collection of fables, which were worked on between 1874 and 1894, and which, had he lived longer, might have become a book. At least he promised to deliver a book devoted solely to them when an editor from Longmans visited him in New York in 1888. Several were published in *Longman's Magazine* (1895) and *McClure's Magazine* (1896); they were printed as a group in an appendix to a new edition of "The Strange Case of Dr. Jekyll and Mr. Hyde" (1896), and they illustrate (in briefer form than the "fables" contained in his Jekyll–Hyde narrative, "Will o' the Mill," and "Markheim") the fable that Stevenson had defined as a genre in his review of Lord Lytton's *Fables in Song*.[1] As Sir Sidney Colvin wrote in a prefatory note, several of these were conceived in "a more mystic and legendary vein,"[2] and evidently all these fables – long and short together – were designed to incorporate elements of moral allegory or apologue.

They are slight efforts – very few biographers or critics mention their existence – but their major interest lies in the problems Stevenson obviously encountered when trying to incorporate a message within the briefest of story-lines. The task he set himself was the avoidance of a tacked-on moral: how might he tell the story so that it commented on its own significance without seeming to do so? In "The Sinking Ship" a captain debates with his first lieutenant the proper course of action to pursue while the danger of a powder magazine about to detonate grows more and more serious. The Captain urges his officer to finish his shave, partly on the ground that "to the philosophic eye there is nothing new in our position: the ship (if she is to go down at all) may be said to have been going down since she was launched." He sees the inevitability of death, and wonderingly speaks of "man's handsome fashion" to carry on as if in every way "he might hope to be eternal." Is he right to ask for a cigar, while doing nothing to save the ship? Is it really for the best that the ship should blow up with "a glorious detonation"? The first lieutenant, bemused by the Captain's indifference, wonders at the philosophic difference "between shaving in a sinking ship and smoking in a power magazine." Stevenson offers no answer; there may be none; but the conundrum, offered playfully, deals with a serious issue: the need to play-act when the alternative proffered by an indifferent God is too terrifying to contemplate.

Some of the fables are too brief to clarify Stevenson's line of thought. "The Tadpole and the Frog" amounts to no more than the exchange between a frog ("Be ashamed of yourself. When I was a tadpole, I had no tail") and a tadpole ("Just what I thought! You never were a tadpole"). Other fables – "Faith, Half Faith and No Faith at All" – run on almost endlessly, and never arrive at the announced destination. Stevenson sometimes is uncertain that the story makes its point ("The House of Eld" and "Something in It"), and appends a blunt "Moral." The *Fables* are unfinished experiments in story-telling, but their objective is clear enough, and here, we understand, is a continuation of the running battle between Stevenson's interest in allowing the imagination free rein and his concern that he might not be serious enough to deserve the attentive respect of his audience. It is – in nineteen separate examples – the same problem that confronted him when Fanny objected to his sheer delight in story at the expense of allegory, at a crucial moment when the first draft of "The Strange Case of Dr. Jekyll and Mr. Hyde" was being considered.

The struggle may be illustrated by stories that fail to make their mark as well as by stories that succeed, for the chasm between them is wider and deeper than it is for most Victorian shapers of the imagination. If we consider the first group, "Will o' the Mill" may serve as paradigm. Leslie Stephen, writing to its author on September 29, 1877, suggested that the story be revised "to make it either more grotesque or more realistic,"[3] though he expressed a willingness to print it without revision in *The Cornhill Magazine*;

Stevenson let it go forward, took his twenty pounds, and saw it into print in the issue of January 1878.[4]

Will's existence "in a falling valley between pine-woods and great mountains" is dedicated to watching others live lives more crowded with incidents than his own. The mill stands near a pass that serves as "a high thoroughfare between two splendid and powerful societies," and yet a war that breaks out "over a great part of the world" seems very remote from Will's daily round of activities. A casual conversation with the miller reveals to him the existence of the sea ("the greatest thing God made," according to the miller), but a surge of desire to see some of the world subsides not long after a traveller tells him that all men are frustrated by their inability to know who inhabits the stars, or to achieve their grandest ambitions. Will does not resist this cold realism, nor does he deny the applicability to his own position of the parable that the traveller, a "fat young man," "plainly one of those who prefer living people to people made of ink and paper," outlines for him. The years pass; Will proposes to Marjory, the parson's daughter, and then thinks better of it ("I do not think getting married is worthwhile . . . But I'll marry if you will"); he does not lament lost opportunities when Marjory suddenly marries somebody else; and, growing old contentedly, he placidly accepts the invitation of a stranger (Death) to accompany him for a turn in his barouche. "One of the servants awoke about this time and heard the noise of horses pawing before he dropped asleep again; all down the valley that night there was a rushing as of a smooth and steady wind descending towards the plain; and when the world rose next morning, sure enough Will o' the Mill had gone at last upon his travels."

Will, for most readers, is a dull stick; his adopted parents are not individualized before they (all too conveniently) die; Marjory seems no less placid than her wavering lover; and even Death, who comes to harvest the soul of a man who has been "prudent and quiet" all his life, is "little more than a shadow at table." Stevenson may mean to suggest that human beings, taking a lesson from the indifference of the stars, should not seek to break from their cages, and surely Will's two unsuccessful efforts to enlarge the horizons of his experience, first by travel and then by marriage, do not affect in any serious way the general self-satisfaction of his life. Nor is this sermon – or moral – substantially different from that contained in "The Sinking Ship," a fable which implies that men must bow before the inevitable, and not trouble themselves about choices between alternative paths of

conduct that lead in all cases to the grave. But it is a puzzling thesis –
Stevenson did not abide by its implications as he worked heroically,
and in great pain, to add something of value to the written record –
and it is not embodied very convincingly by Will o' the Mill, who
leads a vegetable existence, and whose aspirations, even at best, are
not very interesting.

The intention of this story – as revealed by Stevenson to Graham
Balfour – was to argue for a point of view, a philosophy, opposite to
that which he held personally. It was, in brief, an experiment, and,
in Balfour's language, "Will o' the Mill" depicts "the delight of
fruition indefinitely deferred, the prudence of giving no hostages to
fortune, the superiority of the man who suffices to himself."[5] But
Leslie Stephen was right to complain about the uneasy mixture of
styles that blurred a reader's perception of what Stevenson was up
to. The mountain scenery, drawn from Stevenson's memories of his
Grand Tour, taken when he was twelve years old, combined
elements of the Brenner Pass in the Tyrol and the Murgthal in
Baden. And Balfour – who admired the story – admitted that
elements in Will's personality, namely his wisdom, spirit, courage,
and "so much of all that was best in the writer,"[6] contradicted the
explicit sermonizings of both the traveller who visits the Mill, and
Death, who brings the final reckoning.

And what was Stevenson attempting in his "Latter-Day Arabian
Nights," published in seventeen weekly installments in *London* (June
8 to October 26, 1878)? More specifically, in "The Suicide Club,"
which formed the first three of the seven stories, and which has
earned the widest readership of all the units contained in this
particular sequence? Stevenson, who earned £44–12–0 for these
stories, proposed to C. Kegan Paul that they be published as a book;
but the suggestion was turned down because the stories possessed a
"preposterous character."[7] Soon enough after this aborted publication scheme of 1879, "The Suicide Club" was reprinted as part of the
first volume of *New Arabian Nights* (1882); but at least one of the
owners of *London* believed that Stevenson's fantastic fictions turned
away readers, and contributed to the demise of the periodical after
114 issues. It is worth remembering that Stevenson, trapped by the
demands of weekly contributions, held no exaggerated opinion of
the worth of what he wrote for *London*, a magazine that was "rapidly
hustling [him] into the abhorred tomb," as he wrote to Charles
Baxter in 1878.[8] The success of *New Arabian Nights*, a book which
earned him as much money as he had received for both *An Inland*

Voyage and *Travels with a Donkey*, and which, in his own words, was "the first book that ever returned me anything, and ... also established my name,"[9] helped him to forget the artistic problems that had deviled him while he wrote the three stories that, taken collectively, he labeled "The Suicide Club."

These narratives mark a stage in his development as an artist; though severe on their failings as satire ("uneven and incomplete"), one critic finds the sequence "peculiarly instructive as a reflection of an artist's mind in turmoil."[10] It is hard to take this judgment as any kind of commendation.

These adventures of Prince Florizel of Bohemia and his loyal companion, Colonel Geraldine, begin in London, when they meet a young man who has already eaten twenty-five cream tarts and is distributing – in a spirit of mockery – additional cream tarts to patrons of an oyster bar. The Prince wears "false whiskers and a pair of large adhesive eyebrows." The Colonel is "dressed and painted to represent a person connected with the Press in reduced circumstances." The young man introduces them to a society of men unwilling to continue living. The president of the club has depraved tastes, and diabolically engineers the death of young men who no longer believe in the future. The major thrust of the opening pages is directed against the aesthetes and decadents whose artistic credos Stevenson found offensive as the century aged. The members of the Suicide Club smoke, drink champagne, and attempt to sustain "a feverish hilarity," although "sudden and rather ghastly pauses" are inevitable. Stevenson has no use for them: "As in all other places of resort, one type predominated: people in the prime of youth, with every show of intelligence and sensibility in their appearance, but with little promise of strength or the quality that makes success ... some talked well, but the conversation of others was plainly the result of nervous tension, and was equally without wit or purport ... There was little decency among the members of the club ... There was a tacit understanding against moral judgments ..." Stevenson's years of illness had enlarged his sympathetic understanding of pain suffered as a consequence of real grief, genuine loss; but these clubmen, in perfect health, had not earned the right to easeful death.

But "The Suicide Club" is only in part a polemic against the excesses of thought and behavior exhibited by those who read too literally the prose of Pater, the poetry of Swinburne and Rossetti, the epigrams of Wilde. The story of the young man with the cream tarts begins with a social statement, an advocacy (through irony) of a

sane moral position that opposes the worst excesses of the 1880s –
and collapses into the shabby melodrama of the story of "The
Physician and the Saratoga Trunk," with the tiresome carting of a
lifeless body from one address to another (even across the English
Channel); and the dreadfully self-conscious adventure of the
hansom cabs, wherein an elaborately decorated mansion is stripped
bare in order to signify the end of all illusion: "The flowering shrubs
had disappeared from the staircase; three large furniture waggons
stood before the garden gate; the servants were busy dismantling the
house upon all sides; and some of them had already donned their
great-coats and were preparing to depart. It was like the end of a
country ball, where everything has been supplied by contract..." It
is as if Stevenson, who has already found himself unable to continue
the satire of his opening pages, no longer has faith even in the ability
of his fiction to suspend disbelief; the dream has lost its power; the
splendid house that turns out, unexpectedly, not to have "a stick of
furniture nor so much as a picture on the walls" after the revels have
ended can be interpreted – and has been interpreted – as the ruin of a
universe; its creator has abandoned it to an all-too-probable fate.

This dark interpretation may take too seriously a linked sequence
of tales that many readers have enjoyed; but "The Suicide Club" is
representative of much else in the canon, because it lacks consistency
of tone; the major characters (the Prince and Geraldine) disappear
for long stretches, and without explanation; the narrative might be
extended indefinitely or ended abruptly, without apology (there
seems to be no sense of the rightness of form for a particular
adventure); and, although it begins with hostility toward those who
demean the significance of honest work and of life itself, the cavalier
suggestion in the final story that life is a game or masquerade undoes
a reader's faith in the integrity of Stevenson's attitude toward
Haroun Al Raschid, here incarnated as a Prince of that conveniently remote kingdom of Bohemia.

Stevenson's contributions to the short-story genre, however,
should not be under-valued because of a series of problems relating
to structure, characterization, and message (i.e., whether or not to
include one). Nor should the wide-spread belief that Stevenson's
personality, a singularly attractive and ingratiating one, which
dazzled a large number of individuals normally suspicious of charm,
and thus prevented editors from holding Stevenson's stories to higher
standards, distract us from the verifiable history of the widespread
popularity of his fictions during the last decade of his life. Another

way of saying this: Stevenson always wanted to write commercially, and often succeeded; his short stories between "The Strange Case of Dr. Jekyll and Mr. Hyde" and *Island Nights' Entertainment* (published a year before his death) represent – for better or worse – the flourishing of the Victorian short story in the late 1880s and early 1890s. It is time to re-examine the best of Stevenson's work in this genre, and the Jekyll–Hyde story is as good a place as any to begin.

The various versions of the genesis of "The Strange Case of Dr. Jekyll and Mr. Hyde" are not easily reconciled. Inconsistencies from one version to the next are striking enough without further embroidering of what Stevenson read for inspiration, or what he dreamed, or how many versions he drafted, or the extent to which Fanny Stevenson contributed ideas and criticism. It seems clear that Stevenson read an article about the subconscious in a French scientific journal several years before the story took shape (the article has not been identified); was deeply impressed by it; and used it as an intellectual basis for the "hugger-mugger melodrama" that he wrote about Deacon Brodie. It had some weight in the writing of "Markheim" as well, according to Fanny, and her statement suggests that the essay treated the problems of a split personality. "The Travelling Companion," written in 1881, revised in 1883, and destroyed when "Dr. Jekyll and Mr. Hyde" supplanted it, was undoubtedly another dramatization of the same article.

There *was* a dream. Stevenson needed a plot, though he had no specific notion of how it might develop; his financial situation required the sale of a story that first had to be written; and it has been suggested that this, the most famous of all horror stories printed toward the end of the century, answered the request for a shilling shocker made by his publisher.[11] Stevenson had some understandable compunction at the thought that such a story would be aimed at the Christmas trade, but the convenient timing of a dream – which Stevenson described in several places, "A Chapter on Dreams"[12] (1888) and an interview for the *San Francisco Examiner* (June 8, 1888) being two of the more notable – led him to clarify his ideas on what the narrative would treat. Stevenson saw, in his sleep, a man being pressed into a cabinet, swallowing a drug, and changing into another person. (In another version of this moment of inspiration, according to Fanny, her husband had a nightmare; she woke him; he was indignant because she had interrupted his dreaming at the transformation scene.)

Stevenson, happily on the right road at last, wrote his first draft –

some thirty thousand words – in three days. So reads one account. Or, if this account seems exaggerated, half the draft; or, again, only a few pages. The only certain element in these conflicting accounts is that he submitted what he had written to Fanny for her criticism (it was his habit to do so), and that she disapproved of the way in which it was developing as a mere "story." She apparently saw the value of an allegorical treatment before her husband did, and though he was disappointed to have met with less than full approval, one should remember that Fanny's disappointment that her husband was writing below his true level of ability and insight could have been no less keen. He burnt his draft, because tinkering would have taken fully as much time as rewriting all that he had done up to that point. He therefore put himself beyond temptation and began fresh; wrote an equal amount in three days; and, without the goad (or the depressing influence) of additional criticism from Fanny, he went over the manuscript carefully, completing the revision in a little over a month.

The instant success of this longish short story may have been exaggerated by several biographers; the forty thousand copies sold during the first six months by Longmans, Green, and Co. – which decided not to compete with Christmas issues of a large number of periodicals, and withdrew the book until January 1886 – were only a preliminary accounting. Its extraordinary success developed only after *The Times* printed an editorial praising both its theme and its art. Sermons were preached everywhere, including one at St. Paul's Cathedral. Playwrights prepared three versions, and these appeared on the boards within a few months. Authorized editions competed with pirated publications.

The passing of time has intensified the damage done by Fanny to Stevenson's original desire to tell a story pure and simple. Hollywood (which made all four of the famous film versions) has broadened and vulgarized Hyde's character so that he lives out the brutal, criminal, and heavily sexual fantasies of Dr. Jekyll in a far more juvenile manner than Stevenson intended. Marxist interpretations of Hyde as economic man have been paralleled by somber readers of Hyde's meaning as some kind of political commentary. It is difficult not to agree with one reader who, shaking his head, writes, "Hyde is usually described in metaphors because essentially that is what he is; a metaphor of uncontrolled appetites, an amoral abstraction driven by a compelling will unrestrained by any moral halter. Such a creature is, of necessity, only figuratively describable;

for his deformity is moral rather than physical. Purposely left vague, he is best described as Jekyll-deformed – dwarfish, stumping, ape-like – a frightening parody of a man unable to exist on the surface."[13]

Stevenson's "message" has been interpreted in a variety of ways. Jenni Calder argues that the narrative strikes at hypocrisy, "the bland but relentless outside of a hypocritical society that forces Jekyll first to hide his inclinations for what were probably relatively innocent pleasures, and then to free himself from his own sense of guilt by giving himself up to evil." This approach almost inevitably attempts to fortify its critical bias by some allusion to the author's personal experience: Stevenson "had led a double life himself. The writing of *Jekyll and Hyde* may well have been a cathartic experience for its author."[14] Christopher Harvie, fascinated by what Stevenson probably knew about Gladstone's solicitude of London prostitutes, and by what Stevenson undoubtedly knew about the disparity between the statesman's "Christian high-minded politics" and his allowing of General Gordon's murder at Khartoum (1885), and by Stevenson's championing of Home Rule for Ireland at the same time that Irish terrorism was claiming one victim after another (the Phoenix Park murders took place in 1882), claims that "The Strange Case of Dr. Jekyll and Mr. Hyde" possessed for its contemporary audience more than the psychological interest of the human dualism worked out in the events of that story; "it appealed to the book-reading public because it provided a parable as well as a convenient metaphor for the politics of their time."[15] Edwin Eigner rejects the popular view that the story is "an allegory of the evil in man swallowing up the helpless good," and develops the thesis that it is "a story of a whole man driving one part of his nature to depravity until the entire ego is destroyed."[16] He points out how strongly Stevenson denied that Hyde was a "mere voluptuary,"[17] and how carefully the author traces the degeneration of Hyde's actions, from conscience-less acts of brutality to more violent deeds, including murder.

It may be that Stevenson's new draft still retains signs of indecision as to how best the narrative should unroll; there are, after all, four points of view in addition to that of Dr. Jekyll (who speaks for himself only in the final quarter of the story). Within a relatively brief compass, these are not only an unexpectedly large number of narrators but more than Stevenson used in any other story, including his novels. The diversity of perspectives enables us to put together a composite (or social) attitude toward the baffling secret of

Dr. Jekyll, one that is based largely upon observable behavior, before the truth comes out in "Henry Jekyll's Full Statement of the Case." Also, not knowing the explanation for the cruel, baffling actions that begin with Hyde's trampling calmly over a child's body and leaving her "screaming on the ground," a reader, intrigued by the story-teller's self-assurance that these actions will ultimately be explained, fully and satisfactorily, but not until due time has been given to the whole business, appreciates the suspense that multiple viewpoints create. Moreover, Mr. Gabriel John Utterson, the sober lawyer who is only tangentially involved in Dr. Jekyll's life, reassures us – by his unshakable sense that English society remains under the control of rational human beings – that all will come right. More than one Victorian reader shares with Andrew Lang a shudder of anticipatory delight when he comes to that moment in the narrative describing Utterson's reaction to the discovery of a "neat array of papers," on top of which lies a large envelope bearing his name. Utterson looks at the servant, "and then back at the papers, and last of all at the dead malefactor stretched upon the carpet." His head "goes round." Now, holding all these enclosures, he must return home and read them in quiet; he promises to return before midnight, when they shall send for the police; and off he trudges to his office, closes the door, and begins to read "the two narratives in which this mystery was now to be explained."

There is a secret in the story, and its relevation requires time and space. To appreciate its full dimensions, we must regain the innocent eye. Stevenson manipulated the reader's desire to know; it was his privilege to do so, since the reader needed to be led carefully from one crux of narrative to the next; and the delay of introducing the final confession is artfully contrived. If we had come closer to Dr. Jekyll, if we had known more intimately the details of his struggle with the malign forces destroying his respectable facade, we could not have sweated with Dr. Utterson; the stillness of his study would not have seemed so sinister; the dreadfulness of Dr. Jekyll's confession would not have been so overpowering. The allegorical element is not introduced until the final thousand words, but this is not as damaging to the thrill of the story as it might have been at an earlier stage: "He had now seen the full deformity of that creature that shared with him some of the phenomena of consciousness, and was co-heir with him to death: and beyond these links of community, which in themselves made the most poignant part of his distress, he thought of Hyde, for all his energy of life, as of something not only hellish but inorganic. This was the shocking thing; that the slime of the pit seemed to utter cries and voices; that the amorphous dust gesticulated and sinned; that what was dead, and had no shape, should usurp the offices of life. And this again . . ." – spelling out that which the story has already embodied, that which has already been dramatized.

Formal criticism has had a rather hard time trying to apply rigorous criteria of form or content to Stevenson's short stories; contemporary disdain for the shilling shocker has obscured the importance that this type of story assumed in late Victorian periodicals. Stevenson's best stories sometimes become the target of hostile critics, and his least artistically successful stories bring out devoted admirers by the dozens. Fanny's anxiety that Stevenson not write below his true level of ability has been shared by generations of readers; but where that true level may be fixed is not clear after the passage of a near-century since his death.

Several observations may be made at this point, despite the probability that each is an arguable proposition. First, Stevenson's stories were written originally for periodicals. For the sake of acceptance, Stevenson had to study the market; as he understood it, that market flourished when the literary commodity sold by the periodical was escapist, highly colored, and unobtrusively moral in its implications. He had to imagine himself as a member of the reading public served by any periodical to which he intended submitting a particular manuscript.

Second, the stories so seldom turned out completely satisfactorily that Stevenson encountered difficulties in explaining, either to himself or to his friends, why he had not done better. Of "Thrawn Janet" he wrote, in a preface to *The Merry Men* begun in 1887, that it suffered from being "True only historically, true for a hill parish in Scotland in old days, not true for mankind and the world."[18] Disgusted by the horridness of the tale, he put one draft of "The Body Snatcher" to a side before trying again, this time for a collection entitled *The Black Man and Other Tales*, and submitting it to an editor for the *Pall Mall* Christmas "Extra" (December 1884). He was not pleased by *The Merry Men*; according to Fanny, he believed that he had failed to get a real grip on his story despite his conviction that he had succeeded in giving the terror of the sea.[19] As for "The Travelling Companion," he sent it to an editor who remarked that it was a work of genius, and indecent, hence unpublishable; Stevenson concurred ("it is a foul, gross, bitter ugly daub ... a carrion tale!"), and burned it. "Markheim," which Stevenson withdrew from Charles Morley's consideration for the *Pall Mall Gazette*, was characterized by its author as not being his best work, and worth ten pounds less than the forty pounds originally agreed on ("The Body Snatcher," ugly enough, in Stevenson's haunting phrase, "to chill the blood of a grenadier," was printed in place of "Markheim," which, in addition to the problems of inferior style felt so keenly by its author, proved to be not long enough for the assigned space in the periodical). He recognized the falseness of "Olalla," but only after it was printed, and, as he confessed in a letter to Lady Taylor (January 1887), "'Markheim' is true; 'Olallah' false; and I don't know why, nor did I feel it when I worked on them." He expressed some unease about the heterogeneousness of the collection called *The Merry Men and Other Tales and Fables* (1887). *The Wrong Box*, a work written in collaboration with Lloyd Osbourne, was regarded, from the beginning, as a "silly," "gay," "absurd" draft of a tale; he wanted to rewrite an important section in May 1889, because he had there "overdone confusion, the meaning is obscure, and the joke does not tell, in consequence."[20] But Scribner's, anxious to exploit Stevenson's name, rushed the uncorrected proofs into print by mid-June, and the second- and third-thoughts of Stevenson's pen never were incorporated in later editions of this novella. (Stevenson was in the anomalous position, more than once, of wanting to rewrite, while his editor or publisher refused to wait patiently for copy, and hurried his work into print.) Even at the end of his life, Stevenson, uncertain of his own acuteness in evaluating his fiction, read stories aloud at Vailima, and accepted, with greater trust than perhaps the situation warranted, remarks about the quality of such stories as "The Waif Woman," which he omitted from *Island Nights' Entertainments*, published in 1893. (Incidentally, this last-named volume sold only 2,348 copies of the cloth edition and 1,500 copies of the paper-covered edition during its first nine months; Stevenson, noting in a letter to Colvin dated November 1893, that *The Merry Men* had sold even fewer copies, remarked with some resignation, "The short story never sells.")[21]

Although Stevenson expressed similar sentiments about his novels while he worked on them, the note of diffidence struck for one short story after another seems stronger, and may be heard more often. One becomes convinced that he is sincerely confessing inadequacy; he was never wholly convinced that he had mastered the form. All of which leads to a final generalization: Stevenson's natural bent was to let a story tell itself, and his later tinkerings, after the first draft had been completed, did not necessarily amount to improvements, or to more sophisticated elucidations of his intention. Several critics have already documented this view in terms of his collaborations with Henley, and Stevenson's suspicion that it was true may have contributed to the deterioration of that friendship, although the nominal cause was Henley's accusation that Fanny had committed plagiarism by publishing as her own a story based upon a manuscript written by Katharine Stevenson de Mattos, a cousin of Stevenson. Closer inspection of those stories to which Stevenson appended a moral, or, in Fanny's endearing term, an allegory, may confirm the charge. Perhaps this is no more than a judgment about Stevenson's recurring problem in defining a relationship between form and content, i.e., a judgment that his art suffered frequently because he did not know where, in advance, he wanted his story to lead his reader. His efforts to pretend otherwise, once the story came into print, were often disingenuous; at any rate, seldom convincing; and more than one story was attributed – by Stevenson – to two, and sometimes three, sources, and possessed more than one objective. Such was the case, for example, with one of his popular efforts, "The Bottle Imp," which was, at various times, said to be "the centre-piece of a volume of Märchen" that he intended, slowly, to elaborate; or the result of reading (rather than seeing on the stage) Richard Brinsley Peake's *The Bottle Imp*, which had been acted by Richard John ("Obi") Smith in 1828; or a story designed from the very beginning for translation into Samoan, with appropriate compromises for that audience worked throughout the fabric of the story.

Stevenson's distaste for literary criticism is well known, even though he wrote several essays in this field. "There is nothing more disenchanting to man," he wrote in "On Style in Literature: Its Technical Elements" (published in *The Contemporary Review*, April 1885), "than to be shown the springs and mechanism of any art." He sincerely believed that it was much easier for men "of equal facility to write fairly pleasing verse than reasonably interesting prose," because "in prose the pattern itself has to be invented, and the difficulties first created before they can be solved."[22] A writer of prose had to keep "his phrases large, rhythmical, and pleasing to the ear, without ever allowing them to fall into the strictly metrical."[23] It is not surprising, therefore, that Stevenson regarded the dominant movement of the nineteenth century – toward an increasing realism, toward the inclusion of more factual details, toward the use of a "local dexterity"[24] in a "technical method"[25] – with some dismay; he preferred to labor (difficulties and all) on fiction, that was "philosophical, passionate, dignified, happily mirthful, or, at the last and least, romantic in design."[26] He sought "truth to the conditions of man's nature and the conditions of man's life"[27] rather than "a photographic exactitude in dialogue." This idealistic view, he granted, would not produce perfect or wholly trustworthy literature, if only because the rendering of any "fact" was closely related to the imperfect sensibility of the author who committed it to print; but Stevenson went further. "The health or disease of the writer's mind or momentary humour forms not only the leading feature of his work, but is, at bottom, the only thing he can communicate to others."[28] He preached a generous and catholic faith in the possibilities of human existence; a writer cannot afford to ape or conceal a sentiment. "Any book is wrong that gives a misleading picture of the world and life."[29] And, for the editor of the *British Weekly* who had requested a list of books which had proved influential over the years, Stevenson wrote that works of fiction that did not pin a reader to a dogma ("which he must afterwards discover to be inexact") or teach a reader a lesson ("which he must afterwards unlearn"[30]) had pleased him most. Apart from poets, playwrights, and essayists whom we might expect to turn up on Stevenson's list (Shakespeare, Whitman, Wordsworth, Montaigne, Spencer), there are the novelists: Dumas ("Perhaps my dearest and best friend outside of Shakespeare is D'Artagnan – the elderly D'Artagnan of the *Vicomte de Bragelonne*,"[31] Bunyan, Meredith, and perhaps unexpectedly, Algernon Bertram Freeman Mitford, whose book *Tales of Old Japan* (1871) taught Stevenson for the first time the proper attitude of any rational man to his country's laws. (Mitford's life, in several respects, paralleled that of Stevenson, and was one of the most romantic lives led by any Victorian diplomat.) This essay, of considerable interest to any friend of Stevenson's idealistic turn of mind, repeats several old themes, in that the function of art is again seen to be a repetition, rearrangement, and clarification of the lessons of life; fiction in this sense instructs fully as much as a work of non-fiction, say, the Gospel according to St. Matthew, Lewes's life of Goethe, or Marcus Aurelius's *Meditations*. But it also emphasizes "the improvable reader,"[32] who benefits from seeing another side of the argument in print; and Stevenson's relationship to his audience, increasingly close as the 1880s gave way to the final decade of the

century, became increasingly important to him. "The slightest
novels are a blessing to those in distress, not chloroform itself a
greater ... To please is to serve; and so far from its being difficult to
instruct while you amuse, it is difficult to do the one thoroughly
without the other. Some part of the writer or his life will crop out in
even a vapid book; and to read a novel that was conceived with any
force is to multiply experience and to exercise the sympathies ... The
writer has the chance to stumble, by the way, on something pleasing,
something interesting, something encouraging, were it only to a
single reader."[33]

How rigorously does Stevenson live up to his own dicta in the
short stories that he wrote (some of them a full twenty-five to thirty
thousand words in length)? The answer must be that he does so
inconsistently. Some of his stories are grimly realistic to a degree that
would have pleased Flaubert or Zola, and conventional, mildly
patronizing assessments of Stevenson as "a lesser Scott" – based in
part on his essays of literary criticism – must be revised upward.
Stevenson was an artist in his own right, and not a day-dreamer in
the Scott-imitators' mode; as a writer, he concerned himself with the
more serious romantic conventions that had already been exploited
by Hugo – for whom "moral significance" served as an organizing
principle.[34] Stevenson's high regard for the educative function of
fiction is not always borne out by a particular story, and, for that
matter, his demand for an open-minded, intelligent, and judicious
audience could not always be met. Indeed, Stevenson frequently
spoke with some chagrin of the newspaper-reading public as non-
serious, even though his short stories were written for a substantial
fraction of that audience.

There is no question that Stevenson's brand of moral romance
would have palled by the middle years of the Great War;
reputations of romantic story-tellers that loomed large in the 1880s
and 1890s were destroyed forever by the horrors of trenches dug for
some five hundred miles along the Western Front; and even the
dedicated singers of an imperial destiny – G. A. Henty, Alfred
Austin (the Poet Laureate), and Rudyard Kipling, as well as lesser
lights – spoke about "noble duty" to an increasingly skeptical
public.[35] Yet even if Stevenson exploited imperial emotion and
moved many of his fictional characters against imperial backdrops,
an integrity-bound tough-mindedness prevented him from senti-
mentalizing "fortitude," "loyalty," and "adventure" in the manner
of a Henley, or a Haggard, or a Henty.

Stevenson was at his best in his horror tales, and three of these may be taken as representative: "The Body Snatcher," "Thrawn Janet," "Markheim." They have retained their popularity over a full century, and they serve to identify important characteristics of Stevenson's craft. They are, rather surprisingly, not the product of sudden inspiration (the effortlessness of the narration is deceptive, but easy reading, as professionals know, comes usually from hard writing). "The Body Snatcher" required several months of work at Pitlochry in 1881, went through several drafts, and got into print only after three years had elapsed.

"Thrawn Janet" took longest of all. Stevenson certainly intended to write a story about her when he prepared *A Covenanting Story-Book* in 1868–9, and listed "The Story of Thrawn Janet" as one of his entries; perhaps he did write a draft at that time; but not until 1871, when he bought a copy of *Satan's Invisible World Discovered*, by George Sinclair (1685), did he acquire a readily accessible source for a major part of his story (another source being the Reverend Robert Wodrow's *Analecta*, 1842–3). But the story was not accepted for publication until June 1881, when Leslie Stephen approved it for inclusion in the *Cornhill Magazine*, and it is impossible to say how many versions it went through before a final metamorphosis.

"Markheim" was drafted in 1881, but not sent to an editor until December 1884, and then as a replacement for "Oliver Leaf," a story insufficiently blood-curdling for the taste of Charles Morley of the *Pall Mall Gazette* ("Oliver Leaf" was never published). "Markheim" thus was aimed at a specific audience of readers who knew – from advertisements prepared by Morley – that the Christmas "Extra" issue would contain exciting and even shocking stories. Stevenson distrusted his judgment as to its merits, and – as we have seen – willingly accepted ten pounds less for "The Body Snatcher" than Morley had agreed to pay for "Markheim." He tried again in 1885, revising "Markheim" extensively, in response to Henry Norman's request for a story in Unwin's *Christmas Annual*; it was published as one of the items in Norman's *The Broken Shaft: Tales in Mid-Ocean* (1885, but dated 1886). Similar lengthy periods between genesis and completion of a satisfactory draft may be traced for most of Stevenson's short stories.

The basic situations of all three stories are contrived, melodramatic, and even outrageously improbable; in none of them does the plausibility of the plot matter excessively. They are relatively brief; the limited space concentrates Stevenson's mind wonderfully. They all deal with death, and the possibility that for evil spirits death is not final. The stories seem to be told for their own sake, their issuing-forth to be *compelled*. They are tales of horror, and, in Hardy's memorable phrase, exceptional enough to justify the telling. Nor – despite our observation that two of the three stories take place in a more remote time ("The Body Snatcher" is based upon the doings of Burke and Hare in the eighteenth century, while the climactic scene of "Thrawn Janet" is precisely dated as taking place on August 17, 1712) – a reader may not take comfort; evil is all around us, and never goes out of fashion.

The popularity of these tales (a term perhaps more suitable than that of short stories, since they all partake of the marvelous) was enhanced, at the time of publication, by a large number of sandwich boards. Stevenson was not convinced that the tales helped his reputation among readers whose opinion in such things he trusted, and he wavered between pride and disgust when he alluded to them. But he under-estimated their narrative values and their allegorical weight. "The Body Snatcher" strikes a note of awed conviction that men's natures can become satanic, which assumes some importance in Stevenson's later fiction; "Thrawn Janet" is his first mature piece of Scottish fiction, heavy in atmospherics; and "Markheim," for all its heavy-handed symbolism, invites serious comparison with Dostoyevsky's treatment of a murder in *Crime and Punishment*, and offers a more substantial and believable treatment of the psychology of the Doppelgänger than does "The Strange Case of Dr. Jekyll and Mr. Hyde."

Two of these stories are traceable to a dispirited summer of heavy rain, when the Stevensons lived in Kinnaird Cottage, Pitlochry, in the Vale of Atholl. Space was at a premium; the cottage was small, and divided into two flats (the second was occupied by Stevenson's parents); and the weather, foul and gloomy throughout the supposed vacation-period, provoked a classic exchange between Fanny ("When will spring begin?") and her mother-in-law ("This *is* the spring!").[36] But it also allowed Stevenson time to listen to the grim ghost tales recounted by Mrs. Sims, the owner of the cottage, a cook, and a true-bred Scot, and it revived a flagging sense of dedication to the fictionalizing of his Scottish heritage.

"The Body Snatcher" begins with a brief description of four men who like to meet in a hotel-parlour at Debenham: an undertaker, a landlord, an old drunken Scotsman named Fettes, and the man who recounts the events of the narrative. The description of a terrifying ride over a deeply rutted road with a macabre travelling-companion is prepared for by a sober-sided, calm narrator. Though we learn next to nothing about him – not even his occupation – we are reassured by his manner; by his interest in the strange behavior of Fettes; by his willingness to investigate the reasons underlying Fettes's belligerent accosting of a doctor who has come to visit a patient at the hotel. "It is no great boast," he writes in a confidential manner, "but I believe I was a better hand at worming out a story than either of my fellows at the George; and perhaps there is now no other man alive who could narrate to you the following foul and unnatural events ..."

"Thrawn Janet" begins, similarly, with a quiet review of the impeccable reputation as orator enjoyed by the Reverend Murdoch Soulis, minister of the moorland parish of Balweary, in the Vale of Dule, and a masterful description of the strip of causeway down which Mr. Soulis walks, "sometimes groaning aloud in the instancy of his unspoken prayers." This introductory passage, of approximately a thousand words, is rendered in standard English; again, the strange events to be recounted must be seen first from an unhurried perspective. Many members of the parish do not know about the weird events marking the early years of Mr. Soulis's tenure in Balweary; those who do might be reticent, or shy. "Now and again, only, one of the older folk would warm into courage over his third tumbler, and recount the cause of the minister's strange looks and solitary life." From this point on the narrative continues in fairly broad Lallans, as an experiment in language that Stevenson seldom undertook.

"Markheim" is told from Markheim's point of view (in the third person); and, we soon learn, he has mixed motives, and a conscience that ultimately will lead to a decision to turn himself in to the police. The dealer whom Markheim murders is not a particularly agreeable person, nor is meant to be; but the brutality of the act, once committed, leads Markheim to thoughts that confirm his original terror, morbid predisposition, and resolve, and that accentuate his physical repulsion at war with his "fascination." Images accumulate to vivify his knowledge of self-guilt: the door that stands ajar, peering into the shadows "with a long slit of daylight like a pointing finger"; the striking of many clocks (time has "become instant and momentous for the slayer"); the multiple reflections of his own face in the mirrors scattered through the shop, "as it were an army of spies," with his own eyes meeting and detecting himself; and the candle that he carries from room to room, causing "the gross blots of darkness" to swell and dwindle "as with respiration." Markheim speaks to a visitant who reviews with him the nature of evil. "Evil, for which I live, consists not in action but in character," he tells Markheim. "And it is not because you have killed a dealer, but because you are Markheim that I offered to forward your escape ..." He goes on to warn Markheim that he can never change. The tale turns upon the issue of free will, for Markheim is determined to cheat his tormenter by exercising his one alternative option: to cease from action, to refuse to kill the maid who even now is ringing the doorbell. He wins an inner battle with his debased instincts as well as the outer debate. One of his last statements is that he has still his hatred of evil, and from that he "can draw both energy and courage." He thus makes a *rational* choice to accept full responsibility for the murder of the dealer.

All three tales are insistent on their suggestion that evil, though suffering one fall after another, is so deeply rooted in human nature that it will rise again, and often higher than before. "The Body Snatcher" ends with a pouring rain ("it was no easy matter to make a light in such a world of wet and darkness"), and the discovery by Fettes and Dr. Macfarlane that the body of a sixty-year-old woman has changed, within its "dripping sack," into the body of Gray, who long since had been cut up by K——, the extramural anatomist. But Wolfe Macfarlane, who began his medical career as "a high favourite among all the reckless students, clever, dissipated, and unscrupulous," has had no more than a momentary scare at the moment of discovery; the beginning of the story has informed us that he became a great London physician after that eerie ride; and, when we first see him, he enters "richly dressed in the finest of broadcloth, and the whitest of linen, with a great gold watchchain, and studs and spectacles of the same precious material"; and Fettes's confrontation only momentarily disconcerts him. He escapes from Fettes's grasp; from his hoarse whisper, "Have you seen it again?" – and his only loss is a pair of "fine gold spectacles," which remains behind, broken on the threshold.

"Thrawn Janet" is, in effect, the story of a conversion, for Dr. Soulis (to Stevenson the best name in all the world, which he would gladly have used again if this story had not ruined its possibilities for other narratives)[37] begins as a mild-mannered religious believer ("fu' o' book-learnin' an' grand at the exposition, but, as was natural in sae young a man, wi' nae leevin' experience in religion"), and undergoes tremendous shock when he learns that Janet M'Clour, the "auld limmer" whom he hires as maid despite the disapproval of many Balweary citizens, is indeed "sib to the de'il," just as they have said. The real question here is what Dr. Soulis is converted *to*, after he has seen her body hanging "frae a nail beside the auld aik cabinet," with her head lying on her shoulder and her tongue projecting from her mouth, and her heels two feet above the ground (this is an apparition); and after the devil, in Janet's form, comes slowly toward the terrified minister to torment him. Dr. Soulis escapes; indeed, the devil never again appears in Balweary. "But it was a fair dispensation for the minister; lang, lang he lay ravin' in his bed; an' frae that hour to this, he was the man ye ken the day." His conversion, apparently, is to a soul-wrenching faith in the devil's capabilities to wreak mischief; in the *reality* of the devil. Because he did not recognize the signs of possession when they appeared (he was newly graduated from college, and had no patience with the superstitions of the townsfolk when he came to Balweary), he was fated to undergo a crisis of the soul; and, with the passage of fifty years after the singular death of Thrawn Janet, turned into "a severe, bleak-faced old man, dreadful to his hearers," exactly the kind of minister whom Stevenson personally distrusted as being over-dogmatic.

"Markheim," too, poses an unresolved question at story's end. Stevenson intended it for a Christmas market, but it provides no Christmas cheer. Markheim is not saved by his confession to the maid, or by his decision not to murder her, any more than his presence on the platform of a revival meeting some three years back meant that God's grace had descended upon him at that time. Salvation is denied to a thirty-six-year-old man who has squandered great gifts on the foolish pursuit of pleasure; even at year's end, when the birth of the child Jesus promises a washing-clean, when Markheim truly repents and says, with passion, that "there is no good thing nor true thing on earth" that he does not love from his heart, when he has absorbed the lessons of the dark man, when he has looked within and seen himself for what he truly is, he is not worthy of forgiveness, nor will he receive it. If moral there be, it is that God cannot or will not look past Markheim's acts to approve his repentance; and it is clear that Markheim is correct in his conviction that the "creature" with whom he debates "was not of the earth and not of God."

The "crawlers," in brief, are complicated inventions, and possibly Stevenson's lasting legacy to the genre. Stevenson understood that morality in the modern short story would have to be more diffused than it had been in previous generations of stories; the merely fabulous had lost its audience because of a progressive centralization of modern thought. The price was high: the story-teller had lost much of his innocence, the kinds of stories he loved to tell (humorous, fantastic, occasionally even trivial) had fallen from favor. There was, he believed, less humanity in the modern short story. Stevenson's contribution to this field was thought to be – and may still be assessed as – notoriously uneven; Stevenson knew it, and blamed his failures partly on the changing conditions of the relationship between publisher and author; between the author and his public. But there were moments of satisfaction, when he knew he had done well. "Thrawn Janet," after all, was a story that he read to Fanny in their bedroom, when only a single candle illuminated the page; while outside the rain poured heavily down. At story's end the author took his wife's hand, and, both frightened of the dark, they crept downstairs.

To Sidney Colvin Stevenson wrote, in June 1881, "'Thrawn Janet' is off to Stephen, but as it is all in Scotch he cannot take it, I *know*. It was *so good*, I could not help sending it."[38] But Stephen liked it too, accepted it without hesitation, and doubtless wished that Stevenson might live forever to continue writing such tales.

7

Rudyard Kipling: the Anglo-Indian stories

Kipling's appearance at the age of twenty-five on the London scene was one of the more dramatic events of a decade marked by newness in all the arts. He immediately became known as a young man worth knowing; his stories were kicking up dust in all directions within three months of his arrival (in October 1889). Ninety-day wonders are often never heard from again, but Kipling turned out to have staying power.

He had earned for himself in India – where he had served "seven years' hard" as a journalist and sub-editor – a reputation for writing up, in vivid and sometimes luridly colored prose, the routines of an extraordinary class of civil servants, soldiers, and adventurers who were ruling a subcontinent with some success. The story of William Ernest Henley's dancing around a room on his wooden leg to express his glee at the receipt of the manuscript of "Barrack Room Ballads. 1 Danny Deever" – here was poetry at last for the pages of Henley's *National Observer*! – is a pretty anecdote, and a true one. There followed into print "Tommy," "Fuzzy Wuzzy," and "Loot" (March); "The Widow at Windsor" (April); "Gunga Din" and "Mandalay" (June). Cockney accent and all, these poems opened up new vistas of experience and feeling; it was as if an entire genre had been invented. England was entertainingly reminded of what it owed its colonial administrators.

Nor did Kipling rest while gathering the laurels of a poet. He was drumming up business for reprintings of his short stories, which had appeared over a period of several years in two Indian papers, the *Civil and Military Gazette* of Lahore and *The Pioneer* of Allahabad. These had been printed as "turnovers," whereby a story would begin on the last column of page one, and continue to page two; the initials "RK" certified its quality; and readers throughout northern India looked forward to each new turnover. Kipling believed, justly, that he could win a larger audience, one that counted more for an aspiring writer, if only he could break free of the journalistic routines of India, and go to England.

These stories, like those of Stevenson, were written to order. Their length, a modest two thousand words apiece, meant that little time could be spent on characterization or conventional plot. Kipling, as one-half the editorial staff of the *Civil and Military Gazette*, gathered thirty-nine of these turnovers, written between November 2, 1886, and June 10, 1887. (Approximately six may not have been written entirely by himself; other members of his family had writing talents, and family collaboration was frequently indulged in.) He reprinted them as *Plain Tales from the Hills*.

It may be that Kipling's art could flourish only after Stephen Wheeler, exhausted and ill, left the editorship, and Kay Robinson, his successor, came aboard to encourage Kipling in the writing of both poetry and fiction. Kipling appreciated Wheeler's stress on the business-end of journalism – which events had to be reported, which Government publications had to be translated into "journalese," and which sentences had to be rewritten or struck out – and claimed, in later years, that his apprenticeship had been thorough, and badly needed. Still, he did not speak with nostalgia of his years under Wheeler's strict tutelage, and during the years that his longer stories (three to five thousand words) appeared in the *Pioneer*'s magazine supplement, the *Week's News*, he could not have been ignorant of their improving literary quality. He wrote more short stories than he collected, to be sure, and he gave excellent value for his salary of £420 a year. (He had started at £100.) He wrote on everything, in all kinds of literary forms. His first book-success was *Departmental Ditties*, which scored heavily in India in 1886; his first collection of short stories, issued by the Calcutta firm of Thacker Spink & Co., was also a best-seller there.

Efforts to interest the English public in these stories proved unavailing. The thousand copies that Thacker Spink sent on to its London branch failed to sell, though a notice in the *Saturday Review* moved some copies off the shelves of bookstores; trying to win acceptance by long-distance maneuvering simply did not work. General Ian Hamilton, who served with distinction in India for a full quarter-century, and who admired Kipling's turnovers greatly, sent to his brother Vereker the manuscript of a story (later to be titled "The Mark of the Beast"), suggesting that he show it first to Andrew Lang and William Sharp, and then to editors of two magazines.

Lang's response to Vereker's request for a critical judgment was blistering: "I would gladly give Ian a fiver if he had never been the

11   Portrait of Rudyard Kipling by P. Burne-Jones, 1899

means of my reading this poisonous stuff which has left an extremely disagreeable impression on my mind." He added that Kipling would be well advised not to make a start in English literary circles with a story "of this nature . . . supposing, even, he could get anyone to touch it," which Lang "very much doubted."[1] Sharp, who customarily differed strongly from Lang, wrote to Vereker something to this effect: "I would strongly recommend your brother's friend instantly to burn this detestable piece of work. If I would not be considered to be going beyond my brief, I would like to hazard a guess that the writer of the article in question is very young and that he will die mad before he has reached the age of thirty."

The two editors fired back the story to Vereker as soon as they had a chance to inspect it. Vereker, chagrined, read the story to several of his friends, among them Charles Furse and William Strang, fellow-students who were to become famous artists. They agreed that "there was a strong flavour of the horrible in the tale," but they admired "the originality of the theme and the style in which it was narrated."[2] Even so, this was *private* appreciation. Kipling, hungry for public success, was understandably annoyed when the manu-script came back to him in India, not only unprinted and unaccepted, but assessed (and assailed) as unprintable.

Kipling knew better. The Indian reception of his stories, after all, was the needed stimulus for his resolve to return to England; and certain special circumstances of the stories' publication guaranteed that his arrival on the London scene would not be wholly unprepared for. Not only did publication of the turnovers in their original form reach a substantial number of well-educated readers spread across vast distances, but Kipling's contributions to the supplements of the *Pioneer* were gathered, in six paperback volumes of the Indian Railway Library series, for sale at a rupee apiece on railway bookstalls. These volumes – *Soldiers Three, The Story of The Gadsbys, In Black and White, Under the Deodars, The Phantom 'Rickshaw,* and *Wee Willie Winkie* – were picked up by travelers throughout India and carried to far-distant destinations, including England. It was not merely *Plain Tales from the Hills* that guaranteed Kipling's success when it was reprinted in the land to which he was returning. Sampson Low, Marston & Co. reprinted the Indian Railway Library volumes in 1890. Kipling's flamboyant personality, his successful interviews with countless editors and publishers, and his swift writing of *The Light that Failed* in the intervals between social engagements, made him the literary lion of more than one season.

We are talking here about sixty-seven short stories, written within a five-year period. Many of them are almost beyond criticism. Very few are "dated," dull, or obvious in structure or sentiment, dismissible as the easy-to-spot maunderings of a youthful author who had not yet reached the age of thirty (when, according to Sharp, he would go mad). During the 1890s short stories remained his favorite medium of artistic expression. Unlike most short-story writers of the decade, he found that his hard-bound collections sold

SOLDIERS THREE

A.H. WHEELER & Co's
No. 1
INDIAN RAILWAY LIBRARY

BY

Rudyard Kipling

ONE RUPEE.

MAYO SCHOOL OF ART LAHORE

12 Cover of the Indian Railway Library edition of *Soldiers Three* by Rudyard Kipling. Design supervised by John Lockwood Kipling (Mayo School of Art, Lahore)

THIRD EDITION.

SOLDIERS THREE,

A COLLECTION OF STORIES

Setting forth certain Passages in the Lives and Adventures of Privates Terence Mulvaney, Stanley Ortheris, and John Learoyd.

DONE INTO TYPE AND EDITED BY

RUDYARD KIPLING.

" We be Soldiers Three——

Pardonnez moi, je vous en prie."

A. H. WHEELER & Co.,

ALLAHABAD.

1889.

13   Title page of the Indian Railway Library edition of *Soldiers Three* by Rudyard Kipling

well. Some stories appeared in that odd assortment of materials, *From Sea to Sea*, which came out as a book in England in 1900, even though it had all been written ten years earlier. Other titles included *Life's Handicap* (1891), eleven stories; *Many Inventions* (1893), fourteen stories; *The Jungle Book* (1894), seven stories; *The Second Jungle Book* (1895), eight stories; *The Day's Work* (1898), twelve stories; and *Stalky & Co.* (1899), nine stories. During the first decade of the twentieth century Kipling published: *Just So Stories* (1902), twelve stories; *Traffics and Discoveries* (1904), eleven stories; *Puck of Pook's Hill* (1906), ten stories; *Actions and Reactions* (1909), eight stories; and *Rewards and Fairies* (1910), eleven stories. To complete the record, even though we go well past the Edwardian era, we should add *A Diversity of Creatures* (1917), fourteen stories; *Land and Sea Tales* (1923), eleven stories; *Debits and Credits* (1926), fourteen stories; *Thy Servant a Dog* (1930), three stories; and *Limits and Renewals* (1932), fourteen stories. If we add to this total the 121 "uncollected" stories that are printed in volume v of R. E. Harbord's edition, *The Reader's Guide to Rudyard Kipling's Work* (1970), and keep in mind that even this grand sweeping-up represents an uncertain total – the rediscovery of all the fiction that Kipling published anonymously during his Indian years is still going on – we have well over 350 short stories. All these in addition to the poetry, several novels, reams of vivid journalism, travel books, formal addresses to various societies, clubs, and distinguished gatherings, and an autobiography (incomplete, but still a substantial fragment)!

It is impossible to group the stories to show a steadily developing skill. Kipling did not "improve" from first to last; some of the *Plain Tales* are as brilliant as any contained in the stories of the late, or darker, period, written while Kipling fought waves of pain, periods of depression, and the gloomy certainty that the war to end wars (H. G. Wells's phrase) had paved the way only for a new international conflict. Despite the fact that Kipling's early stories were often denounced as gossip, inaccurate depictions of military life and slang, unreasonably cynical for someone Kipling's age, and a set of slanders about real people who were doing their best for England – even Charles Carrington, whose authorized biography is strongly supportive, wrote, damagingly, that Kipling's tone in his turnovers "was always that of smoking-room conversation"[3] – their art was seldom called into question.

Grouping the stories by subject-matter, even so, enables us to see that only a generous number of (sometimes overlapping) categories will account for all of Kipling's interests: stories about children (far many more than stories written *for* children), soldiers and sailors in wars fought in several different centuries, life in modern England (with special emphasis on Sussex), and weird or supernatural events. I want to concentrate here on Kipling's investigations of how Englishmen behave when they are sent far from home and must interact with Indian natives who, for understandable reasons, doubt that their best interests are being protected. These stories about India include anecdotes of marital infidelity, bloody revenge, sudden death, and ghosts. They do not preach the white man's burden in any simple way, and Kipling's sympathy for the Indian point of view is an important element in his characterization of those Anglo-Indian administrators who fail to respect it. Louis Cornell has argued that Kipling's views about India, developed during childhood, are those of an Anglo-Indian, "echoing the race and class prejudices not only of his own caste but of his Indian friends and servants as well,"[4] but in later chapters of his study he concedes that it would be inadvisable to think of Anglo-Indian attitudes as fixed, as unaffected by political and historical changes; Kipling's tough, sardonic tone in his early poetry is not sustained; and the short stories are far more than the fictional working-out of attitudes held by members of the Punjab Club. Those members detested the reformist tendencies of the Ilbert Bill, proposed by Lord Ripon in 1883, which would have severely modified the "right" of a European resident in India to be tried by a European judge. Kipling became deeply involved in the fight. When the *Civil and Military Gazette* decided to end its active opposition, he was blamed for the change in editorial policy. Members of the Punjab Club hissed him, and Kipling, not yet twenty years old, and startled by the intensity of feeling aroused by Lord Ripon's legal initiative, must have thought quite seriously from then on about racial problems. Whether the views that he held for the rest of his life were unswervingly conservative is not to be answered glibly. He certainly believed in a responsible imperialism. His fictions identified, lucidly and sympathetically, the problems that Anglo-Indian administrators confronted, and fumblingly attempted to solve. The Indians who have written about Kipling most recently[5] do not accept over-simplified views of him, though, for various reasons, they do not approve of much that is in his stories about India. Even the harshest of Kipling's critics, those who find his false knowingness insufferable, concede that his openness to experience and understanding of Indian ways of thinking are handsomely illustrated by "Lispeth," "Without Benefit of Clergy," "The Tomb of his Ancestors," "The Miracle of Puran Bhagat," and the novel *Kim*.

Kipling never could remember who originated the idea of turnovers, or who suggested that he write a series of them. He knew only that he liked the way in which a predetermined length affected his concept of the structure of a short story. His news stories forced him to stress accuracy and interest in his reporting, "but first of all accuracy" (he was more disturbed than he cared to admit by the "visible and often brutally voluble critics at the Club"). These concerns carried over into his fiction.

More than many writers at the beginning of an apprenticeship, he enjoyed the sheer physical setting-down on paper of the words and images that flooded his mind: "This made it easier to throw away anything that did not turn out well: and to practise, as it were, scales."[6] Kipling wrote with the honest intention of including everything, and rewrote by shortening ("first to my own fancy after rapturous re-readings, and next to the space available"). As a consequence, his Anglo-Indian tales were originally a good deal longer than when they appeared in print. The "Higher Editing," as Kipling explained the process, consisted of using a camel-hair brush, awash with well-ground Indian ink, to black out "where requisite" in a final draft. The amount of brushwork was directly affected by both the length of the tale and the "lie-by," the time-intervals between re-readings. (This explanation must be kept in mind when reading complaints by even Kipling's admirers that too much has been blacked-out in the stories written during the last two decades, as – for example – "Mrs. Bathurst.") The habit of using the brush at more frequent intervals became stronger, while the inspiration provided by "the Personal Daemon" turned into a more infrequent visitor, as Kipling aged. The Daemon could not be coerced. "My Daemon was with me in the *Jungle Books*, *Kim*, and both Puck books," Kipling wrote, "and good care I took to walk delicately, lest he should withdraw. I know that he did not, because when those books were finished they said so themselves with, almost, the water-hammer click of a tap turned off . . . *Note here*. When your Daemon is in charge, do not try to think consciously. Drift, wait, and obey."[7]

Admirable as the craft of his late manner may be, many lovers of Kipling respond at the deepest level to stories in which strong emotions flash lightning-like, unexpectedly, across otherwise hum-drum lives. These stories seem to proliferate during the Indian years, and though the greatest of them illustrate the swiftness with which Kipling mastered problems of technique (rapid shifts in point of view, for example, and the clarification of dislocations of time – backward and forward), their appeal lies more in what they tell us Kipling knew about human beings. "Without Benefit of Clergy" first appeared in *Macmillan's Magazine* (June 1890), and *Harper's Weekly* (June 7 and 14, 1890), before being printed in Harper and Brother's editions of *The Courting of Dinah Shadd and Other Stories* (1890); it affords a reader an opportunity to revalue the conventional view that Kipling saw Indian life from the perspective of a journalist committed whole-heartedly to the doctrine of the White Man's Burden (a phrase he invented). It is appropriate that the story should begin with preparations for the coming of a child. John Holden, who has entered into a secret relationship with Ameera, a native woman, may have bought his mistress ("from her mother, who, being left without money, would have sold Ameera shrieking to the Prince of Darkness if the price had been sufficient"), but no church has sanctified the marriage. In one sense, the deaths of both Ameera and her child serve as the formal notification of a due payment made to the gods. Kipling stresses the notion of fate. The "red and heavy audit" that Nature exacts – through cholera, the endless rains, famine, inadequate supplies of medicine, bad sanitation, and fever – is described in some of the most eloquent passages of Kipling's early career. (Kipling's being sent to spend an unhappy childhood in what he called the house of desolation at Southsea, with Aunty Rosa, had one blessing at least; it allowed the writer to live to manhood. His parents were determined that he should not die as a child in India, a country in which infant-mortality statistics were appalling.) Ameera's passionate attempt to determine whether she herself is to blame for the death of her son Tota – "Perhaps I did not take sufficient heed ... Say that there is no blame on me, or I shall die – I shall die!" – is countered by Holden's stern reply: "There is no blame, – before God, none. It was written, and how could we do aught to save? What has been, has been." Still, lurking at the back of his mind is the thought that he should not have believed in the permanence of happiness; that in some measure he was impious.

The novelty of "Without Benefit of Clergy" does not lie in the catchpenny doctrine that hard work can compensate for personal tragedy because it forces one to pay attention to bureaucratic routine. The *new* note which marks his distinctive contribution to the short-story genre, and his arrival as a literary force to be reckoned with, is not struck by his "getting into" Ameera's "skin" (her speeches are warm-hearted, shrewdly perceptive, and passionately female to a degree that makes us yearn for more such characterizations of native women). Rather, it comes at the moment that Holden, awed by his introduction to the fact of the physical existence of his son, reaches out to touch the hand of Tota, and learns something new about himself.

Holden found one helpless little hand that closed feebly on his finger. And the clutch ran through his body till it settled about his heart. Till then his sole thought had been for Ameera. He began to realise that there was someone else in the world, but he could not feel that it was a veritable son with a soul. He sat down to think ...

The author of *that* has imagined greatly. Kipling, who was not to marry for another two years, or to have a child for three, was accurately describing Holden's ensuing mood, "full of riotous exultation, alternating with a vast vague tenderness directed towards no particular object, that made him choke as he bent over the neck of his uneasy horse." Kipling's best short stories, many of which were written at the beginning no less than at the end of a career that spanned a full half-century of literary production, are not so much a series of revelations about a character already formed as a succession of actions that show a character in the process of change, and very frequently of growing in his or her understanding.

This distinguishes between the teller of a tale, who works with materials largely received (folklore, twice-told narratives, often stressing the strange and irrational, and embodying elements of oral tradition), and the writer of a short story, who perforce must begin afresh and invent more. Both kinds of author may work with a single center of consciousness, if only because the available time and space do not permit full development of two centers. But the tale-teller has a tendency to cite himself as the authority for the fiction, to serve as omniscient commentator, and to feel confidence in his position because the tradition to which he proudly belongs is widely recognized as having connections with the universal elements of story in all lands and in all ages. He is no stranger to the traditions embodied in Homer, the *Rigveda*, the *Thousand and One Nights*, the *Gesta Romanorum*, and Perrault; he can be recognized as a blood-brother to those who re-tell *märchen* and popular myths. Kipling, on the other hand, works harder at becoming someone or something other than what he is, and many of his fictional characters –

particularly in the Indian period – are caught at moments of transformation. Hardy's "Interlopers at the Knap" is indeed a Wessex *tale* because its characters do not change as they age; they simply move from one situation to the next. Kipling's "Without Benefit of Clergy" is more recognizably a modern short story because Holden is continuously learning about himself, and changing. "The first shock of a bullet is no more than a brisk pinch," the narrator writes (after the death of Tota). "The wrecked body does not send in its protest to the soul till ten or fifteen seconds later. Holden realised his pain slowly, exactly as he had realised his happiness, and with the same imperious necessity for hiding all trace of it." There follows a poignant passage describing Holden's reaction to the boasts of his (white) colleagues about the accomplishments of their children: "He could not declare his pain. He had neither help, comfort, nor sympathy . . ." He is not granted the boon of sufficient time to recover; Ameera dies next from the black cholera; and only three days later, Holden, returning for one last look "at the house wherein he had been master and lord," discovers that heavy rains have so aged the dwelling-place and grounds that they look "as if the house had been untenanted for thirty years instead of three days." India has not changed. Ameera's mother is still whining and avaricious. Durga Dass, who owns the home, wants to exploit the property for the betterment of "the Municipality." But Holden has become a different man. Though larger in his sympathies, his capacity to give love is blocked by the indifferent Powers that rule the universe, which have twice betrayed him.

Henry James, in his introduction to Kipling's *Mine Own People* (1891), was among the first to recognize the over-simplification inherent in the notion that Kipling was "wonderful" about India because India had not yet been "done." He saw that Kipling's appeal to critics and to other serious readers lay in something else: "the surprise of his skill and the *fioriture* of his form, which are so oddly independent of any distinctively literary note in him, any bookish association."[8] Another way of saying this is that Kipling's explosive originality of self benefited from his choice of the short story as a suitable genre for his "many inventions." James, who admired "The Courting of Dinah Shadd" as a masterpiece, wrote that the talent which had produced it was "eminently in harmony with the short story, and the short story is on our side of the Channel and of the Atlantic, a mine which will take a great deal of working . . . In a word, he appreciates the episode . . ."[9]

James was right, of course. But this emphasis on Kipling's

greatness in handling "the episode" was less interesting to readers in the 1890s than the possibility that Kipling's stories about India, containing as they did a startling number of unpleasant opinions, spoke directly for the author, and maligned not only the well-connected members of the Indian Civil Service but all servants of the Queen who believed that they deserved sympathetic treatment in any fiction that might dramatize their lives.[10] Kipling's reputation, for the rest of his life, suffered from this reductionist reading of his art.

To take one example of how Kipling's characterization of a recognizable soldier-type in India exposed him to this kind of censure, "The Taking of Lungtungpen" is a story told by Private Mulvaney, the "born scutt av the barrick-room." Mulvaney mentions coolly, and with no thought that his behavior might be censured, that he uses a "clanin'-rod" to beat needed information out of a prisoner. This is brutal savagery; no defender of Kipling need prettify it. But those who point to this kind of incident as an illustration of Kipling's sadism, jingo imperialist views, moral insensitivity, and aesthetically disgusting art (George Orwell runs all these charges into two sentences;[11] but similar charges have been made in more extended form by Max Beerbohm, Robert Buchanan, and Lionel Trilling) ignore, first of all, Kipling's awareness that Mulvaney never pretends to be better than he is. Mulvaney is a creation, an imagined point of view, who operates by his own best lights. He has been given the charge of discovering and eliminating armed robbers – the dacoits – who operated with impunity in much of nineteenth-century India. He believes in their treachery: "'Tis only a *dah* [a broad-bladed Burmese knife] an' a Snider [a breach-loading rifle] that makes a dacoit." He has been frustrated by long and useless searches, in which his only prizes have been spells of fever, or elephants. When he catches a man who knows the whereabouts of the dacoits, he operates on the assumption that the end justifies the means, and he is not deterred – he is even encouraged – by an instruction given to him by Lieutenant Brazenose, his commanding officer: "Trate him tinderly." "Tinderly" is translated into the use of the "clanin'-rod" to convert a prisoner's jabbering into a confession of some use to "the Intilligince Departmint."

The Lieutenant does not reprimand Mulvaney for beating his prisoner. The possibility that he does not know how Mulvaney discovers the location of the stronghold of the dacoits is not clarified; nor does the reader know whether the Lieutenant cares to learn.

This brings us to another important strand in the story: the need of the Lieutenant to become a better fighting-man, under the guidance of his subordinate Mulvaney. For Mulvaney has little use for an officer who fights by the rules. "I niver thought much av Lift'nint Brazenose till that night," Mulvaney confesses, speaking of the moment when he brings to his superior officer the needed "informashin." "He was shtiff wid books an' the-ouries, an' all manner av thrimmin's no manner av use." Brazenose tries to remind Mulvaney that the "the-ouries av War" require that they wait for reinforcements; but Mulvaney, reminding him that "the nearest throops was up to their shtocks in the marshes out Mimbu way," is able to persuade him to "make an excepshin," and to raid the Burmese town of Lungtungpen that very evening. The Lieutenant supports Mulvaney's strategy, and urges his fighting men to strip and swim across "the shtrame" which blocks their way; in the midst of the chaos of unexpected discovery, with guns firing on the soldiers "like a cat's back on a frosty night," he orders his priorities correctly (from Mulvaney's point of view), and cries, "Go on an' take the town! An' the Lord have mercy on our sowls!" After the skirmish, considerably after (for Mulvaney is about to be "invalided for the dysent'ry to India"), Mulvaney admits that the Lieutenant has emerged nobly from a battle in which he and his men have fought, for all practical purposes, "as nakid as Vanus." He tells the Lieutenant that the latter has the makings in him of a great man (Brazenose accepts this tribute from "an ould sodger"), and forever after he will remember Brazenose, who waltzed through Lung-tungpen "like a Red Injin widout the war-paint," as "a fine upstandin' young orf'cer."

These warriors, far from the amenities of their homeland, must be true to their own code, which alone supports them; they would not understand the line of argument which condemns them for being what they are; they see no need to apologize (and to whom? Kipling might well ask). Bonamy Dobrée, in assessing the scale of Kipling's values held through life, places first the need to accept the world as it is "with no romantic illusions," of playing the man "while the odds are eternally and crushingly against you. It is hopeless to try to alter the world. Even if you are capable of adding to it, if yours is not the appointed time your work will be sacrificed ... But man must not complain, nor ask for life's handicap to be reduced."[12] This is stoic doctrine, in some ways too bleak for optimists, social reformers, and democrats, to accept; the emphasis on work for its own sake, or on a definition of Duty conceived by the individual rather than by the state, cannot easily be accommodated by those who, bemused by Kipling's extraordinary ability to "get inside the skin" of a number of fictional characters unacceptable in conventional social situations, mistake Kipling's creations for Kipling himself. Kipling is partly in each of his creations, in the three soldiers who illustrate the characteristics of the Irish, Yorkshiremen, and Cockneys, but he is not to be mistaken for any of them. (The irritating spellings come, regrettably, from a literary convention, and may have been recorded with surprising carelessness because Kipling was not wholly satisfied with the convention.) His philosophy must be inferred from a whole gathering of stories; it is not clearly or explicitly stated by any individual; perhaps most important, it changes under the pressures of time, and of Kipling's increasingly close acquaintance with the appalling costs of war, self-enforced isolation, and physical debilitation.

Two additional features of Kipling's soldier stories deserve consideration. He rapidly learned how to use a "frame," which usually begins with an incident, no more than an anecdote, that in turn leads on to a memory of a longer story; the incident and the story are subtly, challengingly interrelated, though the former seems to be no more than an excuse to introduce the latter. "On Greenhow Hill" and "Love-o'-Women" may be cited as superior examples of the frame; but Kipling found the device useful for many stories with non-military backgrounds. For example, both "The Man Who Would Be King" and "The Phantom 'Rickshaw" come fairly early. A study of Kipling's frames, including the tailpieces which return us to the present moment, would be as illuminating as any analysis of the ways in which Kipling's prefatory poems, for a large number of stories, suggest, in veiled language, the moral or meaning of each narrative.

The second feature, knowingness, is a matter of tone, of the author's relationship to his subject-matter. The censure of false knowingness applies to much that Kipling wrote during his seven years' hard. But the stories with a military background or with military heroes exhibit a true knowingness. Kipling did, in fact, know a great deal about the mess, the barrack-room, various regiments, subalterns, and ordinary soldiers. Sir Frederick Roberts, the Commander-in-Chief in India (called "that great Little Man Bobs" in "The Taking of Lungtungpen," and, at a later stage of his career, Lord Roberts of Kandahar), consulted Kipling about the morale of the rank and file shortly before the journalist left India for England. What Kipling did not see first-hand, he imagined; he wrote a good deal about war and fighting. Kipling's years in India were years of peace; the North-West Frontier was, taken by and large, a quiet territory in the 1880s. But Kipling could describe the breaking-down of a military formation; the cowardliness of a British infantry regiment during an Afghan campaign ("The Drums of the Fore and Aft"); and many of the less pleasant aspects of military behavior. Though he admired soldiers – Richard Le Gallienne described him, in 1900, as a "war correspondent in love with soldiers"[13] – he did not shirk from his compulsion to tell the truth about two things: what he knew on the basis of experience, and what he felt, bone-deep, was possible. He differentiated between the subalterns, who could articulate their feelings about hardships, who lived by the clear tenets of a code unknown to Englishmen and Englishwomen safe at home, and who all too frequently died in unheroic circumstances, and the ordinary soldiers, who misbehaved, drank and whored and bullied, and fought for the flag, all the while seeking (for the most part unsuccessfully) to find a suitable language for their inchoate, half-formed thoughts. Those readers in the 1890s who resented his knowingness could not deny – convincingly – the truth of what he told them about the sons they had sent to fight in distant lands. Kipling upset them, or at least some of them, because he reminded them of the unpleasant truth that the responsibility of maintaining an Empire was a two-way obligation, and exacted understanding and sacrifice from the English in England. The lesser breeds without the Law could not be civilized unless both were forthcoming.

Before the Great War began, the truth lying behind Kipling's stories about military life was confirmed. Soldiers like Robert Graves and Sir George Younghusband swore that Kipling had shaped the popular image of Tommy Atkins, not only in the minds of the British public but in the mind of Tommy Atkins himself. In Keats's memorable formulation: "The Imagination may be compared to Adam's dream – he awoke and found it truth."[14]

Kipling's earliest contributions to the short-story genre were more than a series of cleverly wrought turnovers. Their subject-matter, after all, was India, a magical, mysterious subcontinent that could be evoked, but never defined with certainty. Kipling himself never ceased to marvel at its wonders, the ineffable and often irrational relationships between gods and men, between animals and the jungle they inhabit, between traditions of unknowable age and modern engineering marvels of bridge and road. Le Fanu had thought of human evil as his essential subject-matter and Dickens had exploited in tales of the supernatural his childhood fears with great gusto; Hardy had adapted, with skill, legends of the Wessex past that suggested how devitalized the modern world was becoming; and Stevenson, writing his shockers, posited their astonishing events against a solidly-specified world of Victorian reality. All of them recognized a distinction between what they fancied and what they knew. But Kipling, with his view of India as a shimmering universe of indeterminate values, and inspired by a Daemon which spoke only to him, benefited tremendously from his conviction that the best of explanations of Indian life cannot, do not, truly explain much.

"The Phantom 'Rickshaw" was, according to Kipling, his first serious attempt to think in another man's skin. It appeared early in his career (in *Quartette*, the Christmas Annual for 1885 of the *Civil and Military Gazette*, to which Kipling, his sister Alice, and his father and mother contributed). It was later used as the lead story in No. 5 of the Indian Railway Library series (1888), and reprinted in the collection *Wee Willie Winkie* of 1890. In the version most commonly used in anthologies, Kipling's added pages, constituting a frame, introduce a narrator who sits with the sick patient Theobald Jack Pansay when Doctor Heatherlegh is away. The "I" of the prologue persuades Pansay to write out "the whole affair" because "ink might assist him to ease his mind." A rational, somewhat skeptical note is struck by the worldly-wise commentator, who begins his story with the sentence, "One of the few advantages that India has over England is a great Knowability." Kipling recognized that this first example of his Daemon at work was not all of a piece, and, in characterizing it for *Something of Myself*, referred to some of it as "weak," and much of it as "bad and out of key."[15]

"The Phantom 'Rickshaw" deals with an apparition – of a jilted sweetheart, "handkerchief in hand, and golden head bowed on her breast," sitting in a 'rickshaw with its hood fallen back, driven by "four *jhampanis* in 'magpie' livery" – in a curiously convincing way. Pansay, who makes no excuse for the fact that his love for Agnes Keith-Wessington has cooled first, or for his brutal behavior toward her when he breaks off the affair, is first distracted, then tormented, driven out of his mind, and finally broken by the vision of an

THE PHANTOM 'RICKSHAW & other EERIE TALES by Rudyard Kipling.

A. H. Wheeler & Co's Indian Railway Library No. 5 | One Rupee | No. 5

MAYO SCHOOL OF ART LAHORE

MUFID I AM PRESS LAHORE

14 Cover of the Indian Railway Library edition of *The Phantom 'Rickshaw* by Rudyard Kipling. Design supervised by John Lockwood Kipling (Mayo School of Art, Lahore)

Avenger, who represents the "Powers of Darkness." Yet Pansay is not all brute. The Kipling who brought him to life knew – even at the age of twenty – that the calloused philanderer also has a point of view, a conscience that can be touched. Pansay accepts his own death as "the last portion" of his punishment. More important, he is drawn to Mrs. Keith-Wessington's spectral form, even though her death had given him relief because "the inexpressible burden of her existence" had been removed (permanently, he thought) from his life. The ordinariness of the 'rickshaw is emphasized: it is "a yellow-panelled, cheap, bazar 'rickshaw." In one of her appearances she even carries a card-case. The preposterousness of the vision is underlined: "One may see ghosts of men and women, but surely never coolies and carriages. The whole thing is absurd. Fancy the ghost of a hillman!" The spectral illusion is more than a "Horror" in the Dickensian sense. It is (we may have to say it for Pansay, because he will not say it for himself) *attractive*. The battle to remain objective about the chimeras of the mind is a losing proposition, and Kipling scores his finest stroke when Pansay, succumbing to the persistence of the "shadow among shadows," wonders whether he and Mrs. Wessington in her 'rickshaw are *real*; whether he, like the Prince in *The Princess*, seems "to move among a world of ghosts"[16]; whether this newly established relationship with the supernatural world does not, in truth, have its own attractions. "It was a ghastly and yet in some indefinable way a marvellously dear experience," Pansay writes in his memoir. "Could it be possible, I wondered, that I was in this life to woo a second time the woman I had killed by my own neglect and cruelty?"

The novelty of Kipling's insights – that another world, coexisting with our own, manifests itself in broad daylight, and that it can be weirdly, cruelly attractive (Pansay wanders, by day, with Mrs. Wessington "almost content") – marks off a number of Kipling's stories of bloody revenge. It is difficult to imagine Edgar Allan Poe undermining Pansay's growing insanity by describing it as "a dim sort of pleasure," or by saying that the commingling of the seen and the Unseen gives rise to a "sensation of dull, numbing wonder."

Similarly, the primary interest of "The Man Who Would Be King" lies not so much in the buccaneering exploits of Peachey Carnehan and Daniel Dravot as in the wondering reactions of the young journalist who narrates the tale. Few of Kipling's stories are as nakedly autobiographical in their depiction of a professional at work; several memoirs, written by Kipling and those who knew him

in the 1890s, attest to the accuracy of this (perhaps unexpectedly)
diffident portrayal.[17] The story-teller informs us immediately that it
has not been his lot in life to be able to change his destiny: "The Law,
as quoted, lays down a fair conduct of life, and one not easy to follow.
I have been fellow to a begger again and again under circumstances
which prevented either of us finding out whether the other was
worthy. I have still to be brother to a prince, though I once came
near to kinship with what might have been a veritable King and was
promised the reversion of a Kingdom – army, law-courts, revenue
and policy all complete. But, to-day, I greatly fear that my King is
dead, and if I want a crown I must go hunt it for myself." The
journalist never goes hunting for his crown (though he would not
mind owning one); he can only watch others, who live dangerously,
reach out for it, and wear it. Nothing that Carnehan or Dravot does
– from pretending to be a mad priest in the Kumharsen Serai to
supervising "peace" negotiations between warring villages, to
pretending to be "Gods and sons of Alexander" to assuming the
Grand-Mastership of "all Freemasonry" in Kafiristan, a fictionalized (but very realistic) inaccessible corner of the world – lies
within his own realm of possibilities.

It is not as if Kipling is describing a hum-drum alternative. The
journalist, in the course of his duties, has visited many of the dark
places of the earth (in the Native States); has done business with
"divers Kings"; has consorted with "Princes and Politicals, drinking
from crystal and eating from silver"; and has done more than his fair
share of "recording and reporting" in one of the most exotic of all
British Dominions. He lives close to sickness and death; the
telephone "becomes a tinkling terror, because it tells you of the
sudden deaths of men and women that you knew intimately," and,
"as the advertisements say, 'must be experienced to be appreciated.'" India, in these terms, is a universe of half-lights; it is not
England; and the story-teller, relieved at one point to learn that
Dravot and Carnehan have gotten beyond the Border, turns back to
his own business: the reporting of the death of "a real King" who has
died in Europe.

It is clear, not far into the narrative, that he vigorously upholds his
own code of ethics. He does not approve of bums pretending to be
correspondents of English-language newspapers, or blackmailing
"one of the little rap-trap states of Central India or Southern
Rajputana," and he takes appropriate steps to insure their deporta-
tion "from the Degumber borders."

But even without Carnehan and Dravot, he lives in an India of pitchy black nights, when a red-hot wind from the west booms among "the tindery trees ... pretending that the rain [is] on its heels." The naked compositors wipe the sweat from their foreheads. The "whole round earth" stands still "in the choking heat, with its finger on its lip, to wait the event." The event waited for turns out to be the sudden materialization of "two men in white clothes," who need factual information about "the top right-hand corner of Afghanistan, not more than three hundred miles from Peshawar."

Although we cannot determine whether the journalist forms any definite attitude toward the story Carnehan has brought back from Kafiristan, we appreciate the professional doggedness of the reporter, who wants the *whole* narrative, as he plies the returned adventurer, a broken Carnehan, with strong drink. "Take some more whiskey, and go on," he says more than once. He does not contradict Carnehan's characterization of what has happened as "*the* most amazing miracles." He shudders when he recognizes – "in spite of defacements manifold" – the "dried, withered head of Daniel Dravot"; he puts Carnehan into a carriage, drives him off to the nearest missionary "for eventual transfer to the Asylum," and two days later hears of his death from the Superintendent of the Asylum. Dravot's severed head has disappeared. "And there the matter rests."

Perhaps Kipling comments here, in subtle fashion, on the folly of Empire-builders who believe that their enterprise will endure forever. But it will not do to be too positive on this point. Dravot and Carnehan, even in their determination to loot the territory, are heroic on a very large scale. The order that they superimpose on the barbarians of Kafiristan is better than the random and savage killing that has terrorized the countryside. At any rate, no editorial attitude comes through clearly, no easy condemnation is registered, no moral superiority of the stay-at-home is recorded. What Kipling stresses is the openness of the journalist – of Kipling himself – to the miraculousness of life in the East, where anything can happen, and very often does.

This, then, is the most fascinating constant in Kipling's art: an openness to experience during a full half-century of creative work. Perhaps too much has been made in Kipling criticism of the knowingness, what Randall Jarrell has described as having "all the unnumbered details of others' guilds, crafts, mysteries, techniques at the tip of his fingers,"[18] and not enough about Kipling's fascination with the possibility of something surprising, wondrous, at almost every turn of human existence. It is more than a simple preoccupation with horrifying detail or the sinister aspects of supernaturalism (though there is enough, and more than enough, in the stories that begin with "In the House of Suddhoo" and "The Mark of the Beast," and continue with "They," "Mrs. Bathurst," "Mary Postgate," "Swept and Garnished," and "The Wish House"). Kipling, for all his lavish attention to details and to facts, never forgets his allegiance to the underlying mysteries; and that allegiance is plain enough, and simultaneously provocative enough, to make the Anglo-Indian stories of his first decade one of the richest achievements of Victorian fiction.

Joseph Conrad and H. G. Wells: different concepts of a short story

By the 1890s magazine editors, authors, and virtually all members of the periodical-reading public knew what the commercial short story had evolved into, and were reasonably well satisfied with its conventions, its length, and its emphasis upon a single point of view. In part, this consensus rested on principles enunciated in a spirited public debate between Henry James and Walter Besant, conducted in 1884. James's emphasis on "felt life" implied that an artist had a right to interpret the impact of experience on his own temperament. This view was not far off from Joseph Conrad's famous contract between author and reader, as expressed in the Preface to "The Nigger of the *Narcissus*": "My task which I am trying to achieve is, by the power of the written word, to make you hear, to make you feel – it is, before all, to make you *see*. That – and no more, and it is everything. If I succeed, you shall find there, according to your deserts: encouragement, consolation, fear, charm – all you demand – and, perhaps, also that glimpse of truth for which you have forgotten to ask."

Two authors may be selected to illustrate directions in which the short story traveled. Joseph Conrad learned how to control the flow of rich detail by developing a persona (Marlow), who knew exactly what the reader knew at a given moment, and did not pretend to know more. H. G. Wells, on the other hand, was so fascinated by the practical applications of new sciences that he found useful – and retained – the concept of an ominiscient narrator. Wells was more successful, commercially, than Conrad, who did not come into his inheritance of a large audience until very close to 1915, the year in which his talents first exhibited unmistakable signs of decay; but both writers were dealing with subject-matter largely new to the Victorian public, and their divergent attitudes toward the telling of a story are worth examining.

Conrad may have originally conceived of "The Nigger of the *Narcissus*" as a novel: it is, after all, longer than "Heart of Darkness." It was not his first, since *Almayer's Folly* (1895) and *An Outcast of the*

Islands (1896) had preceded its publication in 1897. Although sprawling in form and treating more than the simple relationship between the Nigger James Wait and the crew (the will to endure of the Captain, a man named Allistoun, is fully as important), Conrad's concept of a ship sailing through foul weather to its final destination unifies a host of disparate episodes. Conrad was feeling his way toward an assured sense of narrative voice, and betrayed some nervousness about the identity of the teller of his tale. The final pages are told from the perspective of a crew-member, who speaks as a shipmate watching Donkin receive his bad discharge; disengages himself from Belfast's slobbering embrace; bids farewell to his friends near the Tower of London and the Mint; and invokes their memory after several years have elapsed. "You were a good crowd," the crew-member writes in his peroration. "As good a crowd as ever fisted with wild cries the beating canvas of a heavy foresail; or tossing aloft, invisible in the night, gave back yell for yell to a westerly gale."

Conrad had serious difficulty in revising the draft of this story; the manuscript was messier than usual. When Sidney Pawling, an editor at Heinemann, accepted it as a book and passed it on to William Ernest Henley for possible serialization in the *New Review*, Conrad was delighted at Henley's approval; but he knew that not enough had been successfully achieved. A reader of this story has a right to question the ability of the story-teller – if indeed he is meant to be an ordinary sailor – to know what is said in conversations to which he is not privy, or his right to moralize about the thoughts of others that have not taken the form of speech. Conrad undercuts the authority of the narrator when he conducts a running quarrel between Singleton, a man without a voice who belongs to a generation "inarticulate and indispensable," and Donkin, who whines in filthy loquacity, and whose complaints are those of a "consummate artist"; Singleton is obviously cast in heroic mold, Donkin is meant to be distrusted and, ultimately, despised; the more a man talks of himself or of life at sea, the less trustworthy he is. Conrad, as one who deliberately adopts an anti-literary stance, complicates his reader's response.

"Youth" (1898) gives us Charles Marlow for the first time. He reappears in "Heart of Darkness" (1898–9) and *Lord Jim* (1900), and his successive incarnations are demonstrations of Conrad's growing control of a speaking voice. In "Youth" Marlow tells his story to "a director of companies, an accountant, a lawyer," and the narrator; they share memories of professional careers begun in the

15   Photograph of Joseph Conrad

merchant service. They know "the strong bond of the sea, and also the fellowship of the craft, which no amount of enthusiasm for yachting, cruising, and so on can give, since one is only the amusement of life and the other is life itself." The man who sets the scene, introducing the cast of listeners, does not know Marlow well enough to be sure how he spells his name; but at the conclusion of Marlow's chronicle of a long voyage beset by difficulties, one that concludes disastrously, all the listeners know that their memories have aged, along with Marlow's, "together with the youth, with the strength, with the romance of illusions."

Marlow's ship, the *Judea*, was Conrad's *Palestine*, and the difference between the historically recorded facts and Conrad's fictionalized reconstruction of events taking place some two decades earlier are more significant than the similarities. The voyage of the *Palestine* was marked by harrowing problems; but she never collided with a steamship in the waters of Newcastle; she came back to Falmouth only once instead of several times; and the dangers besetting the crew after they abandoned ship were (almost wildly) exaggerated. Conrad was justified in scolding Richard Curle – in 1922 – for over-stressing the autobiographical element in the story.[1]

The greatest refinement of the original material lay in the character of Marlow, who turned into more than the sum of Conrad's memories of his younger self. Marlow was really two men: a younger, cocksure, energetic second mate taking up his commission for the first time ("Fancy! . . . a really responsible officer!"), and an older, wiser, more somber man lamenting "the best time, that time when we were young at sea." The double perspective amounts to an awareness of two levels of time. The more experienced Marlow, breaking into his narrative periodically to exult over a lost youth or to request a passing of the bottle, sometimes jarringly breaks the spell of immediacy which the younger Marlow has so vividly conjured up.

Conrad, in the 1890s, had traveled much, but there was more than a little fantasizing in his lending to Marlow the aura of a mariner whose achievements were recognized by other successful professionals. Conrad had been an exile on the face of the earth, a Polish outsider in more than one alien culture, an intellectual in one after another semi-literate society of sailors, a would-be writer in a painfully acquired second language with its own great literary tradition; and here he was inhabiting the mind of a sophisticated, cosmopolitan raconteur, pretending to more wisdom of the ways of the world than he actually possessed, well along into his fifth decade. Moreover, Marlow's command of English – capable of colloquial abruptness, rhetorical effects, and dramatic inflection – seemed, to many of Conrad's friends, to be superior to the English Conrad used, years later, at Capel House, where he and Jessie lived (from 1910 to 1919).

The romance and magic of what Marlow went through are remembered with affection; but the chosen vantage point – that of a mature voyager who can see how the adventures of his twenty years fit into a larger whole – enables Conrad to comment, unsentimentally, upon his mistaken judgments and his limited understanding of an earlier day. Marlow becomes more than the narrator of a frame story, as in Dickens's *Christmas Books* or Stevenson's *New Arabian Nights*. He learns while he fights the crises created by a ship "all rust, dust, grime – soot aloft, dirt on deck," manned by a sullen crew who eventually abandon her (like the rats), and the conspiracy between Fate and foul weather that ultimately sinks her. The *Judea*'s motto, "Do or Die," proves true: the ship dies. Youth creates illusions, but it also plays tricks; it can be cruel and pitiless, and "more bitter than the sea."

Conrad, at first, did not appreciate the possibility that he had gone beyond the conventions of the "yarn" as told in the Polish *gaweda*, with which he had grown up. Marlow's determination to endure, and to arrive at his Eastern destination, becomes a cheerful mindlessness as the *Judea* lurches through the ocean. The older Marlow never describes his younger self as cheerfully mindless. It is taken for granted that when he was younger, he did what had to be done, and when, twenty-two years later, he recounted his adventure, the proper tone to adopt was that of nostalgia.

What seems much less clear is what Conrad thought about Marlow. The narrator, we remember, introduces Marlow's audience by emphasizing the mahogany table round which they sit. It reflects the bottle, the claret glasses, and their faces as they listen to Marlow. At story's end, the reflection becomes a key image: "And we all nodded at him: the man of finance, the man of accounts, the man of law, we all nodded at him over the polished table that like a still sheet of brown water, relfected our faces, lined, wrinkled . . ." If the reader looks at the reflections to be seen in the polished table, as the narrator does, as Conrad himself may have done, Marlow is seen at one remove. An image is not the reality. What Marlow thinks he has learned from experience is not necessarily what Conrad thinks Marlow has learned.

"Heart of Darkness" has often been treated as a study of the devastation created by imperialist policy on a white man's moral standards. This story, based in large part on Conrad's diary kept for sixty-seven days in 1890, burns with his hatred of what the "emissaries" sent by the Société Anonyme Belge pour le Commerce du Haut-Congo were doing to the natives in order to ensure a steady flow of ivory and precious metals back to Brussels. Conrad's awareness of the work of Henry Morton Stanley, and his meeting with Roger Casement, and his hatred of the greed of Leopold II of Belgium, as well as his use of genuine incidents such as the firing of shells by the French man-of-war *Le Seignelay* into the African bush, a railway under construction at Matadi, and his voyage aboard the river steamer *Roi des Belges*, have led many critics to treat the story as a barely reworked chronicle of personal experience. There are some piquant discrepancies between the records of Conrad's expedition and the "facts" as recounted in the story; rather oddly, the exact dates of Conrad's "command" of a steamer are one of the more obscure elements; and the original of Kurtz – a twenty-seven-year-old Frenchman named Georges Antoine Klein, who died of dysentery aboard the *Roi des Belges* – is so unlike the great fictional character that one can only marvel, again, at the magic wrought by the dyer's hand. Marlow was never misled (as Conrad evidently was) by the "civilizing" propaganda of the Company, and hence his disillusionment caused by the discovery of the true state of affairs in the various trading-posts was less severe than one may find running through several of Conrad's letters to Marguerite Poradowska, Karol Zagorski, and his cousin Maria Tyskowa, written over a six-months' period. Some biographers have inferred, from the reading of other journals kept by Europeans, that Conrad's loneliness during his voyage to the Congo led him to exaggerate the isolation experienced by white men, and to underestimate the population living along the river-banks, not only in his notes of 1890 (more detailed than anything else Conrad ever wrote to use later as the basis of a short story or novel) but in "Heart of Darkness" itself.[2] But the ultimate objective of an aritst is not to present, in however distorted a form, something historical. Conrad did not get along well with the director in Africa, Camille Delcommune; was understandably homesick (he went to Africa soon after a visit to family and friends in Poland); fell ill soon after arriving at Bangala in mid-August (he suffered from intermittent attacks of fever for the rest of his life); and learned, much to his chagrin, that "promises made in Europe are not binding here unless they are in the contract."[3]

Perhaps – this can only be speculation – Conrad found that his unavailing effort to secure a command worthy of respect was being frustrated by the unwillingness of traders already on the scene to allow a foreigner (himself) to share in any of the profits; his observations that the profits were obscenely high, and procured at the cost of every decent instinct, were fairly bitter.

"Heart of Darkness" is, therefore, more than a journal brought up to date, and it is difficult to avoid the suspicion that Kurtz, however important as the human goal toward which Marlow's river-voyage struggles, is significant as more than a fictionalized version of a Frenchman who was taken aboard at Kinshasa, and who died as a passenger on the *Roi des Belges*. Marlow learns, during the course of his voyage, the extravagant and ultimately excessive price that Kurtz has had to pay for his successes as a trading agent: sickness, growing insanity, revulsion at the natives (whom he wants to exterminate), Africa ("Oh, but I will wring your heart yet!" he cries at "the invisible wilderness"), and the universe itself, expressed by the cry with which he concludes his life: "The horror! The horror!" Conrad's emphasis here – in ways more complex than he could master in "Youth," only a year earlier – is on Marlow's understanding of Kurtz's sacrifice, and of the events constituting his African expedition. The visit to the Intended – to Kurtz's fiancée – is the most resonant, and difficult, of all the scenes that trace the maturation of Marlow's understanding.

Marlow has been baffled by the forest, the natives who move within it, and almost every visible sign of an inner truth that he cannot define. Nevertheless, Kurtz's death, in structural terms, has been a necessary development in the narrative. To allow Kurtz to return to civilization in good health, and to be honored as a bringer of light to the heathen, would be unthinkable; Marlow, who admits that lying is a miserable, sickening deviation from civilized standards, must stand diametrically opposed to what Kurtz has become, and his effort to nurse Kurtz takes place aboard a steamer that is returning down the river to more normal, civilized, European values. The inability of Kurtz to "make it," to be redeemed, is essential to the fable. What Kurtz knows, no less than what he did, has cast him forever beyond the pale. We do not know whether Kurtz is more appalled by the horror of what his life has turned into than by the horror of what he believes any man's existence can become; but it is evident that he cannot face, in his final moments, what he thinks to be the truth. Nor does Marlow define for us, in an easy moralizing, his view of Kurtz's spiritual condition. The closest he comes to it is a rhetorical question: "Did [Kurtz] live his life again in every detail of desire, temptation, and surrender during that supreme moment of complete knowledge?"

While Marlow tells Kurtz's fiancée that her hero died with her name on his lips, he yields to the temptation to lie for idealistic reasons. He cannot bear to crush her right to mourn – more than a year after Kurtz's fever-stricken death – a lover who was true to her. Conrad's effort to inform the reader of a sea-change in Marlow's understanding of his obligations to himself – of his own ethical position – may be judged as unsuccessful, or problematic, if we are not sure what Marlow has learned, or what his lie to the Intended signifies.

Did Conrad's strategy of ellipses fail at a critical moment in the text? Conrad does not end "Heart of Darkness" with the lie, nor with Marlow's perception that the Intended has believed the truth of his falsehood. The story continues (as life, in fact, must, and would). Marlow is relieved to escape before the skies collapse on his head; but, as he wryly notes, "The heavens do not fall for such a trifle." Perhaps, too, as he feels honor-bound to record, the heavens would not have fallen if he had told the truth, as Kurtz would have wanted ("Hadn't he said he wanted only justice?"). But he knows that he could not have told her: "It would have been too dark – too dark altogether ..." The final image of Marlow repeats the language of the opening of the story, when Marlow, cross-legged and ascetic-looking, first reminded the narrator of "an idol": now, at story's end, Marlow adopts the pose of a "a meditating Buddha." Conrad may intend to suggest by this image that Marlow, having recounted the major adventure of his youth, has apprehended Truth, but does not judge the moral consequences of having lived a lie; the director's remark, "We have lost the first of the ebb," reminds us of how spellbound Marlow's audience has been; and we are reminded, as if we needed it, that Africa's darkness is not far removed from that which overarches the Thames: "The offing was barred by a black bank of clouds, and the tranquil waterway leading to the uttermost ends of the earth flowed somber under an overcast sky – seemed to lead into the heart of an immense darkness."

The last sentence echoes Marlow's observation, in his first speech, "And this also has been one of the dark places of the earth," which draws a parallel between London nineteen hundred years ago and Africa at the turn of the new century. Conrad's Marlow, to be sure, is like his creator in that he despises the values held by the manager of the Central Station, and prefers "the idea at the back of [imperialism]; not a sentimental pretence but an idea; and an unselfish belief in the idea, something you can set up, and bow down before, and offer a sacrifice to..." Kurtz's original goal was to give to the natives some awareness of the benefits of a white man's civilization. The idea had (inevitably, given the nature of imperial practices) been corrupted. Conrad, like Marlow, did not forgive the "methods" – one method being the use of "black, dried, shrunken" heads on stakes set around his house – which Kurtz employed to rack up his impressive totals of ivory. But Conrad also seems to be debating the significance of the moral of his story. The final sentence, eloquent though its limning of a universal darkness at the heart of all things may be, is not enough to convince all readers that Marlow, the "meditating Buddha," has reached any conclusion so sweeping, so grim. He has – after all – witnessed the Intended exult in her "triumph" and "pain" after his lie has reassured her that Kurtz left behind "something – something – to – live with."

The main direction taken by the rigorously crafted short story has been Modernist: stress is placed upon the role of the narrator, who continually measures his distance from the materials of his discourse; irony and paradox suggest the multiplicity of meanings in human motivation and activity; the endings are not so much resolutions as questions for which no easy answers will suffice. Conrad's short stories move inexorably during the late 1890s toward an artistically controlled presentation, in dramatic and human terms, of moral ambiguities, or ethical dilemmas, or baffling mysteries that can only partially be deciphered. Marlow evolves as a point of view from the simplicity of an older man who laments the passing of innocence and youth to the "meditating Buddha" who, knowing more than he tells, hesitates to judge.

"The Secret Sharer" was published in 1909, and may be taken as one of Conrad's last important statements, in short-story form, of a rite of passage conducted at sea. Its content has been controversial from the beginning, although Conrad himself was convinced that he had mastered the genre at last, and written a perfect account in his fictionalized recreation of the *Otego*'s passage through the Torres Strait (between New Guinea and Australia) in 1888. When *'Twixt Land and Sea*, a gathering of three tales ("Freya of the Seven Isles," "A Smile of Fortune," and "The Secret Sharer"), appeared in 1912, Conrad wrote to Edward Garnett, "I daresay Freya is pretty rotten.

On the other hand the Secret Sharer, between you and me, is *it*. Eh? No damned tricks with girls there. Eh? Every word fits and there's not a single uncertain note. Luck my boy. Pure luck."[4]

The first problem is that we do not know whether the young Captain who narrates the story is completely sane. Quite apart from Conrad's occasionally heavy-handed emphasis on Leggatt as the other half of the Captain's personality (many readers, over the years, have found it possible to read the events of the story as psychological revelations of the divided self, because it is known that Conrad originally wanted to call the story "The Secret Self" or "The Other Self"), the Captain behaves in a neurotic, violent way. The Captain, once he has made the decision to hide Leggatt, can do no other than what he does, inasmuch as his own right to command will be taken from him once it is known he is behaving as an accessory to murder. (Leggatt's fate – if caught – is certain: execution. The Captain harbors no illusions on this score.)

The "strain of stealthiness" wears so on the Captain that he cannot clear his mind "of the confused sensation of being in two places at once," and he confesses to feeling "greatly bothered by an exasperated knocking" in his head. He shouts when the person whom he addresses stands mere inches away from him. He cannot sleep or eat: "It was very much like being mad, only it was worse because one was aware of it." The skipper of the *Sephora* – the ship on which the murder had originally taken place was the *Cutty Sark*, aboard which John Anderson, the chief mate, killed a Negro with a capstan bar in 1880 – is baffled, upset, and finally alarmed by the erratic behavior of the young Captain, whose ship he visits in a vain attempt to acquire news of Leggatt. The younger Captain continually wonders about his sanity: "an irresistible doubt of his bodily existence flitted through my mind. Can it be, I asked myself, that he is not visible to other eyes than mine?" He startles his chief mate (at the beginning of the story) by taking on himself a five hours' anchor watch (the first sign of erratic behavior); and he gravely alarms all aboard (at story's end) by sailing the ship much closer to the blackness of Koh-ring than Leggatt, a proven strong swimmer, requires for his safe escape. The Captain has – by his own admission – moved "as near insanity as any man who has not actually gone over the border."

Pointing to this pattern of remarks is not the same as demonstrating that Leggatt is a figment of the Captain's fevered, and perhaps not wholly healthy, imagination. But the chosen perspective is odder than many readers appreciate. The Captain denies, at one point, that Leggatt resembles himself, because "there was nothing sickly in his expression," a remark which implies a sickliness within the Captain himself. Difficulties are inherent in any simplified interpretation of the Captain's behavior, or in the view of Conrad's contemporaries that "The Secret Sharer" is an adventure yarn. Moreover, Leggatt is an enigma. Conrad, alarmed by the critics who had characterized Leggatt as a murderer pure and simple, emphasized Leggatt's potential for good by toning down the viciousness of John Anderson's homicide. But Leggatt, a mirror image of the Captain (as the Captain is of Conrad), provides Conrad with an opportunity to explore the question of how far both Leggatt and the Captain should turn out faithful "to that ideal conception of one's own personality every man sets up for himself secretly." Leggatt is not a passive personality, even though he obeys whatever commands the Captain gives him. Leggatt committed an act of mutiny by setting the *Sephora*'s foresail to save the ship in heavy seas before murdering "one of those creatures that are just simmering all the time with a silly sort of wickedness. Miserable devils that have no business to live at all. He wouldn't do his duty and wouldn't let anybody else do theirs. But what's the good of talking! You know well enough the sort of ill-conditioned snarling cur –" Leggatt does not provide enough information to allow the reader to evaluate the basis of his hatred of the man he murders; but some unsettling details about Leggatt's behavior must be considered. Leggatt, exhausted by the strain of sleeplessness and the need to keep the ship afloat, fells his enemy "like an ox," grapples with him, seizes his throat, and holds on to it, under crashing seas, for a full ten minutes. "It's clear that I meant business, because I was holding him by the throat still when they picked us up. He was black in the face." Leggatt can be (he is shown as) a violent man. He says, without pride but factually, quietly, that if he had been restrained in his effort to get out of his locked cabin aboard the *Sephora*, he would have killed again. He compares himself to Cain. "That's all right," he tells the Captain, who has been listening quietly. "I was ready enough to go off wandering on the face of the earth – and that was price enough to pay for an Abel of that sort." He adds, as coda to his description of how he escaped by swimming away from the ship in which he had been imprisoned, the revealing confession: "Do you see me being hauled back, stark naked, off one of these little islands by the scruff of the neck and fighting like a wild beast? Somebody would have got killed for certain ..."

There is so much pain in the story, so much heart-felt anguish contained in the feelings of inadequacy expressed by both the Captain and Leggatt, that one can hardly believe in the promise implicit in the Captain's final sentence: Leggatt, his "second self," becomes "a free man, a proud swimmer striking out for a new destiny." Not only has Leggatt's freedom been purchased at the cost of another man's life (a crime that the Captain refuses to judge harshly, and that "the shore people" will never be allowed to judge), but the true meaning of the young Captain's assumption of the full command of his vessel – after having sailed foolhardily close to the coast of Koh-ring – is difficult to decipher. It is easier to see what the Captain has been saved from (permanent feelings of inadequacy, doubts about his ability to command) than what he has been saved *for*, or returned *to*. Leggatt's existence aboard the Captain's ship has been a secret, and – the Captain himself has suggested it – possibly a figment of the imagination. Is the Captain wholly sane? When he bids farewell to his mysterious "secret double" and inhales deeply to enjoy "the perfect communion of a seaman with his first command," is the decorum of conventional behavior, shorn of its imaginative energies, being praised by Conrad? If so, does the rapturous description of Leggatt's liberation from the crippling fear of being caught undermine Conrad's characterization of the Captain as a man returning to normalcy?

Conrad, as recent biographies have made clear, did not enjoy a brilliant career of seagoing command, nor did he have much cause to regret his decision, in January 1894, to leave the sea as a way of life. He was not highly thought of by his employers; he did not like most of his ships or many of the individuals in the crews he sailed with. Rather surprisingly, he detested English sailors as much as (perhaps more so than) those of any other nationality, and the stolidity and courage of English sailors in his short stories and novels must be regarded, by and large, as idealizations. Such information should be taken into account when we recall that critics greeted the publication of "The Secret Sharer" with unanimous praise. The story was not (at first) considered difficult; it showed none of Henry James's "lamentable" influence; it was repeatedly described as a straightforward, enjoyable story of the sea. But, it was written after an extended period of depression (eighteen months) that alarmed James B. Pinker, Conrad's agent (Pinker's other authors included Oscar Wilde, Stephen Crane, Henry James, Arnold Bennett, and H. G. Wells); it is chock-a-block full of ambiguities and unresolved tensions;[5] its two major characters are not clearly defined; its concluding lines pose serious problems of interpretation; and recent biographers and critics do not agree on how autobiographically based Conrad's depiction of the young Captain may be.

Conrad discovered his true path after a number of false starts, disappointing encounters with editors and publishers, and intermittent periods of failed inspiration. His work on "The Nigger of the *Narcissus*" may not have suffered too much because of his sensitivity to the harsh reviews that had judged *An Outcast of the Islands* (published in 1896) as over-plotted, over-written, and gloomy; but the negotiations for a decent price for the manuscript with his publisher, T. F. Unwin, collapsed when Unwin, having made its offer of a £50 advance and a low royalty, refused even to consider Conrad's request for a £100 advance and a higher royalty-rate. Conrad also failed with Smith Elder, and found congenial and sympathetic help only when he turned to William Heinemann's publishing house, and to Henley's *New Review*. Yet, even before serialization began, Conrad ran out of money, and began the first of a series of borrowings that placed him in debt that lasted for a drearily extended fifteen years. The critics emphasized the brutality of the incidents recounted in "The Nigger of the *Narcissus*." *The Spectator*, for example, noted that Conrad's "choice of themes, and the uncompromising nature of his methods," made the Polish author's future popularity a chancy business.[6] "Youth" was one of the very few things Conrad was able to complete or publish during 1898; he was falling even more deeply into debt; and his delicate health recoiled from the hammer-blow of a rheumatic attack. "Heart of Darkness," his 38,000-word masterpiece, appeared in three installments in *Blackwood's Magazine*, beginning in February 1899, only days after Adolf Krieger had insisted on a loan-repayment (Conrad, his back against the wall, was rescued by a £100 advance – sent in addition to a £60 advance – from Blackwood); Krieger, who had lent Conrad £150, never did get back his entire loan. Indeed, it is difficult to consider the history of Conrad's short stories without acknowledging the importance of the problems created by Conrad's highly developed debts, neuroses, and illnesses.

Conrad's history contrasts poignantly with that of Herbert George Wells, who published most of his short stories between 1894 and 1906, and whose income soared from a modest £250 – earned from journalistic pieces and short fiction – in 1894 (before the publication of his first "literary" book) to more than £1,500 in 1897. Wells did serve a period of literary apprenticeship, though whether it ran as long as a decade (his own estimate) is debatable. Wells, once he found the secret of what would *sell*, wrote with greater facility, and on an infinitely wider range of subject-matter, than Conrad. His *Textbook on Biology* (1893) was an early effort at popularized pedagogy, but he wanted larger sales, and soon enjoyed them. He wrote humorous sketches for the *Pall Mall Gazette*, reviewed plays in 1895 (cut short by a siege of bad health), and books for Frank Harris's *Saturday Review* (1895–7).[7] Most important for his commercial success were the short stories and scientific romances that – beginning in 1894 – poured forth at the rate of one book plus thirty stories or articles every six months, for a total of a million words by the end of 1899.[8] Wells's short stories, which appeared first in periodicals, were collected in *The Stolen Bacillus and Other Incidents* (1895), *The Plattner Story and Others* (1897), *Thirty Strange Stories* (1898), and *Tales of Space and Time* (1898). In 1895 alone, he published four books (under four different imprints: those of Dent, Heinemann, John Lane, and Methuen), and his canny negotiations with publishers improved his finances far faster than Conrad was able to do during an entire lifetime. It is more than an odd detail, it is symptomatic, that Wells was able to take "The Chronic Argonauts" – written originally for the *Science Schools Journal*, a periodical that he edited while still a student – and rewrite it as a serial (in article-form) in six parts for the *National Observer*, under the name of the *The Time Traveller*. When Henley lost control of the *National Observer*, he asked Wells one more time to rewrite his time-travel concept in fictional form and this became *The Time Machine*, which appeared in the *New Review* in five installments. Wells earned 100 guineas for the serial rights; when it was printed in book-form (1895), it sold 6,000 copies within six months. The mass-circulation market existed, and no writer of the 1890s understood better than Wells how to appeal to its imagination, its interest in science, its fears and hopes for the future – or how to make it pay. Conrad, forced to fight for modest increases in payments for short stories and novels, saw Wells sky-rocket to international recognition within a matter of months; more important, to princely rewards for his fertile imagination – £200 for *The War of the Worlds* (serialized in *Pearson's*), five guineas for a short story, and (by 1903), when he had book-publishing contracts with both Harper and Macmillan, a £500 advance on 15 percent royalties.

While Conrad placed more weight upon the hoped-for profits from novels than upon the payments to be earned from the selling of

16   H. G. Wells, from *The Graphic* (7 January, 1899)

short stories to periodicals, Wells discovered ways of making his serialized novels improve the scale of payments for his short stories. Both Conrad and Wells knew that a volume of short stories would attract little notice, and no reviews, unless their novels first established the existence of an audience willing to read almost anything they might write.

Conrad was, understandably, dazzled by the highly visible successes of a man destined to become his near-neighbor on the Kent coast. Warmed by the favorable review of *Almayer's Folly* that Wells published in the *Saturday Review* of June 15, 1895, he wrote to Wells, thanking him for his first "important" recognition, and on December 4, 1898, sent another letter: "I suppose you'll have the common decency to believe me when I tell you I am always powerfully impressed by your work. Impressed is *the* word, O Realist of the Fantastic! whether you like it or not. And if you want to know what impresses me it is to see how you contrive to give over humanity into the clutches of the Impossible and yet manage to keep it down (or up) to its humanity, to its flesh, blood, sorrow, folly. *That* is the achievement!"[9] But Wells, preoccupied with his own concerns, busy with getting and spending, had little time for Conrad's art, which had "gone literary with a singleness and intensity of purpose that made the kindred concentration of Henry James seem lax and large and pale."[10] Wells could never forget Conrad's *foreignness*: "We never really 'got on' together. I was perhaps more unsympathetic and incomprehensible to Conrad than he was to me. I think he found me Philistine, stupid and intensely English ..."[11]

Conrad's concern for form, for deeper meaning, made Wells impatient. The Polish writer's dismay that Wells wanted to fictionalize social and political issues in order to demonstrate a thesis arose from a sense that Wells was not *writing*, that Wells was sacrificing his reputation for the sake of a philosophy or a world outlook. "'My dear Wells, what is this *Love and Mr. Lewisham about?*'" he would ask. But then he would ask also, wringing his hands and wrinkling his forehead, 'What is all this about Jane Austen? What is there *in* her? What is it all *about?*'"[12]

This is humorously recorded, and does not resemble Wells's humiliation and anger caused by Henry James's seignorial dismissal of his talent. But then, Wells thought of Conrad as "impulsive, uncoordinated, wilful," and "uneducated," whose "abundant, luminous impressions were vastly more difficult to subdue to a disciplined and co-ordinating relationship" than his own.[13]

Still, Wells was not always trying to prove something in his fiction, and practically all his seventy-odd short stories were published before 1903, the fateful year in which George Bernard Shaw and Beatrice and Sidney Webb invited him to join the London Fabian Society; his five-year stint of work for this organization proved destructive to the exuberantly imaginative romances – scientific and otherwise – that he had been able to write so easily during the preceding decade.

Lewis Hind, in 1894, provided the initial stimulus by requesting a number of "single sitting" stories for the *Pall Mall Gazette*, which he edited; but Wells responded with so much energy and enthusiasm that his stories soon were appearing in more than two dozen periodicals. By 1901, as Wells wrote to Arnold Bennett, *The Strand* was paying him as much as £125 for a story[14] (this series was subsequently collected as *Twelve Stories and a Dream*, published by Macmillan in 1903), though he disliked the editor's stolid tastes in fictional subject-matter.

Wells had ample opportunity to consider the framing convention, and its potential usefulness as a means of deepening the significance of the time-traveller's account, before writing *The Time Machine*. The Traveller himself is not named, and neither is "the Psychologist," "the Provincial Mayor," "the Medical Man," "Blank, and Dash, and Chose," "the Very Young Man," "the Editor," "the Journalist," "the Silent Man," or, for that matter, the Narrator who connects the frame to the main narrative. (Only Filby, "an argumentative person with red hair," is named, but here, as elsewhere, Wells is exploiting stereotypes, in this case the reader's preconception of the temperament of the kind of person who grows red hair.) The story begins with an extended argument about the nature of Time: "only a kind of Space," the Time Traveller says. Those who listen to the Time Traveller are instinctively suspicious: "Things that would have made the fame of a less clever man seemed tricks in his hands. It is a mistake to do things too easily. The serious people who took him seriously never felt quite sure of his deportment: they were somehow aware that trusting their reputations for judgement with him was like furnishing a nursery with egg-shell china ..." The distrust deepens when several members of the original party, reassembled for a dinner at Richmond, greet the Time Traveller after his return from his first journey. The Editor is thinking in terms of a headline: "Remarkable Behaviour of an Eminent Scientist." The Journalist wonders whether the Traveller "has been doing the Amateur Cadger." The Psychologist, who moved the lever that sent the (unmanned) Time Machine into "future Time," believes only that he had witnessed an "ingenious paradox and trick," and he waits, with skepticism, for the Time Traveller to tell of his new "tricks."

The assembled audience does not believe the news about the grim evolutionary prospects of the human race – Morlocks versus the Eloi at one stage of the future, no humans at all at a later stage (thirty million years ahead) – brought back by the Time Traveller. The

Editor stands up, "with a sigh," and regrets that the Time Traveller is not a professional writer of fiction. The Journalist, alarmed by the lateness of the hour, wonders how he will get home. The Medical Man requests the flowers, which he does not recognize (the Time Traveller refuses to give them to him), and asks, "Where did you really get them?" Not long after, speaking "with a certain hesitation," he diagnoses the Time Traveller's problem as one that derives from overwork, and the Narrator, for his own part, is "unable to come to a conclusion." After the final trip takes place, and the Time Machine and the Time Traveller both disappear, Wells adds an Epilogue: "One cannot choose but wonder . . ." The Narrator speculates on whether the Traveller has gone backward or forward in time. If into the future, the vision is cheerless. The Traveller has seen "in the growing pile of civilization only a foolish heaping that must inevitably fall back upon and destroy its makers in the end." The narrator declares his personal conviction: "If that is so, it remains for us to live as though it were not so." He promptly confesses his own uncertainty: "But to me the future is still black and blank – is a vast ignorance, lit at a few casual places by the memory of his story. And I have by me, for my comfort, two strange white flowers – shrivelled now, and brown and flat and brittle – to witness that even when mind and strength had gone, gratitude and a mutual tenderness still lived on in the heart of man."

This response to the thrilling events recounted in the Traveller's tale seems inadequate. Marlow's image of a meditating Buddha is, we recall, cryptic in that we cannot pronounce, with much certainty, on what Marlow has learned from his encounter with Kurtz. But we are invited to speculate; Conrad's story opens up, it exfoliates. But in Wells's stories the frame is simply a means of getting into the narrative: "The Door in the Wall," "The Remarkable Case of Davidson's Eyes," "The Plattner Story," "The Sea-Raiders," "The Grisly Folk," "The Truth about Pyecraft," and "The New Accelerator," among many others, use a frame, but each story ends with only the barest of hints that what has just been told is so remarkable, so hair-raising or wonderfully speculative, that it must surely have altered the Narrator's life as well as that of the individual to whom extraordinary things happen.

There are corollary implications, having to do with the imaginative laziness of Wells in devising a Narrator – for story after story – who is seldom interesting in his own right, never expresses unorthodox opinions, and seems to be consistently conceived as a middle-aging professional man long on common sense, a good listener, and a willing amanuensis. The endings of stories signify, by their abruptness, that Wells has used up his material, or has tired of a particular effort. The unexpected death of Lionel Wallace in "The Door in the Wall" – he opens a small doorway, and crossing the threshold drops into a deep excavation – may be a convenient way to round off a series of frustrated efforts to rediscover the magical world of childhood (when he passed through a green door set in a white wall, and saw two tame panthers, played games with lovely people, and knew what the word "love" meant); but at story's end all the Narrator can tell us is: "My mind is darkened with questions and riddles ... Was there, after all, ever any green door in the wall at all? I do not know. I have told his story as he told it to me ..." A story that ends with a shrug – as in "The Remarkable Case of Davidson's Eyes," when the narrator dismisses various vague explanations of Davidson's remarkable experiences with disgusted exclamations, "mere nonsense to me ... The reader may grasp this argument, but I certainly do not ... But the whole of his theory seems fantastic to me" – is less than satisfying. "The Plattner Story" concludes with a characteristic passing-on of responsibility to the reader: "One other thing, even at the risk of an irksome repetition, I must insist upon lest I seem to favour the credulous superstitious view. Plattner's absence from the world for nine days is, I think, proved. But that does not prove his story. It is quite conceivable that even outside space hallucinations may be possible. That, at least, the reader must bear distinctly in mind." Since the situations are set up with considerable skill, we want to learn more. But Wells will not tell us what happened to Elstead when he descended once more into the depths of the ocean ("In the Abyss"); the story breaks off with the sentence, "So the matter rests for the present ..." The "horrible creatures" who make such a spectacular appearance off England's southern coast disappear as abruptly as they originally appeared ("The Sea-Raiders"): "This is the last fact to tell of this extraordinary raid from the deeper sea. Whether it is really the last of these horrible creatures it is as yet premature to say ..."

Wells was doubtless too busy writing new fictions to spend much time rewriting what he had already set down on paper. He remembered, in his *Autobiography*, one conversation as he and Conrad lay on the Sandgate beach, looking out to sea. How – Conrad demanded – would Wells describe a boat in the water? "I said that in nineteen cases out of twenty I would just let the boat be there ... But it was all against Conrad's oversensitized receptivity that a boat could ever be just a boat."[15] The differing views of how to make an object significant, how to make sure that the reader perceived the significance of its being there, were miles apart.

Once, and only once, did Wells drastically change the ending of a short story to clarify his intention, and he did so after the lapse of some thirty-five years. Written first in 1904, "The Country of the Blind" dramatized Plato's Allegory of the Cave. Wells was attempting to show that those who cannot or will not see (the act of seeing being an infinitely extendable metaphor for the elements that, taken together, constitute civilization) are permanently locked into a barbaric culture that satisfies them because it is all they know, or wish to know. Nunez, "a mountaineer from country near Quito," learns, to his dismay, that the proverb "In the country of the blind the one-eyed man is king" is untrue. Though he tries his best to adjust to the ways of a community in which every man, woman, and child is blind, and falls in love with Medina-sarote, a woman of the village, he cannot – for the sake of "getting along" – permit them to operate on his eyes, to make him blind, so that he will no longer be different from the villagers. He flees from the community, leaving Medina-sarote behind, and the last sentence of Wells's original version, written as the summation of Nunez' admiration of a brilliant sunset, reads: "The glow of the sunset passed, and the night came, and still he lay peacefully contented under the cold stars."

By 1939, however, Wells was depressed by the approach of the new World War, which he had gloomily, and accurately, foreseen. He altered the story's ending for a limited press run (280 copies) at the Golden Cockerell Press, London. Nunez, in the new version, escapes with Medina-sarote and takes her to his own country; he becomes the father of four children. Nunez, able to see, and his wife, blind for the rest of her days, are satisfied with their respective lots. Because the final words are hers, they assume great importance. She argues that knowing the truth about the world – being able to see – "must be terrible."[16] Wells seems to be arguing that the coming devastation of the world will not matter quite so much if a man and his woman can cling to each other. It is – taken all in all – an unconvincing thesis, and not an improvement of the original ending.

Wells was as impatient to get his latest story into print as his public was to read it. During the 1890s he did not have to search hard for his basic situations. "I found," he wrote in a note prefacing an edition of

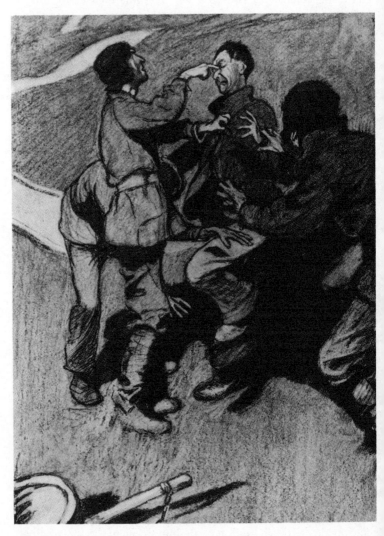

17   Drawing of *The Country of the Blind* by H. G. Wells, from *The Strand Magazine*, vol. xxvii (April 1904)

18 Another drawing of *The Country of the Blind* by H. G. Wells, from *The Strand Magazine*, vol. xxvii (April 1904)

"The Country of the Blind," "that, taking almost anything as a starting-point and letting my thoughts play about it, there would presently come out of the darkness, in a manner quite inexplicable, some absurd or vivid little incident more or less relevant to that initial nucleus. Little men in canoes upon sunlit oceans would come floating out of nothingness, incubating the eggs of prehistoric monsters unawares; violent conflicts would break out amidst the flower-beds of suburban gardens; I would discover I was peering into remote and mysterious worlds ruled by an order logical indeed but other than our common sanity ..." The fertility of Wells's inventions, the sense of a bubbling talent set free to play in the fields of the Lord, impressed contemporary reviewers, even though many observed the seriousness of Wells's failure to follow through on original and potentially first-rate premises. The reasons for the popularity of Wells's short stories, most of them approximately five thousand words in length, may be briefly enumerated: they were evidence of a new talent, and they introduced novel subject-matter, in a decade when the word "new" became a shibboleth; they were imaginative (in Frank Swinnerton's phrase, Wells was always asking, "What if – ?");[17] they were easy to get through, and entertaining; they were so good-humored, for the most part, that even the satire was acceptable.[18]

Almost single-handedly he made the sub-genre of science fiction fashionable, but there was, in truth, less science in the technical discussions that preceded most of his narratives than in the romances of Jules Verne. He used scientific terminology – as in "The Lord of the Dynamos," "The Cone," and "The Stolen Bacillus" – but did not stress it, though he had studied under Huxley, and was the best-trained scientist writing fiction during his lifetime. Many readers associate Wells's fiction with the widespread curiosity, in the first half of this century, with the abstract concept of a fourth dimension, and there is justice in the association, for Wells talks about it in "The Strange Case of Davidson's Eyes" and "The Plattner Story" as well as in *The Wonderful Visit* and his various versions of *The Time Machine*.

Wells's short stories, crammed into a decade of furious activity, pointed the direction for hundreds of writers in the twentieth century. They were not formulaic, but could be easily analyzed by other creative writers, and they were to be widely imitated. The short story attracted Wells, and many of his contemporaries, because acceptance for publication generally paid better than acceptance of an article (so Wells wrote to his father on August 10, 1894), and they were "much more profitable in the end because they can be republished as a book."[19] Conrad's more troubled and experimental short stories, which enjoyed only a fitful critical enthusiasm, and were never as lucrative as Wells's narratives, represented a different path chosen. We remain grateful to both men for their originality, and their vision, and their successes in two radically different approaches to the short-story genre.

Epilogue: the triumph of a genre

A creative writer often imagines that his fiction is the end-product of a free imaginative exercise – but he may suffer from a delusion. The triumph of the short-story genre in the final years of the nineteenth century was made possible by a powerful concatenation of circumstances. I will concentrate on three new factors in late Victorian life: a broadening of the educational base, mechanization of printing, and the development of mass-circulation periodicals specializing in fiction.

Though the extent of the revolution in literacy created by the Elementary Education Act of 1870 was much exaggerated by the champions of that Act, it was clear, within less than a decade after its passage, that the concept of a truly national education, based on compulsory attendance, and with provisions made for paying the way of needy students out of the rates, had taken hold. Despite the necessary compromises made to secure the passage of the original Act – including the Cowper–Temple clause that forebade the teaching of any religious catechism or formulary "which is distinctive of any particular denomination" – the number of children who attended inspected day schools, and thereby received efficient elementary instruction in reading, writing, and arithmetic, rose from 2,000,000 to 3,500,000 in only six years; that fraction of the population governed by school boards rose some thirty percent; the annual grants increased from £894,000 to £1,600,000. Employers who hired children under ten were liable to penalties; moreover, they had to be careful that they did not hire children between ten and fourteen who had not obtained a required certificate of proficiency in reading, writing, and arithmetic, and who had not attended a certified efficient school. The inevitable consequence of the Act was that the ranks of literate Englishmen and women – of "common readers" – swelled tremendously by the mid-1880s. A steady series of Education Bills – 1876, 1880, the work of the Cross Commission in 1887, the Technical Institution Act of 1890, the rise of the new university colleges in the last quarter of the century, the

Secondary Education Commission of 1894, and the Board of Education Act of 1899 – implemented, once and for all, the idea of an "educational ladder."

By the mid-1880s, changes in the printing industry were radically altering the markets for which fiction-writers toiled. Perhaps only individuals professionally concerned can appreciate the fact that the printing industry did not advance much for its first three and one-half centuries; one criterion is the production-rate – no more than several hundred sheets a day – of a late eighteenth-century printer working with a screw press.[1] But hot-metal composing machines that printed reading matter, and photo-engraving techniques that speeded-up the reproduction of pictures, moved printers into a new universe of production values. Ottmar Mergenthaler invented the linotype in 1885 (many had worked on it before him, but none had perfected the mechanical concepts), and Frederic Ives devised the crossline screen, or the half-tone, which Max Levy improved in 1890. Printing on rotary principles was in itself ample matter for amazement: these new web-fed magazine presses could damp (if required), feed, print on both sides, cut, fold, paste, wrap (when required), and count, all steps being conducted automatically. Webs of any width could be printed, at speeds of up to 100,000 feet of paper per hour. A periodical running between 32 and 192 pages could be printed, in thousands of copies, in less than an hour. When, in 1900, Henry A. Wise Wood developed the autoplate – a machine for rapidly and automatically casting curved stereotype printing plates for rotary presses – newspapers as well as periodicals could be produced at fantastic, hitherto impossible speeds. Several machines, working with duplicate sets of the same plates, could be run simultaneously. These improvements in mechanization reduced the costs of production to mere fractions of what they had been.

The change-over from steam, gas, and water to electricity as the power-source for printing houses also drove down costs dramatically.[2] Entrepreneurs interested in the book trade saw their opportunity. The 1880s was an especially lively decade for the introduction of new publishing houses: George Allen, Swan Sonnenschein & Co. (merging with Allen in this century), George Hutchinson, T. Fisher Unwin, Joseph Malaby Dent, William Heinemann, and Algernon Methuen Marshall Stedman. The 1890s witnessed the growth of Edward Arnold, the revival of Constable, and the first commercial successes of John Lane and Elkins Matthews (The Bodley Head), Grant Richards, the Studio, the

Temple Press, and Gerald Duckworth.³ And in any review of the history of the book-publishing industry, one must note the astonishing market that developed for series of inexpensive reprints: the Pseudonym Library, the Temple Shakespeare, the Temple Library, the Temple Classics, the International Library, "The sixpenny Blacks," and The Dumpy Books may be cited. Just before the Great War, each of Dickens's works – complete in one volume – was available for the astonishing price of 1d. More important than these, however, were five "library" series. Cassell's National Library, founded in 1886, brought out 209 volumes in four years that sold for 6d. in a cloth binding, and 3d. in paperback. Each title averaged more than 30,000 copies; the grand total of the series came to 7,000,000 in some fifty years of publishing. Cassell's People's Library, founded in 1907, specialized in fiction, and sold 900,000 copies of its 85 titles at 8d. each over the same time-period. Nelson's New Century Library (1900, becoming Nelson's Classics in 1905) sold fifty million copies in half a century. Grant Richards founded the World's Classics, which Oxford University Press took over in 1905; the 550 titles of this series sold 12,500,000 copies. Collins Pocket Classics (1903) sold 25,000,000 copies of its 300 titles by 1950. Dent's Everyman's Library, with more than a thousand titles, sold some 43,000,000 copies by the middle of the twentieth century.⁴ The venerable tradition of the three-decker at 31s. 6d. – dating back to the first decade of the Waverley Novels – died undramatically in 1894, when Mudie's and W. H. Smith's decided that 10s. 6d. a volume was more than they wished to pay.

The six thousand separate titles published in 1900 did not contain more than a scattering of volumes of short stories, and the approximately eight hundred booksellers in London (admittedly several of them highly specialized, dealing with medical, engineering, architectural, agricultural, botanical, or nautical literature) found them, in general, hard to sell. The primary market – indeed, almost the entire market – for short stories lay in the periodical press, which had been multiplying to feed the appetite for reading matter. The most notable of them included *Macmillan's Magazine* (1859–1907), the *Cornhill Magazine* (beginning in 1860, and soon reaching a circulation of 100,000), *Temple Bar Magazine* (1860–1906), *Longman's Magazine* (1882–91), *Blackwood's* (known familiarly as "Maga"), and, of course, *The Strand Magazine*.

By the year Victoria died (1901), more than 2,500 newspapers were being published annually in the British Isles, more than one-fifth of them appearing in London. Though several of these were very specialized, and over half of them were weeklies, they formed an important market for the perfection of writing talents in the fields of entertaining information, light-hearted essays, and brief fictions. In London alone nineteen morning newspapers and ten evening newspapers competed for readers; during the Edwardian years, the number increased by another ten.[5]

The most representative of these periodicals was *The Strand*. George Newnes, a young businessman in Manchester, was struck – in 1881 – by an item in the *Manchester Evening News*, which described the astonishing fourteen-mile run (in seventeen minutes) of an out-of-control eight-carriage train that finally ended as a wreck in a tanners' building, but did no harm to the five children of a station-master who were huddling within the central portion of the train. He thought that a paper filled with minor stories like that – *Tit-Bits* – might find its audience. The first issue of this singularly dull-looking periodical – despite its lack of a cover, illustrations, and advertise-ments – sold five thousand copies in two hours, as newsboys (who wore hatbands marking them as "The Tit-Bits Brigade") ran shouting through the streets of Manchester. Because it came out on Saturday and could be read more leisurely on a Sunday, because it was cleaner than the blood-and-thunders that W. H. Smith's had already found repellent, and because it packaged entertainment in bite-sizes, the periodical proved ideal for a new generation of readers, who had already benefited from the Education Act of 1870, the telegraphic system of the General Post Office,[6] the cancellation of paper duties, the development of new manufacturing techniques for the production of paper, and the invention of the rotary press. It did not take much longer than a year before the circulation of *Tit-Bits* exceeded 100,000; indeed, Newnes – even before the Harmsworths and the *Daily Mail* and the *Daily Express* – was an important agent in forming the concept of a new journalism that appeared to millions of readers for the first time. In less than a decade Newnes, who described himself as "the average man," earned some thirty thousand pounds annually from *Tit-Bits*, and astonished the publishing world with successful circulation drives based upon "free insurance," hidden treasure, prize competitions, and Christmas Numbers written by contributors (who sent in more than three hundred mailbags filled with entries).

Newnes was more responsible than W. T. Stead (the editor of the *Pall Mall Gazette*, and his partner) for the concept of what proved to be the successful *Review of Reviews*, a digest of serious-minded journalism and various articles and essays in periodicals. Despite endorsements from various statesmen, ecclesiastics, and intellectuals, the magazine seemed too risky in its coverage of controversial and possibly libellous material for Newnes, who bowed out from its editorship in less than a year, and turned it over to Stead.

His next scheme proved less of a headache and more successful. *The Strand*, a new monthly based partially upon the successful format of *Harper's* and *Scribner's*, emphasized short stories far more than any periodical appearing before its first issue (January 1891), when it sold 300,000 copies at sixpence each, and went on to a circulation of 500,000 a month. Each issue contained 112 pages of articles and stories, or 62,000 words of text. It was a distinctive, original contribution to the reading matter of Victorians, well-rewarded by advertisers, and an attractive periodical to read, with numerous illustrations, a free colored print (from the Royal Academy show of the year before), and self-contained stories that no longer required a six-thousand-word minimum appearing serially.

The Strand enjoyed the largest circulation of any English or American periodical during the years before the Great War, and influenced greatly the development of a mass-market interest in shorter fiction. The illustrations which accompanied the stories were meant to be popular art, and succeeded in fixing in the minds of readers images of the fictional characters who kept reappearing in successive issues. Sidney Paget's concept of Sherlock Holmes is often cited as the classic matching of illustrator with author (Doyle was delighted with the "excellent" drawings of the artist selected for him by the art editor of *The Strand*). Altogether some twenty artists working in black and white enlivened the pages of *The Strand* on a more or less steady schedule.

The magazine published much of Arthur Morrison's grim record of life in the East End, sketches that were later collected in that minor Victorian classic, *Tales of Mean Streets*, as well as Morrison's series of stories about Martin Hewitt, the first important imitation of Sherlock Holmes. Kipling published here, and so did W. W. Jacobs (becoming famous as a consequence), H. G. Wells (among other stories, one in 1903, about "land ironclads," that has often been called a prophecy of tank warfare), E. W. Hornung, A. E. W. Mason, E. [Edith] Nesbit, W. Somerset Maugham, P. G. Wodehouse, Barry Pain, Anthony Hope, Max Pemberton, H. Seton Merriman, Robert Barr (an American who lived with

Kipling in Villiers Street, Strand), Morley Roberts, as well as Baroness Orczy and a flock of women writers – Mrs. L. T. Meade, "Rita" (Mrs. Humphreys), Winifred Graham, Mrs. Baillie Reynolds, Mrs. C. N. Williamson, and Coralie Stanton, all of whose writings earned approximately five guineas a thousand words. After the turn of the century the fiction department changed its policy, and was no longer hostile to serials. Fortunate indeed the magazine that could print novels like *Brass Bottle* (F. Anstey), *The Hound of the Baskervilles* (Doyle), *First Men in the Moon* (Wells), *A Master of Craft* (W. W. Jacobs), and *Puck of Pook's Hill* (Kipling).

This extraordinary record of fiction was made possible, first, by the assembling of an enormous reading public that enjoyed Newnes's formula of interviews, art-work, hero-adulation, jingo-patriotism, and readable stories with recurring characters; second, by Newnes's willingness to pay large sums for what satisfied him (and, in turn, the public); and third, by the emergence of such literary agents as J. B. Pinker and A. P. Watt. (Watt handled Hope and Doyle.) Perhaps the three most highly paid writers of *The Strand*'s pre-war period were Doyle, Stanley Weyman, and S. R. Crockett. Two of these three names have gone into a long eclipse, but Weyman's historical fiction – in its day – won the devotion of Wilde, Gladstone, and Kitchener (among hundreds of thousands of readers), and Crockett's glorification of Scotland – particularly Galloway – in forty novels delighted Robert Louis Stevenson). Doyle's rate of return from the mid-1890s on – a minimum of £100 a thousand words from *The Strand* – was royal indeed. Authors received a fixed rate per thousand words, so that W. W. Jacobs might earn £63 13s. 4d. for "The Grey Parrot," and £86 13s. 4d. for "The Madness of Mr. Lister," while H. G. Wells would earn £83 6s. 4d. for "Mr. Brasher's Treasure," and £125 for the longer story, "The Truth about Pyecraft."[7]

If *The Strand* is taken to be the Victorian general-interest periodical at its most representative, and most commercially successful, Arthur Conan Doyle must be considered its most successful contributor, partly because of his ingratiating personality (nobody disliked him), and partly because he was so successful in correcting what he believed to be the great deficiency of most detective stories, the ability of a sleuth to arrive at his results "without any obvious reason." Before he became a regular contributor to *The Strand*, he had been accustomed to payments averaging £5 per thousand words. Doyle, a doctor himself, played fair with his readers by identifying clearly and sequentially the reasoning process used by Holmes in solving each of his cases. The readers of *The Strand*, grateful for his trust in their intelligence, and most of all pleased by the rapid movement of an interesting self-assured narrative, repaid him by their loyalty. Newnes never regretted the high rates he paid for Doyle's contributions. When Doyle wearied of Holmes as a distraction from what he considered a higher goal in fiction (a series of historical romances that were to engross him for a full decade), young men in the City wore crepe in their silk hats to mourn the passing of the Baker Street detective, as described in "The Adventure of the Final Problem" (November, 1893).

Most literary histories of the late Victorian era over-stress the importance of "decadent" fiction. Most of the journals in which such stories were printed had very short lives, seldom lasting more than three or four years. A closer look at the contents of *The Albemarle*, *The Yellow Book*, *The Savoy*, the *Anti-Philistine*, *The Butterfly*, *The Hobby Horse* (an important inspiration for the Arts and Crafts movement at the turn of the century), *The Pageant*, and the *Quarto*, will confirm what has often been suspected: fictions focusing on human and supernatural depravity were less important – and less numerous in those periodicals – than carefully wrought illustrations, highly colored impressionistic essays, and stories emphasizing the values of art in everyday life.[8]

The common reader refused to support a large number of laments about the lot of women, hopeless acknowledgements of the indifference of the universe, and explorations of perversity (as in Aubrey Beardsley's "Under the Hill"). The genteel, middle-class, largely female readers of mid-Victorian monthlies that specialized in short stories – *Argosy*, *Belgravia*, *Cassell's*, *Cornhill*, *Gentleman's Magazine*, *Macmillan's Magazine*, *New Monthly Magazine*, *St. James's Magazine*, *St. Paul's Magazine*, *Temple Bar*, *Tinsley's Magazine*, and *Victoria Magazine*[9] – were being added to continually as the number of monthly journals, weekly journals, and magazines sold in weekly parts, proliferated. Relatively few of these new periodicals had intellectual or educational pretensions. The concept of the tit-bit carried all before it. *The Strand* must be considered not only as a phenomenon in itself (before the Great War a single issue might well have enjoyed two million readers), but as typical of a larger class of periodicals that emphasized action over introspection, adventure over analysis, doing over thinking, and appreciation over depreciation.[10]

More than sixty periodicals used illustrations, and the lavishness of pictures printed as dramatizations of moments in short stories was a phenomenon of the times. A decision was made, for every general-market publication in the book-trade, as to whether or not to include photographs etched on metal, drawings, engravings, and reproductions of colored wood-blocks. One example (not isolated) may be cited: *The Adventures of Sherlock Holmes* appeared in 1892 as a large octavo volume, made up to resemble an issue of *The Strand,* and was printed on thick, gilt-edged paper. More than one hundred illustrations accompanied the three hundred pages of text. The price – 4s. 6d. – still allowed the publisher to make a profit, though one art historian, arguing that the book was "ugly," may have believed it was over-priced.[11] And it is not as if *The Strand* enjoyed a monopoly: *Windsor* began publishing in 1895, and *Pearson's* in 1896. Indeed, the *Illustrated London News,* established in 1842, had begun its career with sixteen pages of letterpress and thirty-two woodcuts; between 1850 and 1870, the great age of skilled wood-engraving, and 1870 and 1890, the years of exploitation of the process camera, publishers of periodicals had accustomed the public to expect the lavish use of illustrations as accompaniment to printed texts.

In 1910 the United Kingdom printed 2,795 "magazines" and "reviews" (the number partly depends on who is defining the terms). In London alone, 797 monthlies and 155 quarterlies were being printed; but it is impossible to tell, three-quarters of a century later, how many of the professional-class publications (691) and how many of the juvenile periodicals (218) in the U.K. printed fiction. The market for short stories was enormous, and apparently insatiable. For a writer who could learn how to master the secrets (or, less grandiloquently, the tricks) of commercially viable fiction, bliss was it then to be alive.

It is all the more surprising, therefore, that an age of controversy over the proper aims of fiction concentrated almost wholly on the novel, ignoring the short story as a genre that might differ in intentions, technical devices, or ultimate effect upon a reader. Henry James's scattered observations about the short-story form, growing out of his unhappiness at having to supply editors with the kinds of stories they wanted for their periodicals, were acute and very much to the point, but essentially they restated Edgar Allan Poe's dicta. James did not concentrate on the short story in any single essay, preferring to make his observations in reviews of novelists and novels, or in brief comments written as parts of longer letters to his friends. The dog that did not bark in the night becomes an even more intriguing phenomenon when the few histories of the genre that were written before the outbreak of the Great War are reviewed.[12] In general, they persist in treating Poe as the progenitor of the short story on both sides of the Atlantic, despite the fact that Poe's review of Hawthorne's *Twice-Told Tales*, in which most of his observations about the aesthetics of the short-story form are contained, was printed first in *Graham's Magazine* in May 1842, and was largely, if not completely, ignored by English editors and writers of fictions for fully half a century. (James's essay on Guy de Maupassant, published in the *Fortnightly Review* in 1888, may be taken as the first serious effort by a major creative writer to think about the short story as a distinctive genre; but its acknowledgement of the debt owed by American short-story writers to Hawthorne, Poe, and Bret Harte is swiftly overtaken by James's homage to the greater debt owed by himself to various French practitioners.)

Moreover, these literary histories, which persist in beginning their review of the evolution of a genre in the last two decades of the nineteenth century, never attempt to demonstrate why the thousands of stories published in periodicals prior to the 1880s are uniformly uninteresting or irrelevant to their considerations; they fail to review the implications of the fact that some of England's greatest short-story writers were happily active, and reasonably well-reimbursed for their short stories by magazine editors (by themselves, as in the case of Dickens and Trollope), long before the demise of the three-decker novel, when, according to their interpretation, the short story emerged from relative obscurity; and, as I have sought to show, some larger considerations in the history of the nation must also be considered if the development of the genre is to be accounted complete.

Perhaps this is saying no more than that the best thinking about short stories may be found in the essays of creative writers like Arnold Bennett, D. H. Lawrence, H. E. Bates, V. S. Pritchett, Katherine Mansfield, Virginia Woolf, Somerset Maugham, Elizabeth Bowen, and Frank O'Connor, all of which appeared during the inter-wars period. But that, as Kipling might say, is another story.

Notes

Introduction

1. Benjamin Boyce, "English short fiction in the eighteenth century," *Studies in Short Fiction*, v (Winter, 1968), p. 97.
2. Wendell V. Harris, *British Short Fiction in the Nineteenth Century* (Detroit: Wayne State University Press, 1979), p. 10.
3. Robert D. Mayo, *The English Novel in the Magazines 1740–1815 with a Catalogue of 1375 Magazine Novels and Novelettes* (Evanston: Northwestern University Press, 1962), p. 222.
4. *Ibid.*, pp. 208–72, *passim.*
5. *Ibid.*, p. 223.
6. Louis James, *Fiction for the Working Man 1830–1850* (London: Oxford University Press, 1963), p. 10.
7. Walter Graham, *English Literary Periodicals* (New York: Thomas Nelson and Sons, 1930), pp. 271–310, *passim.*
8. Margaret Dalziel, *Popular Fiction 100 Years Ago* (London: Cohen and West, 1957), pp. 5–10.
9. Scott Bennett, "Revolutions in thought: serial publication and the mass market for reading," in *The Victorian Periodical Press: Samplings and Soundings*, ed. Joanne Shattock and Michael Wolff (Leicester University Press, 1982), pp. 225–57.

1: William Carleton: elements of the folk tradition

1. Patrick Kavanagh, *The Autobiography of William Carleton* (London: MacGibbon and Kee, 1968), p. 9.
2. Robert Lee Wolff, *William Carleton, Irish Peasant Novelist* (New York and London: Garland Publishing, Inc., 1980), p. 10.
3. Thomas Flanagan, *The Irish Novelists 1800–1850* (New York and London: Columbia University Press, 1958), p. 256.
4. "Briefer" is a relative term. Carleton's "The Poor Scholar," printed in the Second Series of *Traits and Stories*, is as long as Conrad's "Heart of Darkness."
5. Wolff, in his "notes" (numbers 1, 3 and 7 particularly, pp. 129–131), is severe on bibliographical errors made by Richard J. Finneran, André Bond, and William Butler Yeats, as well as *The New Cambridge Bibliography of English Literature*, III, 2nd edition (Cambridge University Press, 1969).

6. *Autobiography*, p. 198.
7. *Ibid.*, p. 233.
8. *Ibid.*, p. 15.
9. *Ibid.*, p. 23.
10. *Ibid.*, p. 34.
11. *Ibid.*, p. 37.
12. *Ibid.*, pp. 46–7.
13. *Ibid.*, p. 80.
14. *Ibid.*, p. 86.
15. *Ibid.*, p. 177.
16. *Ibid.*, p. 189.
17. *Ibid.*, p. 157.
18. *Ibid.*, p. 70.
19. *Ibid.*, pp. 71–2.
20. *Ibid.*, p. 138.
21. *Ibid.*, p. 160.
22. *Ibid.*, p. 147.
23. *Ibid.*, pp. 91–2.
24. *Ibid.*, p. 91.
25. *Ibid.*, p. 67.
26. *Ibid.*, pp. 68–9.
27. *Ibid.*, p. 88.
28. *Ibid.*, pp. 98–100.
29. *Ibid.*, p. 108.
30. *Ibid.*, p. 115.
31. *Ibid.*, pp. 120–1.
32. *Ibid.*, pp. 154–5.
33. Carleton, *The Fawn of Spring-Vale* (New York and London: Garland Publishing, Inc., 1979), vol. I, p. viii.
34. Carleton, *The Tithe Proctor* (New York and London: Garland Publishing, Inc., 1979), p. vi.
35. *Ibid.*, p. vii.
36. *Ibid.*
37. Carleton, *Traits and Stories of the Irish Peasantry*, ed. D. J. O'Donoghue (London: J. M. Dent and Co.; New York: Macmillan and Co., 1896), vol. I, p. xxv.
38. *Ibid.*
39. *Ibid.*, p. xxviii.
40. *Ibid.*, p. xxix.
41. *Ibid.*, p. xxviii.
42. *Ibid.*, p. xxix. Carleton is referring to *Essay on Irish Bulls*, by Richard Lovell and Maria Edgeworth (London, 1802).
43. *Ibid.*, pp. xxix-xxx.
44. *Ibid.*, p. xxxii.
45. *Ibid.*, p. xxxiv.
46. *Ibid.*, p. xxxvii.
47. *Ibid.*, p. xxxviii.

48. *Ibid.*, p. liv.
49. *Ibid.*, p. xliv.
50. *Ibid.*
51. *Ibid.*, pp. xliv-xlv.
52. *Traits and Stories*, vol. I, p. 11.
53. *Ibid.*, p. 67.
54. *Traits and Stories*, vol. IV, p. 15.
55. *Ibid.*, p. 20.
56. *Ibid.*, p. 46.
57. *Ibid.*, p. 56.
58. *Ibid.*, p. 70.

2: Joseph Sheridan Le Fanu: developing the horror tale

1. "The Watcher," in *Ghost Stories and Tales of Mystery, The Collected Works of Joseph Sheridan Le Fanu* (Dublin: James McGlashan, 1851; rpt., New York: Arno Press, 1977), p. 9.
2. *The Purcell Papers* (London: Richard Bentley and Son, 1880; rpt., New York and London: Garland Publishing, Inc., 1979), vol. II, p. 254.
3. Printed under the title, "The Watcher" in *Ghost Stories and Tales of Mystery*.
4. *The Purcell Papers*, vol. I, pp. 96–7.
5. W. J. McCormack, *Sheridan Le Fanu and Victorian Ireland* (Oxford: Clarendon Press, 1980), p. 244.
6. More than two thousand short stories designed to shock, terrify, or thrill readers with the activities or influence of forces beyond human comprehension were printed in Victorian periodicals. The large audiences interested in this sub-genre attracted the talents not only of major writers like Wilkie Collins, Thomas Hardy, H. G. Wells, Henry James, and Rudyard Kipling, but stimulated a significant fraction of the work of secondary figures like Saki (H. H. Munro), W. W. Jacobs, Fitz-James O'Brien, M. R. James, Arthur Machen, Robert Hichens, E. F. Benson, Algernon Blackwood, Oliver Onions, Walter de La Mare, and A. E. Coppard. Very few of these stories sought to provide an intellectual substructure for the horrifying and supernatural events recounted. An honorable effort to marry a genuine point of view with some extraordinary happenings may be found in Bulwer Lytton's "The Haunters and the Haunted" (a story referred to on p. 53); the English novelist postulated the existence of a brain of "immense power" that can set matter into movement, that is malignant and destructive, and that has no distinct volition, though what occurs as a consequence of its activity "reflects but its devious, motley, ever shifting, half-formed thoughts." Bulwer Lytton's interest in exploring the behavior of a twisted occult power possessed by an individual who has learned how to concentrate his will was not successfully integrated within his narrative. The last quarter of the story, dropped from all reprintings after the story's original appearance in *Blackwood's Magazine* in 1859, was not rejoined to the

main narrative until 1944. In general, Victorian readers did not care to find a "message" in stories of this kind.

3: Charles Dickens: establishing rapport with the public

1. Deborah A. Thomas, *Dickens and the Short Story* (Philadelphia: University of Pennsylvania Press, 1982), p. 2.
2. Robert L. Patten, *Charles Dickens and his Publishers* (Oxford: Clarendon Press, 1978), p. 50.
3. Charles Dickens, *Sketches by Boz*, National Library Edition (New York: Bigelow, Brown and Co., Inc., 1920), vol. I, pp. xiv-xv.
4. Thomas, *Dickens and the Short Story*, p. 61.
5. Charles Dickens, *Christmas Books*, National Library Edition, vol. XIV, p. xi.
6. Margaret Dalziel, *Popular Fiction 100 Years Ago: An Unexplored Tract of Literary History* (London: Cohen and West, 1957), pp. 60–3.
7. Thomas, *Dickens and the Short Story*, p. 153.
8. *Sketches by Boz*, pp. xi-xii.
9. Edgar Johnson, *Charles Dickens: His Tragedy and Triumph* (New York: Simon and Schuster, 1952), vol. I, p. 165.
10. *Ibid.*, p. 532.
11. *Ibid.*, p. 520.
12. *Ibid.*, p. 521.
13. *Ibid.*, p. 530. Johnson notes, on p. xliiii, "There is no such comment in the *Westminster Review*; Dickens's remark is either a joke or an error of memory."
14. Norman and Jeanne MacKenzie, *Dickens: A Life* (New York: Oxford University Press, 1979).

4: Anthony Trollope: baking tarts for readers of periodicals

1. Anthony Trollope, *Autobiography* (Edinburgh and London: William Blackwood and Sons, 1883, rpt., New York: Dodd, Mead and Company, 1905), p. 292.
2. *Anthony Trollope, The Complete Short Stories*, ed. Berry Jane Breyer, vol. II (Fort Worth: Texas Christian University Press, 1979), p. 77.
3. *Ibid.*, p. 78.
4. *Ibid.*, p. 79.
5. *Ibid.*, p. 82.
6. *Ibid.*, p. 85.
7. *Autobiography*, p. 120.
8. *Ibid.*, p. 178.
9. *Ibid.*, p. 182.
10. *Ibid.*, p. 193.
11. *Ibid.*, p. 196.
12. *Ibid.*, p. 199.
13. *Ibid.*, p. 201.

14. *Ibid.*, p. 61.
15. *Ibid.*, pp. 144–5.
16. Quoted by Michael Sadleir, *Trollope, A Commentary* (London: Constable and Co., 1927), p. 344.
17. *Ibid.*, p. 346.
18. *Autobiography*, p. 347.
19. *Ibid.*, p. 318.
20. *Ibid.*, p. 250.
21. *Ibid.*, p. 216.
22. *Ibid.*, p. 211.
23. Sadleir, *Trollope, A Commentary*, p. 176.
24. *Ibid.*, p. 177.
25. *Autobiography*, p. 250.
26. Bradford A. Booth, *Anthony Trollope, Aspects of His Life and Art* (Bloomington: Indiana University Press, 1958), p. 144.
27. *Autobiography*, p. 225.
28. *The Complete Short Stories*, vol. I, p. 22.
29. *Ibid.*, p. 65.
30. *Ibid.*, p. 188.
31. Booth, *Anthony Trollope*, p. 46.
32. *Autobiography*, p. 126.
33. *The Complete Short Stories*, vol. I, p. 97.
34. *Ibid.*, p. 102.
35. *Autobiography*, p. 217.
36. *Ibid.*, p. 225.
37. Sadleir, *Trollope, A Commentary*, p. 352.

5: Thomas Hardy: an older tradition of narrative

1. Michael Millgate, *Thomas Hardy: A Biography* (Oxford University Press, 1982), p. 305.
2. Florence Emily Hardy, *The Life of Thomas Hardy 1840–1928* (London: Macmillan and Co., 1928, 1930; rpt., 1962), p. 227.
3. Richard Little Purdy, *Thomas Hardy: A Bibliographical Study* (Oxford University Press, 1954), p. 65.
4. *The Collected Letters of Thomas Hardy, Volume One, 1840–1892*, ed. Richard Little Purdy and Michael Millgate (Oxford University Press, 1978), p. 93.
5. *Ibid.*, p. 189.
6. Preface to *Wessex Tales* (London: Macmillan and Co., 1888; rpt. 1952), p. vi.
7. Preface to *Life's Little Ironies*, reprinted in *Thomas Hardy's Personal Writings*, ed. Harold Orel (Lawrence, Kansas: University of Kansas Press, 1966), p. 30.
8. Preface to *A Group of Noble Dames* (London: Macmillan and Co. 1891; rpt., 1952), pp. v-vi.
9. *Thomas Hardy's Personal Writings*, p. 128.

10. *Ibid.*, pp. 132–3.
11. *Ibid.*, p. 128.
12. See John Paterson, *The Novel as Faith* (Boston: Gambit Incorporated, 1983), pp. 40–68 *passim*.
13. *Thomas Hardy's Personal Writings*, p. 114.
14. *Ibid.*, p. 117.
15. *Ibid.*, pp. 111–12.
16. *Ibid.*, p. 125.
17. Kristin Brady, *The Short Stories of Thomas Hardy: Tales of Past and Present* (London: Macmillan Press Ltd., 1982), p. 48.
18. *The Life of Thomas Hardy*, p. 252.
19. As quoted in William Archer, *Real Conversations* (London: Heinemann, 1904), pp. 369–70.
20. *The Life of Thomas Hardy*, pp. 228–9.
21. *Wessex Tales*, p. 195.
22. *Ibid.*, pp. 286–7.
23. Brady, *Short Stories of Thomas Hardy*, p. 169.
24. *Thomas Hardy's Personal Writings*, p. 112.
25. *Ibid.*, p. 120.
26. *The Life of Thomas Hardy*, p. 53.
27. *Thomas Hardy's Personal Writings*, p. 9.
28. Desmond Hawkins, *Hardy's Wessex* (London: Macmillan, 1983), pp. 1–11.
29. *A Group of Noble Dames*, pp. 48–9.
30. *Ibid.*, p. 50.
31. *Ibid.*
32. *Ibid.*, p. 236.
33. Brady, *Short Stories of Thomas Hardy*, pp. 90–1.
34. *Thomas Hardy's Personal Writings*, p. 118.
35. *Ibid.*, p. 137.
36. *Ibid.*, p. 45.
37. *Ibid.*, p. 114.
38. Norman Page, "Hardy's short stories: a reconsideration," *Studies in Short Fiction*, XI (1974), 75–84.
39. Brady, *Short Stories of Thomas Hardy*, p. 197.
40. Evelyn Hardy, *Thomas Hardy: A Critical Biography* (London: Hogarth Press, 1954), pp. 183–4.
41. See Hardy's letter to Harry Quilter, July 8, 1888, in *The Collected Letters of Thomas Hardy, Volume One, 1840–1892*, ed. Richard Little Purdy and Michael Millgate (Oxford: Clarendon Press, 1978), p. 178.
42. *One Rare Fair Woman: Thomas Hardy's Letters to Florence Henniker*, ed. Evelyn Hardy and F. B. Pinion (London: Macmillan Press Ltd., 1972), p. 118.
43. *Ibid.*, pp. 36–7.
44. *Thomas Hardy's Personal Writings*, p. 7.
45. *Life's Little Ironies* (London: Macmillan and Co., 1894; rpt., 1952), p. 43.

46. *Ibid.*, p. 52.
47. *Ibid.*, p. 41.
48. *Ibid.*, p. 49.
49. *Ibid.*, p. 39.
50. *Ibid.*, p. 42.

6: Robert Louis Stevenson: many problems, some successes

1. *Fortnightly Review*, n.s. Vol. xv (June, 1874), pp. 817–23.
2. *Works*, South Seas Edition (New York: Charles Scribner's Sons, 1925), vol. x, p. 93.
3. *A Stevenson Library Catalogue of a Collection of Writings by and about Robert Louis Stevenson, formed by Edwin J. Beinecke, compiled by George L. McKay* (New Haven: Yale University Library, 1958), vol. iv, p. 1592.
4. Collected in *The Merry Men and Other Tales and Fables*, 1887.
5. Graham Balfour, *The Life of Robert Louis Stevenson* (New York: Charles Scribner's Sons, 1901), vol. i, p. 191.
6. *Ibid.*
7. Quoted by Roger G. Swearingen, *The Prose Writings of Robert Louis Stevenson: A Guide* (Hamden, Connecticut: Archon Books, 1980), p. 31.
8. Quoted by James Pope Hennessy, *Robert Louis Stevenson* (London: Jonathan Cape, 1974), p. 107.
9. Swearingen, *The Prose Writings*, p. 78.
10. Robert Kiely, *Robert Louis Stevenson and the Fiction of Adventure* (Cambridge, Mass.: Harvard University Press, 1964), p. 126.
11. Dr. Thomas Bodley Scott, "Memories," in *I Can Remember Robert Louis Stevenson* (Edinburgh: W. and R. Chambers, Ltd., 1922), p. 213.
12. *Scribner's Magazine*, iii (January, 1888), pp. 122–8.
13. Irving S. Saposnik, *Robert Louis Stevenson* (New York: Twayne Publishers, Inc., 1974), p. 101.
14. Jenni Calder, *Robert Louis Stevenson: A Life Story* (New York: Oxford University Press, 1980), p. 223.
15. Christopher Harvie, "The Politics of Stevenson," in *Stevenson and Victorian Scotland* (Edinburgh University Press, 1981), p. 122.
16. Edwin M. Eigner, *Robert Louis Stevenson and Romantic Tradition* (Princeton University Press, 1966), p. 160.
17. *Ibid.*, p. 150.
18. *Works*, Tusitala Edition (London: William Heinemann, 1924), vol. viii, p. xv.
19. *Ibid.*, vol. viii, p. xiii.
20. Quoted by Swearingen, *The Prose Writings*, p. 126.
21. Robert Louis Stevenson, *Vailima Letters, Being Correspondence Addressed by Robert Louis Stevenson to Sidney Colvin, November, 1890 – October, 1894* (New York: Charles Scribner's Sons, 1896), vol. ii, p. 191.
22. Robert Louis Stevenson, *Essays of Travel and in the Art of Writing*, Biographical Edition (New York: Charles Scribner's Sons, 1923), p. 261.

23. *Ibid.*, p. 276.
24. Stevenson, "A Note on Realism," *op. cit.*, p. 285.
25. *Ibid.*, p. 281.
26. *Ibid.*, p. 286.
27. *Ibid.*, p. 280.
28. Stevenson, "The Morality of the Profession of Letters," *op. cit.*, p. 296.
29. *Ibid.*, p. 299.
30. Stevenson, "Books which have Influenced Me," *op. cit.*, p. 316.
31. *Ibid.*, p. 318.
32. *Ibid.*, p. 324.
33. *Ibid.*, pp. 300–1.
34. Eigner, *Stevenson and Romantic Tradition*, p. 246.
35. James Morris, *Pax Britannica: The Climax of an Empire* (London: Faber and Faber, 1968), p. 343.
36. Hennessy, *Robert Louis Stevenson*, p. 152.
37. Balfour, *Life*, vol. 1, p. 224.
38. *Letters*, vol. 1, p. 238.

7: Rudyard Kipling: the Anglo-Indian stories

1. Ian Hamilton, *Listening for the Drums* (London: Faber and Faber, 1944), p. 203.
2. *Ibid.*, p. 204.
3. Charles Carrington, *Rudyard Kipling: His Life and Work* (London: Macmillan and Co., 1955), p. 91.
4. Louis L. Cornell, *Kipling in India* (London: Macmillan, 1966), p. 12.
5. The most important such works: K. Bhaskara Rao's *Rudyard Kipling's India* (University of Oklahoma Press, 1967); Vasant A. Shabane's *Rudyard Kipling: Activist and Artist* (Southern Illinois University Press, 1973); K. Jamiluddin's *The Tropic Sun: Rudyard Kipling and the Raj* (Lucknow University Press, 1974); and Shamsul Islam's *Kipling's "Law": A Study of his Philosophy of Life* (London: Macmillan, 1975).
6. Rudyard Kipling, *Something of Myself: For My Friends Known and Unknown* (New York: Doubleday, Doran and Company, 1937), p. 223.
7. *Ibid.*, p. 227.
8. Quoted in *Kipling and the Critics*, ed. Elliot L. Gilbert (New York University Press, 1965), p. 12.
9. *Ibid.*, pp. 17–18.
10. Oscar Wilde, who praised *Plain Tales from the Hills*, described Kipling, "our first authority on the second-rate," as one who had "seen marvelous things through keyholes." He was promptly attacked by Anglo-Indians residing in England, and had to write a letter to *The Times*, denying that he had described them as being vulgar. (Quoted in Gilbert (ed.), *Kipling and the Critics*, p. 7.)
11. Quoted in Gilbert (ed.), *Kipling and the Critics*, p. 74.
12. Bonamy Dobrée, "Rudyard Kipling," in Gilbert (ed.), *Kipling and the Critics*, p. 41. In addition to this essay, originally printed in *The Lamp and*

the Lute (1964), Dobrée's chapters, "Philosophy for Living" and "The Framework of Living," in *Rudyard Kipling: Realist and Fabulist* (London: Oxford University Press, 1967), are well worth consulting.

13. Michael Edwards, "'Oh, to Meet an Army Man': Kipling and the Soldiers," in *Rudyard Kipling: The Man, His Work and His World*, ed. John Gross (London: Weidenfeld and Nicolson, 1972), p. 38.

14. Letter to Benjamin Bailey, November 22, 1817.

15. Kipling, *Something of Myself*, p. 226.

16. Alfred, Lord Tennyson, *The Princess*, Canto I, line 17.

17. See, for example, reminiscences by Clive Rattigan, E. Kay Robinson, and Michael O'Dwyer, in *Kipling: Interviews and Recollections*, ed. Harold Orel (London: Macmillan, 1983), vol. I, pp. 61–92, *passim*.

18. Randall Jarrell, *The Best Short Stories of Rudyard Kipling* (New York: Doubleday and Company, 1961), p. xi.

8: Joseph Conrad and H. G. Wells: different concepts of a short story

1. Zdzislaw Najder, *Joseph Conrad: A Chronicle* (New Brunswick, N.J.: Rutgers University Press, 1983), p. 77.

2. See, for example, Norman Sherry, *Conrad's Western World* (Cambridge University Press, 1971), *passim*.

3. Najder, *Conrad: A Chronicle*, p. 137.

4. *Letters from Joseph Conrad, 1895–1924*, ed. Edward Garnett (Indianapolis: Bobbs-Merrill, 1928), p. 243.

5. Several problems raised by a close reading are discussed in C. B. Cox's *Joseph Conrad: The Modern Imagination* (London: J. M. Dent and Sons Ltd., 1974), pp. 137–50.

6. Quoted by Najder, *Conrad: A Chronicle*, p. 217.

7. The lessons learned by Wells in his careful analysis of the market for popular journalism are best reviewed by Wells himself, in *Experiment in Autobiography* (New York: Macmillan, 1938), Chapter the Sixth, "Struggle for a Living," pp. 237–311.

8. Norman and Jeanne MacKenzie, *The Time Traveller: The Life of H. G. Wells* (London: Weidenfeld and Nicolson, 1973), p. 116.

9. G. Jean-Aubry (ed.), *Joseph Conrad: Life and Letters* (Garden City: Doubleday Page, 1927), vol. I, pp. 259–60.

10. Wells, *Autobiography*, p. 526.

11. *Ibid.*, p. 527.

12. *Ibid.*, pp. 527–8.

13. *Ibid.*, p. 529.

14. Harris Wilson (ed.), *Arnold Bennett and H. G. Wells* (Urbana: University of Illinois Press, 1960), p. 59.

15. Wells, *Autobiography*, p. 528.

16. For a fuller discussion, see Richard Hauer Costa's *H. G. Wells* (New York: Twayne Publishers, Inc., 1967), pp. 61–3. Costa believes that the new ending conforms to Wells's "growing misanthropy," and that

"Wells appears to be saying that blindness is the only bearable antidote to the coming catastrophe" (p. 63).

17. *The Country of the Blind and Other Stories* (London: T. Nelson, 1911), p. iv.
18. Frank Swinnerton, *The Georgian Scene* (New York: Farrar and Rinehart, 1934), p. 71.
19. Bernard Bergonzi, *The Early H. G. Wells: A Study of the Scientific Romances* (Manchester University Press, 1961), pp. 65–7.

Epilogue: the triumph of a genre

1. Marjorie Plant, *The English Book Trade* (London: George Allen and Unwin Ltd., 1939), p. 269.
2. *Ibid.*, p. 289.
3. Frank Arthur Mumby and Ian Norrie, *Publishing and Bookselling* (London: Jonathan Cape, 1974), *passim*.
4. S. H. Steinberg, *Five Hundred Years of Printing* (New York: Criterion Books, 1959), p. 266.
5. Simon Nowell-Smith, *Edwardian England 1901–1914* (London: Oxford University Press, 1964), p. 320.
6. The story of the telegraphs, transferred to the Post Office in 1870, is important because it brought rural districts closer to the cities. Whereas in 1869 some 6,500,000 messages had been transmitted over telegraph wires, only six years later 20,000,000 were being transmitted annually; by the end of the century, more than ninety million. Other advances in the laying of underwater cables, wireless telegraphy, and indeed the whole field of electric-wave telegraphy, were helping to unify the nation.
7. Reginald Pound, *The Strand Magazine 1891–1950* (London: Heinemann, 1966), p. 74. I am indebted to Pound's history of Newnes's publishing career.
8. E. Lenore Casford, *The Magazines of the 1890's* (Eugene, Oregon: University of Oregon, Language and Literature Series 1, 1929), pp. 37–8.
9. Alvar Ellegärd, *The Readership of the Periodical Press in Mid-Victorian Britain* (Göteborg: Göteborgs Universitets Ärsskrift LXIII, 1957), pp. 32–5.
10. Pound, *The Strand Magazine*, p. 75.
11. Percy Muir, *Victorian Illustrated Books* (London: B. T. Batsford Ltd., 1971), p. 203.
12. Early book-length treatments of the genre include Ethan Allen Cross's *The Short Story: a Technical and Literary Study* (1914), Carl Grabo's *The Art of the Short Story* (1913), Brander Matthews's *The Philosophy of the Short-story* (1901), H. A. Phillips's *Art in Short Story Narration* (1913), and a number of manuals on how to write and sell short stories. Since *all* of these were written by American critics, and printed first in the United States, the relative lack of interest of English critics is all the more astonishing; the United States, despite its century-long love affair with

short stories, offered – in the 1880s – no serious competition to the skills of Stevenson, Hardy, Kipling, Wells, and Conrad. A number of short essays in English periodicals did not amount to much; for a representative bibliography of these, see Valerie Shaw's *The Short Story: A Critical Introduction* (London and New York: Longman, 1983), pp. 276–84. Ms. Shaw's review of the only partially formulated points of view current in both England and America prior to the Great War, contained in her first chapter, " 'Only short stories': estimates and explanations," is well worth reading.

Index

Aikin, John, 8
Ainsworth, Harrison, 90
Albermarle, The, 190
All the Year Round, 54, 56,.59, 63, 64, 65, 74
Allen, George, 185
Amoranda, or the Reformed Coquette, 22
Anderson, John, 169–170
Annual Register, 7
Anstey, F., *Brass Bottle*, 189
Anti-Philistine, 190
apologues, 5
Arabian Nights, The, 1, 22
Argosy, The, 86, 190
Arnold, Edward, 185
Arnold, Thomas, 11
Athenaeum, 8
"Atkins, Tommy," 153
Augustine, *de Curâ pro Mortuis*, 50
Aurelius, Marcus, *Meditations*, 130
Austen, Jane, 82, 175
Austin, Alfred, 131

Balfour, Graham, 120
Bangala, Africa, 165
Banim, John, 27
Barham, R. H. ("Thomas Ingoldsby"), 8
Barnes, William, 101
Barr, Robert, 188
Bates, H. E., 192
Battle of Aughrim, The, 21
Beardsley, Aubrey, "Under the Hill," 190
Beckett, Samuel, 14
Beerbohm, Max, 150
Belgravia, 190
Bennett, Arnold, 171, 176, 192
Bennett, Susan, 34
Bentley's Miscellany, 8, 57, 60, 64
Besant, Walter, 160
Black and White, 100

Blacks, Sixpenny, 186
Blackwood's Edinburgh Magazine, 7, 8, 98, 172, 186
Blomfield, Arthur, 96, 109
Board of Education Act of 1899, 185
Bodley Head, 185
Bolton Weekly Journal, 100, 101
Booth, Bradford A., 91
Boswell, James, 22
Bovington, 109
Bowen, Elizabeth, 192
Boyce, Benjamin, 1
Brady, Kristin, 105, 111
Brenner Pass, 120
Bristol Times and Mirror, 100
British and Foreign School Society, 9
British Weekly, 130
Brodie, Deacon, 123
Brookfield, W. H., 72
Brown, Andrew, x
Buchanan, Robert, 150
bull, Irish, 26–7
Bunyan, John, 130
Burke and Hare, 133
Butterfly, The, 190

Calder, Jenni, 125
Cambrian Quarterly Magazine, 8
Capel House, 164
Carleton, William, x, 4, 8, 12, 13, **14–32**, 96, 101; *Autobiography*, 16–24, 29; "Battle of the Factions, The," 24; 31; "Dennis O'Shaughnessy," 24; "Essay on Irish Swearing, An," 29; *Fardorougha the Miser*, 17, 24; *Fawn of Springvale, The Clarionet, and Other Tales, The*, 25; "Geography of an Irish Oath, The," 29; "Landlord and Tenant, an Authentic Story, The," 31; "Larry M'Farland's Wake," 31; "Ned M'Keown," 30–1; "Party Fight and Funeral," 24;

"Pilgrimage to St. Patrick's
Purgatory, A," 16; "Poor Scholar,
The," 23–4; "Shane Fadh's
Wedding," 24, 30–1; *Squanders of
Castle Squander, The*, 24; *Tales and
Sketches, Illustrating the Character . . .
of the Irish Peasantry*, 20; *Tales of
Ireland*, 18, 20; "Three Tasks, or,
The Little House under the Hill,
The," 30–1; *Traits and Stories of the
Irish Peasantry*, 17, 20, 26, 29, 30, 31;
Tithe Proctor, The, 25; "Tubber
Derg, or The Red Wall," 31;
"Wildgoose Lodge," 18, 24
Carlyle, Thomas, 105
Carrington, Charles, 144
Casement, Roger, 165
Cassell's illustrated Family Paper, 86, 190
Cassell's National Library, 186
Cassell's People's Library, 186
Castle Rackrent, 22
Cervantes, 94
Chambers, William, 10
Chambers's Edinburgh Journal Magazine,
8, 9, 96
Chapman and Hall, 61
character-sketch, 1
Chaucer, Geoffrey, 31
*Christian Examiner and Church of Ireland
Magazine*, 16, 23, 30
Christian's Penny Magazine, 8
Christmas Books, 74
Civil and Military Gazette (Lahore), 138,
139, 145, 154
Clongowes Wood, College of, 23
Collins, Charles Allston, 54, 74
Collins, Wilkie, 59, 63, 82; *The Woman
in White*, 64
Collins Pocket Classics, 186
Colvin, Sidney, 117, 137
Conrad, Joseph, 4, 13, *160–83*;
Almayer's Folly, 160, 175; "Freya of
the Seven Isles," 168; "Heart of
Darkness," 160, 161, 163–8, 172,
177; *Lord Jim*, 161; "Nigger of the
Narcissus, The," 160, 172; *Outcast of
the Islands, An*, 161, 172; "Secret
Sharer, The," 168–72; "Smile of
Fortune, A," 168; *'Twixt Land and
Sea*, 168; "Youth," 161, 166, 172
Constable, 185
Contemporary Review, 129

Corkery, Daniel, 14
Cornell, Louis, 145
Cornhill Magazine, 80, 109, 118–19,
132, 186, 190
Cowper–Temple clause, 184
Crackanthorpe, Hubert, x
Crane, Stephan, ix, 171
Cresserons, Charles de, 34
Crockett, S. R., 189
Cross Commission, 184
Cutty Sark (ship), 169

D'Arcy, Ella, x
Daily Express, 187
Daily Mail, 187
Dann, J. Vann and Roseman T. Van
Arsdel, *Victorian Periodicals: A Guide
to Research*, 4
Davis, Thomas, 16
Dowson, Ernest, x
Defoe, Daniel, 90; *History of the Devil*,
22
Delcommune, Camille, 165
Dent, 173
Dent, Joseph Malaby, 185
Dibdin's Penny Trumpet, 8
Dickens, Charles, 4, 12, 13, 54, **56–78**,
79, 82, 87, 94, 96, 100, 101, 192;
American Notes, 61; "Barbox
Brothers," 74, 78; "Barbox Brothers
and Co.," 74; *Barnaby Rudge*, 57;
The Battle of Life, 61–2; "Black Veil,
The," 57; *Chimes, The*, 61–2, 69–74;
Christmas Books, 59, 61–2, 65, 69, 72,
164; *Christmas Carol, A*, 61–2, 65, 71;
Christmas Stories, 59; "Confession
Found in a Prison in the Times of
Charles the Second, A," 61; *Cricket
on the Hearth, The*, 61–2; *David
Copperfield*, 62; "Doctor Marigold's
Prescriptions," 54, 64; "Dramatic
Monologues," 64; "Drunkard's
Death, The," 57, 67; "First Night of
the Giant Chronicles," 61; *Great
Expectations*, 63, 64; "Great
Winglebury Duel, The," 57; *Hard
Times*, 63; *Haunted Man and Ghost's
Bargain, The*, 61–2, 65; *Household
Words*, 59; "Lazy Tour of Two Idle
Apprentices, The," 63; "Main Line;
Boy at Mugby, The," 76–8; *Martin
Chuzzlewit*, 61; *Master Humphrey's*

Dickens, Charles (cont.)
 Clock, 57, 60–1, 65, 66; "Mr.
 Pickwick's Tale," 61; "Mrs.
 Lirriper's Lodgings," 64; "Mugby
 Boy, The," 78; "Mugby Junction,"
 64, 74–8; *Nicholas Nickleby*, 57, 60,
 64, 66; *No Thoroughfare*, 63; "No. 1
 Branch Line: The Signal Man," 76–
 8; *Old Curiosity Shop, The*, 57; *Oliver
 Twist*, 57, 60; "Pawnbroker's Shop,
 The," 69, 74; *Pickwick Papers*, 2, 53,
 57, 60, 61, 65, 66, 67; "Public Life
 of Mr. Tulrumble Once Mayor of
 Mudfog," 60; *Sketches by Boz*, 57, 59,
 66, 67, 69, 74; *Sketches of Young
 Gentlemen*, 60; "Somebody's
 Luggage," 64, 74; "Story of the
 Bagman's Uncle, The," 53;
 "Stroller's Tale, The," 66–9, 74, 77;
 Tale of Two Cities, A, 63; "Tuggses
 at Ramsgate, The," 57;
 "Uncommercial Traveller, The," 65
Disraeli, Benjamin, 90, 94
Dobrée, Bonamy, 151
Dorset, 100–1
Dostoyevsky, Fyodor, *Crime and
 Punishment*, 133
Doyle, Arthur Conan, 188–90;
 "Adventure of the Final Problem,
 The," 190; *Adventures of Sherlock
 Holmes, The*, 191; *Hound of the
 Baskervilles, The*, 189; "Red-Headed
 League, The," 2; "Scandal in
 Bohemia, A," 2
Dublin and London Magazine, 8
Dublin Evening Mail, 34
Dublin Evening Packet, 34
Dublin University Magazine, 8
Duckworth, Gerald, 186
Duffey, James, 16
Dumas, Alexander, *Vicomte de
 Bragelonne*, 130
Dumpy Books, 186
Duvaun, Paddy, 24

Edgeworth, Maria, 18, 27, 82
Edinburgh Edition (Stevenson), 116
Edinburgh Journal, 9
Edinburgh Monthly, see *Blackwood's
 Edinburgh Magazine*
Education Act of 1870, 187
Education Bills, 184

Edwards, Amelia B., 74
Egerton, George (Mrs. Golding
 Bright), x
Eigner, Edwin, 125
Elementary Education Act of 1870,
 184
Eliot, George, 8, 82, 85; *Scenes of
 Clerical Life*, 2
Eliza Cook's Journal, 63
Emmet, Robert, 34
English Illustrated Magazine, The, 98
Everyman's Library (Dent), 186
Examiner, 83

Fabian Society, 175
Faithfull, Emily, *A Welcome*, 86
Family Herald, 63
Fielding, Henry, 90, 94
Flanagan, Thomas, 20
Flaubert, Gustave, 131
Forster, John, 73
Fortnightly Review, 86, 192
Fraser's Magazine for Town and Country,
 8
Frayne, Pat, 17, 27–8
Furse, Charles, 141

Gaelic language, 14–15, 26, 28
Galloway, Scotland, 189
Galt, John, 8; *Ayrshire Legatees*, 7
Gamble, John, 7
Garnett, Edward, 168
Gaskell, Mrs., *North and South*, 63, 64
gaweda, 164
General Post Office, 83, 85, 187
Gentleman's Magazine, 190
Gesta Romanorum, 148
Gil Blas, 22
Girl's and Boy's Penny Magazine, 8
Gissing, George, x
Gladstone, William, 125, 189
Goethe, 46
Golden Cockerell Press, 179
Good Cheer, 86
Good Words, 86
Gordon, General, 125
Gothic fiction, 6, 109
Graham, Walter, 6
Graham, Winifred, 189
Graham's Magazine, 192
Graphic, The, 86, 89, 101, 108
Graves, Robert, 153

Griffin, Gerald, 27
Grimaldi the clown, 60
Grub Street, 104

Haggard, H. Rider, 131
Hall, Anna, 27
Halliday, Andrew, 74
Hamilton, Ian, General, 139
Hamilton, Vereker, 139–41
Harbord, R. E., *The Reader's Guide to Rudyard Kipling's Work*, 144
Hardy, Evelyn, 112
Hardy, Thomas, 2, 12, 13, 17, 51, 83, **96–114**, 154; "Anna, Lady Baxby," 99; "Barbara of the House of Grebe," 99; "Candour in English Fiction," 2, 102–5; "Changed Man, A," 97; *Changed Man and Other Tales, A*, 97, 101; "Distracted Preacher, The," 98, 107; "Doctor's Legend, The," 100; "Duke's Reappearance, the," 97; *Dynasts, The*, 110; "Enter a Dragoon," 97; *Far from the Madding Crowd*, 109; "Fiddler of the Reels, The," 110; "First Countess of Wessex, The," 110; "For Conscience' Sake," 110, 112; General Preface to the Wessex Edition, 111; *Group of Noble Dames, A*, 97, 99, 100, 102, 110, 111–12; "Honourable Laura, The," 110; "How I Built Myself a House," 96; "Imaginative Woman, An," 97, 110; "Interlopers at the Knap," 107, 149; *Jude the Obscure*, 97; "Lady Icenway, The," 99; "Lady Mattisfont," 99; *Life's Little Ironies*, 97, 100, 102, 112; "Marchioness of Stonehenge, The," 99; "Melancholy Hussar, The," 97, 102; "Our Exploits at West Poley," 97; *Poor Man and the Lady, The*, 97, 112; "Profitable Reading of Fiction, The," 102–5, 108, 110–11; "Romantic Adventures of a Milkmaid, The," 97, 101, 108; "Science of Fiction, The," 2, 111; "Son's Veto, The," 112–13; "Squire Petrick's Lady," 99; *Tess of the d'Urbervilles*, 99, 100, 103, 108; "Three Strangers, The," 106; "Tradition of Eighteen Hundred and Four, A," 97, 106–7; "Tragedy of Two Ambitions, A," 110, 112; *Wessex Tales*, 97, 99, 101, 105, 106, 107, 111; "Withered Arm, The," 101, 107
Harley, George, 45
Harmsworth, A. C. W. and H. S., 187
Harper, 173
Harper and Brother, 147
Harper's, 188
Harper's New Monthly Magazine, 86, 100
Harper's Weekly, 100, 147
Harris, Frank, 173
Harris, Wendell, *British Short Fiction in the Nineteenth Century*, 3
Harte, Bret, ix, 192
Harvie, Christopher, 125
Hawthorne, Nathaniel, ix, 91; *Twice-Told Tales*, 192
Heinemann, 161, 173
Heinemann, William, 172, 185
Henley, William Ernest, 115, 129, 131, 138, 161, 172, 173
Henty, G. A., 131
Herenberg, John Christofer, *Philosophicae et Christianae Cogitationes de Vampiris*, 50
Heseltine, Rose, 83
Hind, Lewis, 175
History of Mrs. Leeson, 22
History of the Chevalier de Faublas, The, 22
Hobby Horse, The, 190
Hogg, James, 7
Hollywood, 124
Home Rule for Ireland, 125
Homer, 148
Hope, Anthony, 188, 189
Hornung, E. W., 188
Household, The, 97
Household Words, 56, 63, 64, 65
Hugo, Victor, 131
Hutchins, John, *The History and Antiquities of the County of Dorset*, 99
Hutchinson, George, 185
Huxley, Thomas, 182

Ilbert Bill, 145
Illustrated London News, The, 86, 100, 191
Independent, The, 100

Indian Civil Service, 150
Indian Railway Library, 141, 154
International Library, 186
Irish Female Jockey Club, 22
Ives, Frederic, 185

Jacobs, W. W., 188; *A Master of Craft*,
189; "Grey Parrot, The," 189;
"Madness of Mr. Lister, The," 189
James, G. P. R., 8
James, Henry, 93, 104, 149, 160, 171,
191, 192; "The Art of Fiction," 3
Jane Eyre, 36
Jarrell, Randall, 158
Jerrold, Douglas, ix, 8
Johnson, Edgar, 67
Johnson, Samuel, 22
Joyce, James, 14

Kavanagh, Patrick, 18
Keats, John, 153
Keenan, Father, 17–18
Kegan Paul, C., 120
Kennedy, Sandee, x
Khartoum, 125
Kinshasa, Africa, 166
Kipling, Rudyard, 3, 4, 13, 131, **138–
59**, 188, 189, 192; *Actions and
Reactions*, 144; "Barrack Room
Ballads, I. Danny Deever," 138;
"Courting of Dinah Shadd, The,"
149; *Courting of Dinah Shadd and
Other Stories, The*, 147; *Day's Work,
The*, 144; *Debits and Credits*, 144;
Departmental Ditties, 139; *Diversity of
Creatures, A*, 144; "Drums of the
Fore and Aft, The," 153; *From Sea
to Sea*, 144; 'Fuzzy Wuzzy," 138;
"Gunga Din," 138; *In Black and
White*, 141; "In the House of
Suddhoo," 159; *Jungle Book, The*,
144; *Jungle Books*, 146; *Just So
Stories*, 144; *Kim*, 146; *Land and Sea
Tales*, 144; *Life's Handicap*, 144;
Light that Failed, The, 141; *Limits and
Renewals*, 144; "Lispeth," 146;
"Loot," 138; "Love-o'-Women,"
152; "Man Who Would Be King,
The," 152, 156–8; "Mandalay,"
138; *Many Inventions*, 144; "Mark of
the Beast, The," 139, 159; "Mary
Postgate," 159; *Mine Own People*,

149; "Miracle of Puran Bhagat,
The," 146; "Mrs. Bathurst," 146,
159; "On Greenhow Hill," 152;
"Phantom 'Rickshaw, The," 141,
152, 154–5; *Plain Tales from the
Hills*, 139, 141, 144; *Puck of Pook's
Hill*, 144, 189; *Rewards and Fairies*,
144; *The Second Jungle Book*, 144;
Soldiers Three, 141; *Something of
Myself*, 154; *Stalky & Co.*, 144; *Story
of the Gadsbys, The*, 141; "Swept and
Garnished," 159; "Taking of
Luntungpen, The," 150; "They,"
159; "Tomb of his Ancestors, The,"
146; "Tommy," 138; *Traffics and
Discoveries*, 144; *Thy Servant a Dog*,
144; *Under the Deodars*, 141; *Wee
Willie Winkie*, 141, 154; "Widow at
Windsor, The," 138; "Wish House,
The," 159; "Without Benefit of
Clergy," 146–9
Kitchener, Lord, 189
Klein, Georges Antoine, 165
Knight, Charles, 10
Krieger, Adolf, 172

Ladies Penny Gazette, 8
Lady's Almanack, The, 22
Lallans, 134
Lane, John, 173, 185
Lang, Andrew, 115, 139–40
Lavin, Mary, 14
Lawrence, D. H., 112, 192
Le Fanu, Joseph Sheridan, x, 4, 8, 13,
14, 32, **33–55**, 101; *All in the Dark*,
37; "Carmilla," 49–52; "Chapter in
the History of a Tyrone Family, A,"
36; *Chronicles of Golden Friars*, 51;
"Familiar, The," 37; "Fortunes of
Sir Robert Ardagh, The," 37;
"Ghost and the Bonesetter, The,"
36; "Green Tea," 44–8; "Haunted
Baronet, The," 52; *Haunted Lives*,
37; *House by the Churchyard, The*, 36;
In a Glass Darkly, 12, 36–52; "Mr.
Justice Harbottle'," 42–4; *Purcell
Papers, The*, 52; "Room in the
Dragon Volant, The," 37, 48–9;
"Strange Event in the Life of
Schalken the Painter," 36; *Tenants
of Malory, The*, 37; "Watcher, The,"
38–42

Le Gallienne, Richard, 153
Leopold II, Belgium, 165
LeRow, Pam, x
Lever, Charles, 37–8; *A Day's Ride: A Life's Romance*, 65
Levy, Max, 185
Lewes, George Henry, *Life of Goethe*, 130
Life, 86
Life of Edward, Lord Herbert, The, 22
Light: A Journal of Criticism and Belles Lettres, 86, 100
Literary Magnet of Belles-Lettres, Science, and the Fine Arts, 8
Locker, Arthur, 99–100, 101
Locker, William Algernon, 99–100
Lockhart, John Gibson, 7
London, 120
London Journal, 63
London Magazine, 8
London Monthly Magazine, see *Monthly Miscellany*
London Penny Journal, 8
London Review, 86
Longman's Magazine, 98, 117
Longmans, 117
Longmans, Green, and Co., 124
Lough-derg, 17, 20, 23
Lough Swilly, 24
Lover, Samuel, 8, 27
Lynch family, 24
Lytton, Bulwer, 8, 94; *Fables in Song*, 117; "The Haunters and the Haunted", 53; *Strange Story, A*, 64

McClure's Magazine, 117
McCormack, W. J., 37–8
McCulloch, John Ramsey, 71
McKiernan, Eoin, x
Maclise, Daniel, 71
Macmillan, 173, 176
Macmillan's Magazine, 147, 186, 190
Magia Posthua, 50
Maiden Castle, 106
Manchester Evening News, 187
Manchester Weekly Times, The, 100
Mansfield, Katherine, 192
Marlowe, Christopher, 46
Marryat, Frederick, *Peter Simple*, 8
Marsh's Library, Dublin, 21
Mason, A. E. W., 188
Matthew, Saint, 130

Matthews, Elkins, 185
Mattos, Katharine Stevenson de, 129
Maugham, W. Somerset, 188, 192
Maumbury Ring, 106
Maupassant, Guy de, 192
Maynooth, 21, 24
Meade, Mrs. L. T., 189
Mendip Hills, 98
Menikoff, Barry, 117
Meredith, George, 130; "The Case of General Ople and Lady Camper," 2
Mergenthaler, Ottmar, 185
Merriman, H. Seton, 188
Merrion Square, Dublin, 37
Methuen, 173
Metropolitan, 8
Mitford, Algernon, *Tales of Old Japan*, 130
Modern Language Association, 4
Modernist fiction, 168
Montaigne, 130
Monthly Miscellany, 8
Moore, George, x, 14
Morgan, Lady, 27
Morley, Charles, 128, 132
Morrison, Arthur, *Tales of Mean Streets*, 188
Mudie's, 186
Murgthal, 120
Murphy, Piers, 17, 21, 24
Murray, John, 83
Murray's Magazine, 100

Napoleon, 102, 107
Napoleonic Wars, 7
Nation, 18
National Gallery, Dublin, 29
National Observer, 138, 173
National Society, 9
Naturalism, French, 104
Nelson's New Century Library, 186
Nesbit, E. (Edith), 188
New Monthly Magazine, 190
New Quarterly Magazine, 98
New Review, 161, 172, 173
Newnes, George, 187–8, 190
Norman, Henry, *The Broken Shaft: Tales in Mid-Ocean*, 132
North-West Frontier, India, 153
novel, 3

O'Brien, Fitz-James, 14

O'Connor, Frank, 14, 192
O'Faolain, Sean, 14
O'Flaherty, Liam, 14
O'Kelly, Seamus, 14
Orangeism, 21
Orczy, Baroness, 189
Orwell, George, 150
Osbourne, Lloyd, 128
Osgood, McIlvaine & Co., 102
Osgood, McIlvaine edition of Hardy, 109
Otega (ship), 168
Otway, Caesar, 23
Ouida, ix
Owen, Rebekah, 112
Oxford University Press, 186

Page, Norman, 111
Pageant, The, 190
Paget, Sidney, 188
Pain, Barry, 188
Palestine (ship), 163
Pall Mall, 127
Pall Mall Gazette, 128, 132, 173, 176, 187
Paradowska, Marguerite, 165
Pascal, Blaise, 95
Pater, Walter, 121; "The Child in the House," 12
Patten, Robert L., 56
Pawling, Sidney, 161
Peake, Richard Brinsley, *The Bottle Imp*, 129
Pearson's, 173, 191
Pemberton, Max, 188
Penny Comic Magazine, 8
Penny Magazine, 9, 10, 11
Penzoldt, Peter, 51
Perrault, Charles, 148
Phlegon, *de Mirabilibus*, 50
Phoenix Park, Dublin, 125
Pigott, Richard, 16
Pinker, James B., 171, 189
Pioneer, The (Allahabad), 138, 139, 141
Pitlochry, Scotland, 132, 133
Plato, 179
Poe, Edgar Allan, ix, 3, 156, 191–2
Princess, The, 156
Pritchett, V. S., 192
Proctor, A. A., *Victoria Regia*, 86
Protestant Guardian, The, 34

Pseudonym Library, 186
Public Opinion, 86
Punjab Club, 145

Quartette, 154
Quarto, 190

Rambler, 7
Rebellion of '98, 21
"Red-Haired Man's Wife, The," 28
Reform Bill of 1832, 34
Religious Tract Society, 9
Review of Reviews, 188
Reynolds, Mrs. Baillie, 189
Ribbonism, 21
Ricardo, David, 71
Richards, Grant, 185, 186
Rigveda, 148
Ripon, Lord, 145
"Rita" (Mrs. Humphreys), 189
Roberts, Frederick, Sir, 152
Robinson, Kay, 139
Roi des Belges (ship), 165–66
Rosa, Aunty, 147
Rossetti, Dante Gabriel, 121; "Hand and Soul," 2
Rugby Junction, 76
Russell, Lord, 18

Sadleir, Michael, 89; *Trollope: A Commentary*, 94
St. James's Budget, 100
St. James's Magazine, 190
St. Patrick's College, Maynooth, 18, 23
St. Paul's Cathedral, 124
St. Paul's Magazine, 79, 86, 87, 89, 190
"Saki" (H. H. Munro), x
Samoan language, 129
Sampson Low, Marston & Co., 141
San Francisco Examiner, 123
Sandford, County Dublin, 18
Sandgate, 178
Saturday Magazine, 9, 11
Saturday Review, The, 100, 139, 173, 175
Savoy, The, 190
Science Schools Journal, 173
Scott, Walter, Sir, 82, 131; *Marmion*, 104
Scribner's, 128
Scribner's Magazine, 100, 188

Secondary Education Commission of 1894, 185

Seignelay, Le (ship), 165

Seneca, x

Shakespeare, William, 130; *Othello*, 108

Sharp, William, 139–141

Shaw, George Bernard, 175

Sheridan, Richard Brinsley, 26, 34

Sherwood, 8

Shilling Magazine, 8

Sims, Mrs., 133

Sinclair, George, *Satan's Invisible World Discovered*, 132

sketch, 3

Slattery, W. J., 29

Smith, Adam, 71

Smith, Richard John ("Obi"), 129

Smith, W. H., 186, 187

Smith Elder, 172

Smollett, Tobias, 90; *Sir Launcelot Greaves*, 7

Société Anonyme Belge pour le Commerce du Haut-Congo, 165

Society for the Diffusion of Useful Knowledge, 10, 11

Society for the Propagation of Christian Knowledge, 9, 10

Somerville and Ross, 14

Sonnenschein, Swan & Co., 185

South Seas Edition (Stevenson), 116

Southsea, 147

Spectator, The, 7, 172

Spencer, Herbert, 130

Sphere, The, 100

Stamp Tax, 4, 5

Stanford University Press, 117

Stanley, Henry Morton, 165

Stanton, Coralie, 189

Statesman, The, 34

Stead, W. T., 17

Stedman, Algernon M. M., 185

Stephen, Leslie, 118, 120, 132, 137

Sterne, Laurence, 90

Stevenson, Fanny, 117, 118, 123–4, 129, 133, 137

Stevenson, Robert Louis, 3, 4, 12, 13, **115–137**, 139, 154, 189; *Beach of Falesá, The*, 117; *Black Man and Other Tales, The*, 127; "Body Snatcher, The," 127, 128, 132–5; 'Bottle Imp, The,' 129; "Chapter on Dreams, A," 123; *Covenanting Story-Book, A*, 132; *Fables*, 117–18; "Faith, Half Faith and No Faith at All," 118; "The House of Eld, The," 118; *Inland Voyage, An*, 120–1; *Island Nights' Entertainment*, 123, 128; "Latter-Day Arabian Nights," 120; "Markheim," 117, 123, 128, 134–6; *Merry Men and Other Tales and Fables, The*, 127, 128; *New Arabian Nights*, 120–1, 164; "Olalla," 128; "Oliver Leaf," 132; "On Style in Literature: Its Technical Elements," 129; "Physician and the Saratoga Trunk, The," 122; "Sinking Ship, The," 117, 119–20; "Something in It," 118; "Strange Case of Dr. Jekyll and Mr. Hyde, The," 117, 118, 123–7, 133; "Suicide Club, The," 120–2; "Tadpole and the Frog, The," 118; "Thrawn Janet," 127, 132–7; "Travelling Companion, The," 123, 127; *Travels with a Donkey*, 121; "Waif Woman, The," 128; "Will o' the Mill," 117–20; *Wrong Box, The*, 128

Stoker, Bram, "The Judge's House," 53

Stonehenge, 106

story, 3

Strand Magazine, The, 2, 176, 186, 187–90, 191

Strang, William, 141

Strange Story, A, 63

Stretton, Hesba, 74

Stuart, Dr., 24

Studio, The, 185

Sussex, 145

Swedenborg, 47, 52; *Arcana Caelestia*, 44–5

Swinburne, Algernon Charles, 121

Swinnerton, Frank, 182

Symons, Arthur, x

tale, 3

tale (oriental), 1

Tatler, 7

Tatler–Spectator genre, 1

Taylor, Lady, 128

Technical Institution Act of 1890, 184

Temple Bar Magazine, 186, 190

Temple Classics, 186
Temple Library, 186
Temple Press, 186
Temple Shakespeare, 186
Thacker Spink & Co. (Calcutta), 139
Thackeray, William Makepeace, 2, 8, 72, 80–1, 82, 87; *The Luck of Barry Lyndon*, 8
Thomas, Deborah A., *Dickens and the Short Story*, 56
Thousand and One Nights, 148
Tillotson and Son, 101
Times, The (London), 124
Tinsley, William, 83
Tinsley's Magazine, 190
Tit-Bits, 187
Tithe Rebellion, 25
Tithe Wars, 34
Tom Jones, 22
Torres Strait, 168
Trilling, Lionel, 150
Trinity College, Dublin, 34
Trollope, Anthony, 4, 12, 13, **79–95**, 96, 97, 100, 101, 112, 192; *Autobiography*, 80–6; *Barchester Towers*, 85; *Can You Forgive Her?*, 83; "The Château of Prince Polignac," 94, 95; "Christmas Day at Kirkby Cottage," 90; *The Claverings*, 85, 93; *Clergymen of the Church of England*, 86; *Editor's Tales, An*, 79, 86, 92; *Hunting Sketches*, 86; "Josephine de Monmorenci," 89; *The Kellys and the O'Kellys*, 83; *Lotta Schmidt and Other Stories*, 86; *Macdermots of Ballycloran, The*, 83; "Mary Gresley," 89; "La Mère Banche, La," 94; "Mistletoe Bough, The," 90; *Noble Jill, The*, 83; "Not If I Know It," 86; *Orley Farm*, 84; 'Panjandrum, The," 79–80, 82, 89; "Spotted Dog, The," 87–8, 93, 95; *Tales of All Countries*, 86, 89, 94; *Travelling Sketches*, 86; "Turkish Bath, The," 89; "Two Generals, The," 90; "Two Heroines of Plumplington, The," 86, 92–3, 95; *Warden, The*, 84; *Why Frau Frohmann Raised Her Prices and Other Stories*, 86; "Widow's Mite, The," 90
Twain, Mark, ix
Tyskowa, Maria, 165

Unwin, T. Fisher, 172, 185
Unwin's Christmas Annual, 132
Upper Phillimore Place, London, 113–14

Vailina Edition (Stevenson), 116
Vendée, La, 83
Verne, Jules, 182
Victoria, Queen, 11, 13, 186
Victoria Magazine, 190
Villiers Street, Strand, 13, 189
Virgil, 22

Warder, The, 34
Watt, A. P., 189
Waverley Novels, 186
Webb, Beatrice and Sidney, 175
Week's News (Allahabad), 139
Wells, H. G., 3, 4, 13, 144, **160–83**, 188; *Autobiography*, 178–9; "Chronic Argonauts, The," 173; "Cone, The," 182; "Country of the Blind, The," 179; "Door in the Wall, The," 177, 178; *First Men in the Moon*, 189; "Grisly Folk, The," 177; "In the Abyss," 178; "Lord of the Dynamos, The," 182; *Love and Mr. Lewisham*, 175; "Mr. Brasher's Treasure," 189; "New Accelerator, The," 177; *Plattner Story and Others, The*, 173; "Plattner Story, The," 177, 178, 182; "Remarkable Case of Davidson's Eyes, The," 177, 178, 182; "Sea-Raiders, The," 177–8; *Stolen Bacillus and Other Incidents, The*, 173; "Stolen Bacillus, The," 182; *Tales of Space and Time*, 173; *Textbook on Biology*, 173; *Thirty Strange Stories*, 173; *Time Machine, The*, 173, 176, 182; *Time Traveller, The*, 173; "Truth about Pyecraft, The," 177, 189; *Twelve Stories and a Dream*, 176; *War of the Worlds, The*, 173; *Wonderful Visit, The*, 182
Wessex, 102, 109–12
Wessex Edition (Hardy), 96, 97, 102, 107
Westminster Review, 73
Weyman, Stanley, 189
Wheeler, Stephen, 139
"White Man's Burden" (phrase), 147
Whitman, Walt, 130

Wilde, Oscar, 121, 171, 189
Williamson, Mrs. C. N., 189
Wills, W. H., 63
Wilson, John ("Christopher North"), 7
Windsor, 191
Winfrith, 109
Wodehouse, P. G., 188
Wodrow, Robert, *Analecta*, 132
Wolff, Robert Lee, 18
Woman in White, The, 63
Wood, Henry A. W., 185
Woolf, Virginia, 192

Wordsworth, William, 130
World War I, 131, 192
World War II, 179
World's Classics, 186

Yeats, William Butler, 18
Yellow Book, The, 190
Younghusband, George, Sir, 153

Zagorski, Karol, 165
Zangwill, Israel, 10
Zola, Émile, 104, 105, 115, 131